Microsoft Identity and Access Administrator Exam Guide

Implement IAM solutions with Azure AD, build an identity governance strategy, and pass the SC-300 exam

Dwayne Natwick

BIRMINGHAM—MUMBAI

Microsoft Identity and Access Administrator Exam Guide

Group Product Manager: Vijin Boricha
Publishing Product Manager: Mohd Riyan Khan
Senior Editor: Shazeen Iqbal
Content Development Editor: Rafiaa Khan
Technical Editor: Arjun Varma
Copy Editor: Safis Editing
Project Coordinator: Shagun Saini
Proofreader: Safis Editing
Indexer: Pratik Shirodkar
Production Designer: Ponraj Dhandapani

First published: March 2022

Production reference: 2230222

Published by Packt Publishing Ltd.
Livery Place
35 Livery Street
Birmingham
B3 2PB, UK.

ISBN 978-1-80181-804-9

www.packt.com

Foreword

Over the course of my career, identity has always been an important part of any technical design or architecture. When I worked on the help desk, I can remember creating user accounts, resetting passwords, and adding users to security groups. As time progressed, my skills gravitated toward solution architect scenarios involving Active Directory build outs, upgrades, and maintenance, as well as onboarding solutions such as Azure Active Directory Connect. I am currently a program manager within the identity and network access division at Microsoft. I certainly didn't know my technical foundation would evolve into identity being one of my predominant areas of focus all these years later.

The cloud is here to stay, and is reshaping the common identity scenarios of old. Organizations are extending identities into the cloud, which takes identity outside of the four walls housing any infrastructure. As a result, a different approach needs to be implemented to maintain a secure posture and ensure the right amount of governance is applied.

The focus of this book is on the Microsoft SC-300 exam. Any individual who's studying for this exam should hopefully understand the importance of identity and access management. Perhaps this exam is a requirement for a job or maybe even a way to further prove technical skills and knowledge. One thing is sure: customers need to securely protect applications and user data at the perimeter using Azure identity and access management solutions. IT departments need to defend against malicious login attempts, safeguard credentials, protect identities, and enforce strong authentication options (all without disrupting productivity). This challenge is no easy one, especially with the rate of change in both the security and identity spaces.

Passing this exam means you'll receive the *Microsoft Identity and Access Administrator Associate certification*. You'll be uniquely prepared to design, implement, and operate an identity and access management system using Azure Active Directory. You'll be able to manage tasks such as configuring secure authentication and authorization access to enterprise applications. This role-based cert will provide administrators with ways of implementing seamless user experiences and self-service management capabilities to avoid disturbing end users' daily activities. Identity governance is another key element you should be able to plan for and build out. Additionally, you'll also learn how to troubleshoot, monitor, and configure reporting for the identity and access environment.

After going through studying and passing the certification, you'll find yourself better equipped to handle the ever-evolving identity and security threat landscape. This area of focus and study will kickstart your skills to be a great value addition for any company you work for in the future. Good luck and make sure you give yourself plenty of time to study and prep!

I'd like to quickly thank Dwayne for asking me to write this foreword. I'm honored to be thought of in this space! Dwayne is one of my security gurus and always has a great answer or approach to any situation if a question arises. He'll help you make the most sense out of the exam in a pragmatic way that will help you pass!

Shannon Kuehn

Senior Program Manager

Identity and Network Access

Contributors

About the author

Dwayne Natwick is a Senior Product Manager at Cloudreach, an Atos company and a Microsoft Expert MSP. He has been in IT, security design, and architecture for over 30 years. His love of teaching led him to become a **Microsoft Certified Trainer** (**MCT**) Regional Lead and a Microsoft **Most Valuable Professional** (**MVP**).

Dwayne has a master's degree in business IT from Walsh College, the CISSP from ISC2, and 18 Microsoft certifications, including Identity and Access Administrator, Azure Security Engineer, and Microsoft 365 Security Administrator. Dwayne can be found providing and sharing information on social media, at industry conferences, on his blog site, and on his YouTube channel.

Originally from Maryland, Dwayne currently resides in Michigan with his wife and three children.

About the reviewers

Sathish Veerapandian is a certified microsoft infrastructure/cloud architect with 14 years of international large-scale hands-on experience in planning, designing, and executing IT management of messaging platforms such as Microsoft Teams with Telephony, Skype for Business Voice, Microsoft Exchange, Intune deployment, Microsoft Azure, and Microsoft Security implementations. His dedication to serving the technical community has earned him the title of Microsoft MVP for the past 7 years, and he shares his technical knowledge and skills through local meetups and blogs and participates in Microsoft Ignite sessions. He is well known in the community for his contributions to Office 365 and the Microsoft Teams and Security platforms.

Shabaz Darr is an infrastructure master for Netcompany, based in the United Kingdom. He is a Microsoft MVP in Enterprise Mobility, specializing in Microsoft cloud technologies including Endpoint Manager, Security & Compliance, and Azure Virtual Desktop. He has over 15 years' experience in the IT industry, with 8 of those spent working with Microsoft cloud technologies. During this period, he assisted several global organizations with designing and implementing information protection strategies. He coauthored a book on the SC-400 Information Protection Microsoft certification exam and individually authored a book on the AZ-140 Azure Virtual Desktop Specialist exam, and was also a technical reviewer for the SC-900 Security Fundamentals book. He also has his own YouTube channel called "I Am IT Geek" where he creates video series on various Microsoft cloud technologies.

I would like to thank Packt for asking me to technically review this book, as well as thanking the author, Dwayne Natwick, for asking me to be part of this project. It has been a huge honor to be part of this book.

Bart Van Vugt is a freelance workplace/security architect and owner at BVV Consult. He has over 20 years of experience in the field, acting as a security architect with broad professional experience in enterprise security, identity and access management, information protection, cybersecurity, endpoint management, and cloud security. Guiding companies on their zero trust and cloud journey, providing architecture and security advice, and delivering hands-on deployments are part of the job.

In addition to that, Bart has been a passionate MCT since 2021, holding several certifications.

Bart was also recognized by Microsoft in 2021 by receiving digital badges from their Windows Customer Connection Program and Microsoft 365 Threat Protection Program: Community Member 2021.

Marcel Molenaar is a consultant, developer, solution architect, and an MCT with more than 25 years of experience in IT. As a developer, he has experience in many object-oriented programming languages, such as C++, C#, Java, Node.js, Python, and PowerShell. As a SharePoint consultant, he started working with SharePoint 2003 and implemented SharePoint farms for larger enterprises with lots of customizations and strict security conditions.

With the transition to the Microsoft 365 platform, his field of experience moved to SharePoint Online and the Azure platform. Marcel is fascinated by the cloud and new cloud-related technologies. He also loves the data platform and AI because of his scientific background.

He has worked as an MCT for more than 10 years. He teaches lots of students about Azure, Microsoft 365, security, data, and the Power Platform.

Marcel is self-employed and is the CEO of Marcel Molenaar IT Training. He lives and works in the Netherlands.

Bill Wheeler is a security architect for Avanade, a leading provider of cloud and security solutions delivered through the Microsoft ecosystem. Bill has been working in technology for over 25 years, 20 of which was with the Volkswagen Group of America, with a focus on infrastructure and security. Bill is a U.S. Marine Corps veteran.

Table of Contents

2
Defining Identity and Access Management

Section 2 - Implementing an Identity Management Solution

3
Implementing and Configuring Azure Active Directory

4
Creating, Configuring, and Managing Identities

5
Implementing and Managing External Identities and Guests

6
Implementing and Managing Hybrid Identities

Section 3 – Implementing an Authentication and Access Management Solution

7

Planning and Implementing Azure Multi-Factor Authentication (MFA) and Self-Service Password Reset (SSPR)

8

Planning and Managing Passwordless Authentication Methods

9

Planning, Implementing, and Administering Conditional Access and Azure Identity Protection

Section 4 – Implementing Access Management for Applications

10

Planning and Implementing Enterprise Apps for Single Sign-On (SSO)

11
Monitoring Enterprise Apps with Microsoft Defender for Cloud Apps

Section 5 – Planning and Implementing an Identity Governance Strategy

12
Planning and Implementing Entitlement Management

13

Planning and Implementing Privileged Access and Access Reviews

Section 6 – Monitoring and Maintaining Azure Active Directory

14

Analyzing and Investigating Sign-in Logs and Elevated Risk Users

15

Enabling and Integrating Azure AD Logs with SIEM Solutions

Preface

This book simplifies **identity and access management (IAM)** concepts to help you pass the SC-300 certification exam. Packed with practical examples, you'll gain hands-on knowledge to drive strategic identity projects while modernizing identity solutions, implementing hybrid identity solutions, and monitoring identity governance.

Who this book is for

This book is for cloud security engineers, Microsoft 365 administrators, Microsoft 365 users, Microsoft 365 identity administrators, and anyone who wants to learn about IAM and gain SC-300 certification. You should have a basic understanding of the fundamental services within Microsoft 365 and Azure Active Directory before getting started with this Microsoft book.

What this book covers

Chapter 1, *Preparing for Your Microsoft Exam*, provides guidance on getting prepared for a Microsoft exam along with resources that can assist in your learning plan. This will include helpful links along with steps for gaining access to a trial Microsoft 365 subscription for hands-on practice.

Chapter 2, *Defining Identity and Access Management*, provides an overview of what IAM is and why it is important. This chapter will also discuss the evolution of IAM as cloud technologies have become more prevalent.

Chapter 3, *Implementing and Configuring Azure Active Directory*, focuses on the implementation and configuration of Azure Active Directory for cloud identities. This will include how to configure and verify custom domains and tenant-wide settings.

Chapter 4, *Creating, Configuring, and Managing Identities*, discusses how to plan, create, configure, and manage users, groups, and licenses within Azure Active Directory. This will include the bulk creation of users and dynamic group creation.

Chapter 5, Implementing and Managing External Identities and Guests, discusses how to plan and provide guest user access to Azure Active Directory. This will include how to invite guest users and how to manage access. The chapter will also discuss utilizing existing user identities with B2B and B2C access.

Chapter 6, Implementing and Managing Hybrid Identities, focuses on the planning and implementation of hybrid identity. This will include configuration of Azure Active Directory Connect for Windows Active Directory to Azure Active Directory and determining which synchronization type is the best fit for an organization.

Chapter 7, Planning and Implementing Azure Multi-Factor Authentication and Self-Service Password Reset, discusses the planning and implementation of Azure MFA and SSPR for users and groups. This will include deploying, managing, and configuring MFA for users and groups. This chapter will also cover the differences between verifying identity with MFA and SSPR.

Chapter 8, Planning and Managing Password-Less Authentication Methods, discusses how to plan and utilize password-less authentication methods. It will cover the various methods and how they can be deployed within Azure Active Directory.

Chapter 9, Planning, Implementing, and Administering Conditional Access and Azure Identity Protection, covers conditional access policies. This will include planning for these policies and testing them to verify that they are working correctly and providing the proper controls. In addition, we will discuss Azure Identity Protection and using sign-in and user risk conditions with policies.

Chapter 10, Planning and Implementing Enterprise Apps for Single Sign-On (SSO), focuses on enterprise applications and how to plan and implement SSO. This will include setting up an application proxy for connecting on-premises applications to Azure Active Directory.

Chapter 11, Monitoring Enterprise Apps with Microsoft Defender for Cloud Apps, discusses how Microsoft Defender for Cloud Apps is used to manage and monitor enterprise cloud applications. This includes how to utilize conditional access policies for cloud application access.

Chapter 12, Planning and Implementing Entitlement Management, discusses the planning and implementation process for entitlement management. This includes life cycle management for external users and managing the terms of use.

Chapter 13, Planning and Implementing Privileged Access and Access Reviews, discusses the planning and implementation for user privileged access. This will include how to determine and assign users with privileged access rights on a just-in-time basis. This chapter will also cover planning for access reviews.

Chapter 14, Analyzing and Investigating Sign-in Logs and Elevated Risk Users, discusses how to analyze and investigate sign-in logs and determine risks to elevated users.

Chapter 15, Enabling and Integrating Azure AD Logs with SIEM Solutions, discusses how Azure Active Directory logs can be integrated into SIEM solutions. This will include Azure Sentinel and third-party SIEM.

Chapter 16, Mock Test, provides a final assessment and mock exam questions to complete the final preparations to take the SC-300 exam.

To get the most out of this book

This book will explore configuring a tenant for use of Microsoft 365 and Azure. There will be exercises that will require access to Azure Active Directory. *Chapter 1, Preparing for Your Microsoft Exam*, provides directions for creating a trial license of Microsoft 365 and a free Azure account.

Software/hardware covered in the book	OS requirements
Azure Active Directory	Windows, macOS, or Linux (any)
Microsoft 365 Business trial with E5 License	Windows, macOS or Linux(any)
Azure free account	Windows, macOS or Linux(any)

Download the color images

We also provide a PDF file that has color images of the screenshots/diagrams used in this book. You can download it here: `https://static.packt-cdn.com/downloads/9781801818049_ColorImages.pdf`.

Conventions used

There are a number of text conventions used throughout this book.

`Code in text`: Indicates code words in text, database table names, folder names, filenames, file extensions, pathnames, dummy URLs, user input, and Twitter handles. Here is an example: By selecting the Download button, filtered data can then be downloaded to a .csv or .json file for up to 250,000 records.

Any command-line input or output is written as follows:

```
$PasswordProfile = New-Object -TypeName Microsoft.Open.
AzureAD.Model.PasswordProfile
```

Bold: Indicates a new term, an important word, or words that you see onscreen. For example, words in menus or dialog boxes appear in the text like this. Here is an example: The best way to obtain these features is through an **Enterprise Mobility + Security (EMS) E5** license.

> **Tips or Important Notes**
> Appear like this.

Get in touch

Feedback from our readers is always welcome.

General feedback: If you have questions about any aspect of this book, mention the book title in the subject of your message and email us at `customercare@packtpub.com`.

Errata: Although we have taken every care to ensure the accuracy of our content, mistakes do happen. If you have found a mistake in this book, we would be grateful if you would report this to us. Please visit `www.packtpub.com/support/errata`, selecting your book, clicking on the Errata Submission Form link, and entering the details.

Piracy: If you come across any illegal copies of our works in any form on the Internet, we would be grateful if you would provide us with the location address or website name. Please contact us at `copyright@packt.com` with a link to the material.

If you are interested in becoming an author: If there is a topic that you have expertise in and you are interested in either writing or contributing to a book, please visit `authors.packtpub.com`.

Share Your Thoughts

Once you've read *Microsoft Identity and Access Administrator Exam Guide*, we'd love to hear your thoughts! Scan the QR code below to go straight to the Amazon review page for this book and share your feedback.

https://packt.link/r/1-801-81804-5

Your review is important to us and the tech community and will help us make sure we're delivering excellent quality content.

Section 1 – Exam Overview and the Evolution of Identity and Access Management

This section will focus on the objectives and an overview of what to expect in the exam and an overview of the evolution of identity and access management.

This section of the book comprises the following chapters:

- *Chapter 1, Preparing for Your Microsoft Exam*
- *Chapter 2, Defining Identity and Access Management*

1
Preparing for Your Microsoft Exam

You have decided to take the steps to get **Microsoft certified**. The *SC-300* exam focuses on *identity* and *access* administration. This chapter will provide guidance on getting prepared for a Microsoft exam, along with resources that can assist in your learning plan. This will include helpful links, as well as steps on how to gain access to a trial **Microsoft 365** subscription for hands-on practice. Once you have completed this chapter, you will have the necessary tools to know what is needed to prepare for the exam, follow along in this book, and become an **Identity and Access Administrator**.

In this chapter, we're going to cover the following main topics:

- Preparing for a Microsoft exam
- Resources available and accessing **Microsoft Learn**
- Creating a Microsoft 365 trial subscription
- Exam objectives
- Who should take the SC-300 exam?

Technical requirements

In order to follow along and complete the exercises within this book, you will need to have access to **Azure Active Directory (Azure AD)**. This can be accomplished through a trial subscription of Microsoft 365. Advanced identity and access services will also require an Azure AD *Premium license*. The steps to set up licenses will be covered later in this chapter.

Preparing for a Microsoft exam

There are multiple aspects to preparing for a Microsoft exam. These include the resources available to prepare for the exam, the ability to access a subscription for hands-on learning, and the manner in which you are going to take your exam. If this is your first Microsoft exam, understanding the format that most of these exams will follow is important.

Let's take a closer look at each of these areas.

Resources available to prepare for the exam

There are many resources available to help you prepare for most Microsoft exams. This can be in the form of pre-recorded content from learning companies, live courses from *Microsoft Learning Partners*, and content posted by the community and Microsoft blog articles. Each of these resources is helpful, but the pre-recorded content and live courses will come at a price and may not be within your budget. Community and Microsoft blog articles generally provide a level of direction as to where you need to go for each topic but do not get into specifics.

One of the best resources is Microsoft itself. Microsoft provides detailed documentation on every one of its services with *Microsoft Docs*, which allows you to search freely and find the information that you need. This information is publicly available and free. *Microsoft Docs* is tied very closely to Microsoft Learn content, which will be discussed later in this chapter.

To access and search *Microsoft Docs*, simply go to `https://docs.microsoft.com`.

Access to a subscription

It is highly recommended when preparing for a Microsoft exam that you have had some level of hands-on experience with the services within the objectives. For associate- and expert-level exams (the SC-300 being an associate-level exam), this really should be a requirement. Microsoft courses have a *GitHub* repository for labs that are recommended and available to the public.

The lab guides can be found at this link: `http://www.microsoft.com/learning`.

Microsoft offers trial subscriptions for both Azure and Microsoft 365. The process to create these trials will be provided later in this chapter.

Where to take the exam

Part of the preparation process of taking an exam includes *where* you are going to take it. Traditionally, there has been only an option to take these exams at a proctored exam site. Some may prefer this method because it is a controlled environment. Understanding the location and setup of the site can be helpful in lowering your level of stress on the day of the exam. Making a trip to the site before your exam date can avoid any potential surprises on the day of the exam.

When the role-based exams became available, Microsoft provided an additional option of taking the exam remotely from your home or office, using a **remote proctor**. This may be a preferred option if you are more comfortable using your own equipment and working in a familiar environment. If you do not have the choice when scheduling your exam, then this option has not been made available in your region. If it is available, you will see an option similar to the **Online from my home or office** option shown in the following screenshot:

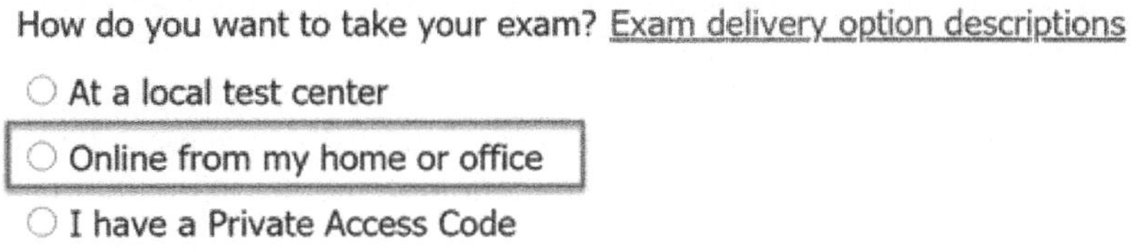

How do you want to take your exam? <u>Exam delivery option descriptions</u>

○ At a local test center

○ Online from my home or office

○ I have a Private Access Code

Figure 1.1 – Selecting a location when scheduling an exam

There are some important steps to prepare for the remote proctor. From an equipment standpoint, you must have a device with a webcam, microphone, and speakers. You can only use one monitor, so be sure to have a high resolution to avoid any issues with viewing the exam. It is highly recommended to test your equipment before the day of the exam to avoid any issues with anti-malware software. The location in which you are going to take the exam must be cleared of any papers, books, pens, and pencils. It must also be a quiet environment where no one will enter while you are taking the exam. You will be required to photograph the location and surrounding area when checking in. A valid form of identification is required as well. During the exam, you must remain within view of the camera. This may feel intrusive and may not be comfortable for some, but others may prefer being within their own environment to take an exam.

Exam format

Microsoft exams are typically made up of four to six question types. These are case studies, multiple-choice, drag and drop, modified true/false, drop-down fill-in, and best-answer scenarios. Let's provide some additional detail on what each of these means, as follows:

1. **Case-study** questions provide a hypothetical company setting with the current environment, proposed future environment, and technical and business requirements. From this scenario, six to eight questions are asked that may cover multiple objective areas of the exam. On most associate-level exams, you could see one to three of these case studies.

2. **Multiple-choice** questions are straightforward questions. Some multiple-choice questions may have more than one answer. Microsoft is generally transparent on how many correct answers need to be chosen for the question, and you will get alerted if you do not choose the correct number of selections.

3. **Drag-and-drop** questions are usually based on the steps of a process to test your knowledge of the order of operations to deploy a service. You are given more selections than required and need to move the steps that apply to the question over to the right column, in the proper sequence.

4. The next type of question is a modified type of **true/false** question. In these questions, you are usually provided some exhibits or screenshots from within the Microsoft portals or tables that show what has been configured. There are then three to four statements about this information, and you need to select **Yes** or **No** for each statement based on whether the statement is correct in terms of the information provided.

5. **Drop-down fill-in** questions are usually where you will find PowerShell or Azure **command-line interface (CLI)** code. You will be asked to complete certain steps within a string of code where the blank sections provide drop-down selections to choose from.

6. **Best-answer scenario** questions are the best test of pure understanding of an objective area. Microsoft will warn you when getting to this section that you no longer have an option to navigate back on these questions. You will be provided a specific scenario that needs to be solved, along with a proposed solution. You will need to determine whether that solution is the best solution to solve the scenario requirements. After selecting yes or no, you may see the same scenario again with a different solution on the next yes-or-no question.

Each of these exam question types tests your level of understanding in different ways, and all go into the weighted exam objectives that will be discussed later in this chapter.

We have covered how to determine an exam location and the types of questions that you may expect. The next sections will cover resources that will help in the process of learning the topics covered within the exam and how to gain access to the solutions to follow along with the exercises in this guide.

Resources available and accessing Microsoft Learn

Earlier in this chapter, some of the resources available for preparing for the exam were mentioned. Microsoft Learn was mentioned along with *Microsoft Docs*, but it requires its own section due to the amount of free content that it provides to help you prepare for an exam.

Accessing Microsoft Learn

Microsoft Learn is a great resource to get your learning path started. All the content on Microsoft Learn is free. When you create an account on Microsoft, learning progress is tracked and you can acquire badges along the way. In addition, Microsoft creates learning challenges periodically with prizes, such as free exam vouchers. Creating a free account is accomplished by selecting the icon on the top right of the page and selecting **Sign in**, as shown in the following screenshot:

Figure 1.2 – Microsoft Learn site profile sign-in

You can sign in with an existing Microsoft account or create one to get started, as indicated here:

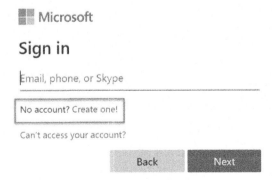

Figure 1.3 – Creating an account or signing in with a Microsoft account

You can get to Microsoft Learn through the following link: `https://www.microsoft.com/learn`.

Finding content on Microsoft Learn

Content on Microsoft Learn can be found in various ways. You can run a search on specific products, roles, or certifications. These options can be found on the selection ribbon at the top of the **Learn** home page, as shown in the following screenshot. The home page also has several recommendations to start your learning:

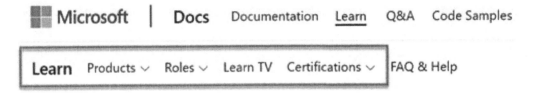

Figure 1.4 – Learn content navigation

From the **Learn** content navigation tabs, select a drop-down arrow to filter for content in the specific **Products**, **Roles**, or **Certifications** areas, as shown in the following screenshot:

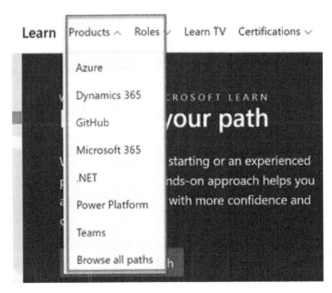

Figure 1.5 – Filtering categories under the Products drop-down arrow

Once you have selected an area of interest or simply chosen to browse all paths, you can then search specific topics and filter even further on individual courses or learning paths, as shown in the following screenshot:

Browse all

Learn new skills and discover the power of Microsoft products with step-by-step guidance. Start your journey today by exploring our learning paths and modules.

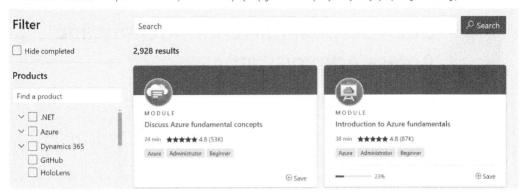

Figure 1.6 – Browsing all content in Microsoft Learn

This section provided the information needed to access Microsoft Learn and browse for modules and learning paths. The next section will assist you in finding content specific to the SC-300 exam.

Exam pages on Microsoft Learn

Another common area within Microsoft Learn is the **exam pages**. For any exam provided by Microsoft, there is an exam page and a certification page that is located within Microsoft Learn. These pages provide an overview of an exam or a certification, the roles of individuals that may be interested in a particular exam, the objective areas for an exam, scheduling an exam, and the Microsoft Learn learning path to prepare for an exam. These pages are extremely helpful when you are preparing specifically for an exam rather than just acquiring general technical knowledge. The following screenshot shows a search for the SC-300 exam:

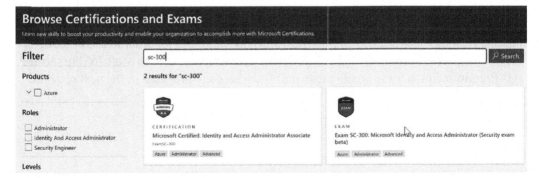

Figure 1.7 – Browsing for the SC-300 exam

This screenshot shows the exam page for the SC-300 exam:

Exam SC-300: Microsoft Identity and Access Administrator

The Microsoft Identity and Access Administrator designs, implements, and operates an organization's identity and access management systems by using Azure Active Directory (Azure AD). They manage tasks such as providing secure authentication and authorization access to enterprise applications. The administrator provides seamless experiences and self-service management capabilities for all users. Adaptive access and governance are core elements to the role. This role is also responsible for troubleshooting, monitoring, and reporting for the identity and access environment.

The Identity and Access Administrator may be a single individual or a member of a larger team. This role collaborates with many other roles in the organization to drive strategic identity projects to modernize identity solutions, to implement hybrid identity solutions, and to implement identity governance.

Part of the requirements for: Microsoft Certified: Identity and Access Administrator Associate
Related exams: none
Important: See details
Go to Certification Dashboard ⬀

Figure 1.8 – SC-300 exam page

As you continue to prepare for the SC-300 exam, it is recommended that you use this exam page as a reference.

You should now have access to log in and browse the content on Microsoft Learn. The next section will provide guidance on signing up for a trial subscription to Microsoft 365 services.

Creating a Microsoft 365 trial subscription

If you are new to Microsoft 365 and Azure, getting hands-on experience is important not just for exam preparation, but also for professional development. If you are getting certified to open doors to new job opportunities, you must understand the administration portals and how to work within them. This book will provide some exercises that will get you familiar with how to work within Microsoft 365 and Azure AD. In order to follow along with the steps, it is recommended that you have a subscription to Microsoft 365 and **Azure AD Premium**. The steps to create these in a 30-day trial are provided in the next sections.

Office 365 or Microsoft 365 trial subscription

Many of the features and capabilities discussed within the exam objectives require an enterprise-level license within Microsoft 365. The enterprise licenses are the E3 and E5 licenses. Microsoft offers 30-day trial licenses of these, so as you prepare for the exam, you can create a trial subscription and will then be able to follow along with the exercises.

To get started, navigate to `https://www.microsoft.com/en-us/microsoft-365/enterprise/compare-office-365-plans` and select **Try for free** under the **Office 365 E5** plan, as illustrated in the following screenshot:

Figure 1.9 – Office 365 trial subscription sign-up

Follow the steps to create an account, as shown in the following screenshot. If you have already created an account previously, you may need to use a different email address to obtain a free trial:

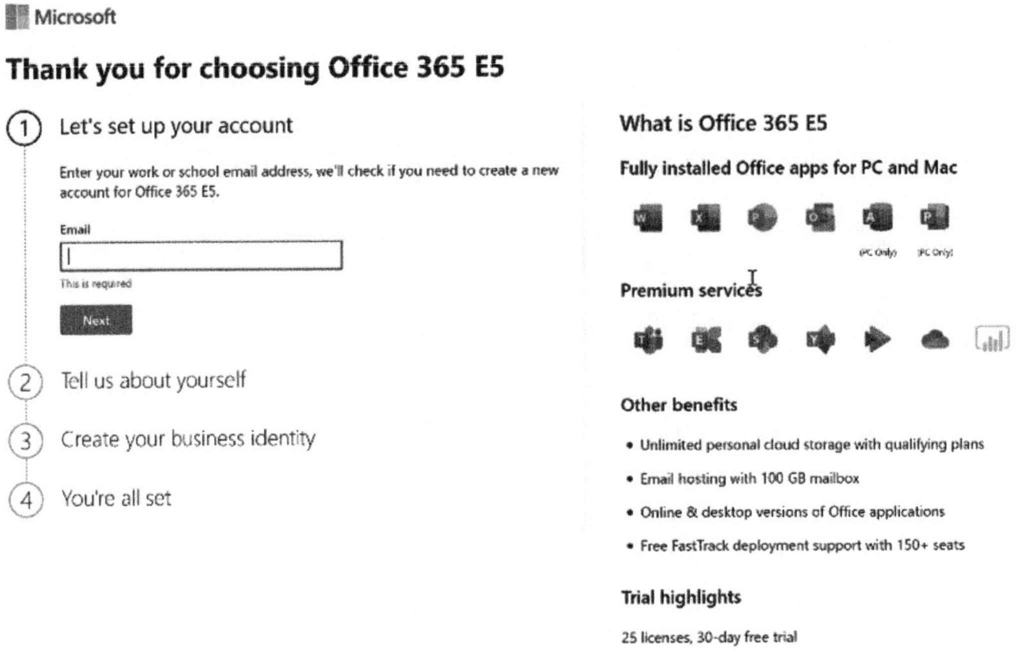

Figure 1.10 – Office 365 E5 subscription sign-up form

After completing the form and creating your Microsoft 365 tenant, you will have access to Microsoft 365 services and the administration panel. The next section will guide you through signing up for an additional add-on service that will be required to follow along with the exercises within this book and to provide full hands-on preparation for your exam.

Azure AD Premium subscription

In addition to the Office 365 E5 trial subscription, you will need access to an Azure AD Premium license for many of the advanced identity and access features that are discussed within the exam objectives. The best way to obtain these features is through an **Enterprise Mobility + Security (EMS) E5** license. Microsoft also offers this as a 30-day free trial. Follow these steps to set this up:

1. To get started, navigate to this link: `https://www.microsoft.com/en-us/ microsoft-365/enterprise-mobility-security/compare-plans- and-pricing`.

2. Then, select **Try now** under the **Enterprise Mobility + Security E5** plan, as shown in the following screenshot:

$14.80
user/month
(annual commitment)

Enterprise Mobility + Security E5

Try now >

Buy E5

Figure 1.11 – EMS E5 trial subscription sign-up

This is an add-on license to Microsoft 365, so you should enter the same email address that you used to sign up for the Office 365 E5 subscription in the box shown in the following screenshot:

Thank you for choosing **Enterprise Mobility + Security E5**

(1) **Let's set up your account**

Enter your work or school email address, we'll check if you need to create a new account for Enterprise Mobility + Security E5.

Enter your email address

Next

(2) Tell us about yourself

(3) Create your business identity

(4) You're all set

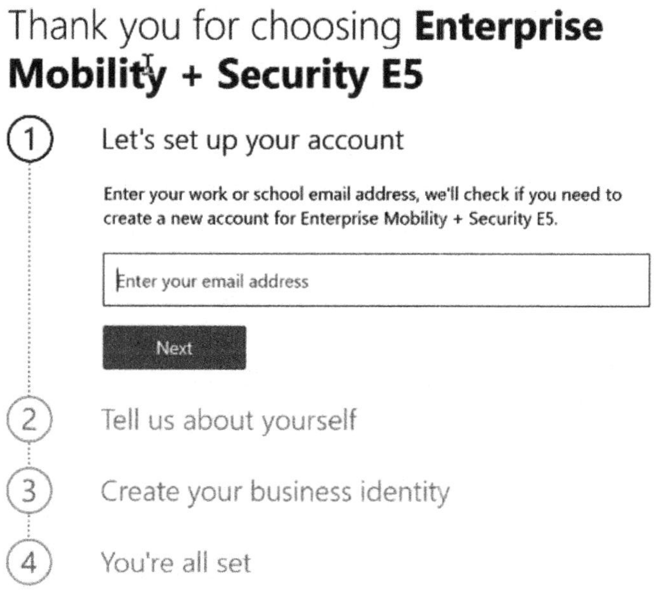

Figure 1.12 – EMS E5 subscription sign-up form

You should now have everything you need for your hands-on exam preparation and to follow along with the exercises within this book. The next section will provide an overview of the objectives that are covered in the exam and throughout this book.

Exam objectives

This book will cover the specific objectives of the *SC-300 Microsoft Identity and Access Administrator* exam. The structure of the book follows these objectives closely within the main sections. However, there is an added section on monitoring and management to provide additional emphasis as you move forward in a career as an *Identity and Access Administrator*.

As is the case with all Microsoft exams, each objective area is weighted differently. The weight of each objective is meant to be used as a guide to understanding the potential number of questions to expect in these areas of the exam. The objectives covered within the SC-300 exam are listed here:

Objective	Weight
Implement an identity management solution	25-30%
Implement an authentication and access management solution	25-30%
Implement access management for applications	10-15%
Plan and implement an identity governance strategy	25-30%

Table 1.1 – Exam objectives

Additional details on the topics that make up these objectives can be found at this link: `https://query.prod.cms.rt.microsoft.com/cms/api/am/binary/RE4Myp5`.

Understand that the weights do not mean that if an objective is weighted at 10%, you will only get 5 questions out of 50 in this area. Microsoft exams use a scoring scale of 1,000 based on the type of question and the objectives covered within the question. Many questions may have elements of multiple objectives and therefore be split into percentages. The weights of the objectives can help to understand the level of importance that is being placed on the objective.

Now that you know the objective areas being covered for this exam, you may be wondering how this exam and certification can assist in professional development and career advancement. The next section provides some insight into the types of roles that this exam highlights.

Who should take the SC-300 exam?

Now that you understand more about Microsoft exams, paths to learning, and the specific areas covered in the SC-300 exam, it is important to think about the roles that someone should have or want before preparing for this exam. The SC-300 exam is the Microsoft Identity and Access Administrator exam, so the focus is on the areas of protecting identities and implementing proper access roles for services within Microsoft 365, Azure, and hybrid infrastructures. The next chapter will go further into the importance of identity and access within cloud infrastructures. Anyone that has the goal of working with Microsoft cloud technologies will benefit from learning the objectives of this exam. This exam could also prepare you for an **Identity and Access Administrator** role as a career, as more organizations are requiring this role as they adopt more cloud-native applications within their environment.

Summary

In this chapter, we covered the areas that will prepare you for the *Identity and Access Administrator* exam and the setup required to follow along with the exercises covered within this book. We also provided an overview of what to expect when taking a Microsoft exam.

The next chapter will discuss the importance of **identity and access management (IAM)** and how it has evolved as cloud technologies have become more prevalent.

2
Defining Identity and Access Management

Now that you have had an overview of the **SC-300 Identity and Access Administrator** exam and what you need to prepare for the exam, it is important to understand **Identity and Access Management (IAM)**. This chapter will provide the foundational information that the topics of this book will be based on and will provide an understanding of where IAM has changed as *cloud technologies* have become more prevalent.

In this chapter, we're going to cover the following main topics:

- Understanding IAM
- Learning IAM use cases
- Understanding the scope of IAM
- The evolution of IAM

Understanding IAM

Before discussing the services and solutions that **Microsoft** has for IAM, it is important to understand the core concepts and why they are important. The concepts of IAM have been around for decades. Any time that you have created a username and a password, you have been engaging in some form of IAM. Let's break down the two components further.

Identity

Identity can be defined simply as *who you are*. Your identity starts with your *username*. This is your digital name for a particular site or application. Just as your first and last name identify you outside the digital world, your username identifies you to the website, application, or email tenant to which you are attempting to gain access. Most usernames are an alias of your actual name. It may be your full first and last name, your first initial with your last name, or something entirely random or custom. In many cases, it could also be an email address. Whatever this username is made of, it is what will identify you to the website, application, or email client.

The second part of your identity is generally a way to verify you are who you say you are. We will discuss different methods for this verification within this book, but the traditional manner of verification has been the use of a password. This verification is similar to a driver's license or a passport when asked to verify your age. The process of verifying your identity is also known as the process of **authentication**.

Access

Access comes after an identity has been verified. After a user has verified their identity, they can then be granted access to the requested resources. What they can view and interact with depends on the level of access, also known as **permissions** or **authorization**.

An example of this is having a *name badge* with your organization that is also used for building access. There may be doors that only certain members of the organization have permission to access with their badges. This is how access to digital services works with the configuration of access within a user's identity. The combination of the user's identity and what they have access to is the foundation of IAM.

The next section will go through some use cases for identity and access.

Learning identity and access use cases

Now that we understand the definitions of identity and access and how they work together, let's explore some examples that will assist in how this takes place.

Shopping websites

If you are reading this book, you most likely purchased it from a shopping website on the internet. It may have been purchased anonymously, without a username and password, but you may have used a site that you have used before that allows you to log in.

The benefit here is that having an identity on this site allows you to search for and save products in a cart. It would also provide you with an account that allows you to view your order history and track orders. Having this identity provides a customized experience when viewing the site that you otherwise would not have. The creators of the site have created the level of access that you have when you sign in with your identity.

Identity and access together provide this experience. The access permissions that are set allow the user to shop, save, and purchase products, but they are not able to see other sensitive information, such as other customer's and sales information, which is only available to users within the organization with access.

Now let's look at the way that identity and access work with an *email account*.

Personal email accounts

As stated in the previous section, identity is in many cases tied to an email address. An email address starts with the username or *alias*, and the second part is the *domain*. In a user's personal email account, this domain is going to be the email provider, such as `outlook.com`.

When you navigate to `outlook.com`, you do not have the ability to see your inbox until you sign in. This is accomplished by providing your username, which is the email address, and password. This the identity and access *verification* that you have the proper *credentials* to view the email account. Once you have provided this verification, you have the permissions of an email user to customize your inbox, calendar, to-do list, and any other services that are provided. You can also change the settings for the account, but you cannot change any application features or permissions for the account.

Within this account, not only is the username/email address the identity that is used to gain access to the inbox and calendar, this email address is a public identity that you can share with others. This is now the identity that you have for others to communicate with you through email.

The following screenshot shows the process of gaining access to an `outlook.com` account using a username, or email address, and password. This is how you would sign into Outlook:

Figure 2.1 – Sign into Outlook

This is followed up by inputting your email address, phone number, or username, as shown in the following screenshot:

Figure 2.2 – Enter your identity

Within the **Sign in** field, note that there is more than one option provided for an identity. As part of the authentication process, enter your password here:

Figure 2.3 – Password to confirm your identity

Once the authentication process is completed, we are then authorized to access our **Outlook** email inbox and calendar, as shown in the following screenshot:

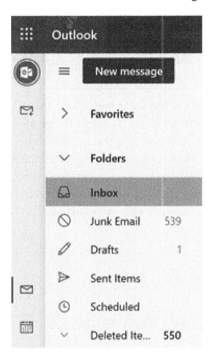

Figure 2.4 – Outlook inbox menu for email and calendar

Verifying your identity and access provides you with the permissions that the application has given to users of their service and the ability to use it to communicate. Let's now look at how identity and access work within a social media account.

Social media accounts

Social media accounts have their own way of utilizing identity. Unlike email accounts and shopping sites, where you typically use an email address for both your identity and access to the site, as well as your profile identity, social media accounts provide a level of separation between the two. With most social media accounts, you have a unique username, or *handle*, that is your public-facing identity. In order to verify that you own this identity and your access permissions, you have an email address tied to this username. This allows you to sign in to your social media account using either the username or email address and provide a password to verify your identity.

As part of your permissions to the social media account, you can customize your privacy settings to hide your email address from the public and only use the username to communicate. This is similar to having an unlisted phone number or address. As for access applied to social media accounts, your account allows you to provide the information that you want others to be able to see. In order to make changes to your account, you must utilize the identity and access mechanisms of username or email along with a password to verify who you are.

The screenshots that follow show the login pages for **LinkedIn**, **Twitter**, and **Facebook**. Similar to Outlook, there is more than one option for using a username for each of these social media accounts. These options include an email address, phone number, account username or alias, and even an identity from a different account type. When using a different IAM account to access a separate account, this is called a **business-to-consumer** (**B2C**), *federated trust* relationship. This will be discussed in more depth in *Chapter 5, Implementing and Managing External Identities and Guests*. The following screenshot is the login page of LinkedIn:

Figure 2.5 – LinkedIn sign-in screen

The next screenshot shows the login page of Twitter:

Figure 2.6 – Twitter sign-in screen

In the following screenshot, you can see what the login page of Facebook looks like:

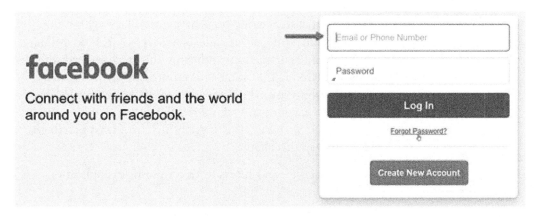

Figure 2.7 – Facebook sign-in screen

Up to this point in this section, use cases have been provided on how identity and access is used within the way that users access various aspects of technology for personal use that require creating an identity to access. The next use case will explain how identity and access are used in a company setting.

Company applications

As far as the objective topics of the **SC-300** exam are concerned, when discussing identity and access, we are usually discussing it in terms of accessing company-provided resources. As you progress in this book, how identity and access work within a company environment will become clear, but we will provide some initial background here.

When you join a company, you provide them with all of your **personal identifiable information** (**PII**) as part of the personnel onboarding. This includes information that makes up your identity, such as your name, address, phone number, social security number, driver's license, passport, and others. Many companies require two specific forms of identification to verify your identity as part of this process. Once you have provided verification of your identity to your company, you are given the ability to access company resources. This may be a badge that allows you to scan and open doors within the office building and your assigned digital identity to access your company *computer* and *applications*.

In the same manner as a personal email account, your digital identity within the company is an email address made of some variation of your name. Common examples include `firstname.lastname`, or your first initial with your last name along with the domain of the company, such as `firstname.lastname@companyname.com`. This becomes your identity for accessing company resources and your identity that everyone will use to communicate with you internally and externally.

What is important to understand is that depending on your status or level within the company, this identity will provide you with a different level of access to resources than others, who may be within a different department or authority. This is all verified when you use your identity in the morning to log into company resources with your email address and password. This verification allows the company systems to pull the level of access that has been assigned to your account and allows you to work with the required resources necessary to complete your job duties. This is the principle of **least privilege**, a concept that will be discussed later in this chapter.

The following diagram shows how identity and access to an on-premises application would take place:

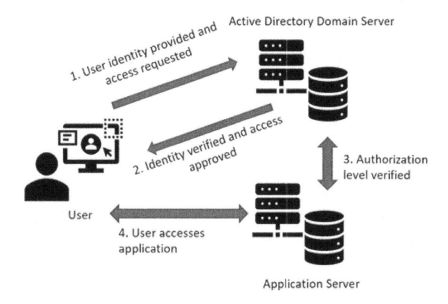

Figure 2.8 – Identity and access to on-premises applications

You should now have a better understanding of what is meant in terms of identity and access, and how it is used in various aspects of our digital lives. Now we will begin to build on that foundation to provide further understanding around the area of IAM.

Understanding the scope of IAM

The topics to this point of the chapter have defined identity and access, as well as provided *use cases* of where identity and access are utilized. In those use cases, the process of identity being verified, and access being granted, is IAM.

Defining IAM

Now that identity and access principles are understood, how do they relate to IAM? IAM is the process by which we assign roles to those users, groups, and resources to determine what permissions they have when they verify their identity. In other words, when a user verifies their identity, they are provided a level of access. IAM is that process of reviewing and providing those access permissions.

This is where the role of **identity and access administrator** becomes important. It is the role of this group to interact with executives and department supervisors to properly plan, define, assign, and test the roles that are required for every task within the organization and provide them with the proper levels of access necessary to perform their duties. Without proper planning and communication, access permissions could be inadequate for users to complete work requirements, or worse, they may have elevated permissions that allow them to access information that they are not authorized to view.

The overall planning and implementation process will be covered in subsequent chapters, but it is important to understand this scope and the importance of properly planning for the access roles required within the company.

Principle of least privilege

When designing and scoping the company roles for IAM, the *principle of least privilege* should always be at the forefront of the discussion. This is the concept that any user or resource only has access to the applications, resources, and information that they require to perform their specific duties. Anything above that could be a vulnerability and a potential threat to the company that sensitive information could be leaked to those that should not be allowed to view it.

The purpose of IAM is to ensure that any user, group, or resource has been properly assigned roles and access that adhere to this principle. This should be properly documented by job title with role assignments, and the roles should be reviewed regularly with department owners to verify that the assignments are still accurate and valid. When we discuss creating users and groups in a later chapter, we will discuss options for creating role assignments in a dynamic, auto-assigned manner, and how to automate the review of these roles.

As you continue through this book and when you perform your duties as an identity and access administrator, you must always be thinking about the principle of least privilege. This is the foundation of IAM.

We will close this chapter by discussing where IAM started and how it has evolved with cloud technologies.

The evolution of IAM

Now that you understand more about IAM, how it is used in our daily lives, and the importance of protecting our resources with IAM, it is important to understand how IAM has changed as people and companies have continued to use more applications and resources in the cloud.

This section will discuss the evolution of IAM at a high level. This will provide a better level of understanding in terms of the importance of IAM and how it is changing with the increasingly growing role of cloud technologies within companies and for personal use. Three stages are discussed when talking about IAM: **traditional**, **advanced**, and **optimal**. We will go through each of these in detail.

Traditional

Traditional IAM is how IAM was handled prior to cloud technologies. As a company, all applications and user identities were within a private *data center*. Users that connected to resources did so through secure **virtual private network** (**VPN**) connections into the data center to access resources. Therefore, the focus of the company was to protect the physical building and *network perimeter* from threats and attacks to protect the applications, data, and identities. All identities were protected within the enclosed private data center, and if *bad actors* did not gain access through the perimeter, physical or virtual, they were protected.

In this scenario, the company is not utilizing cloud applications within the business, so there is no requirement for *single sign-on* for on-premises and cloud applications. IAM for applications was provided through an on-premises server, **Windows Active Directory** in a Microsoft environment, that managed user and group access through *Group Policy* to avoid elevated access. Since IAM was under the full control of the company, usernames and passwords were generally the only form of verification that was used to gain access to applications and data.

Advanced

With the onset and expansion of cloud technologies, companies started to find that their level of control shifted. The physical and network perimeter was no longer the single entry point to company data and identities. The flexibility of the cloud allowed companies to subscribe to business applications rather than making large investments in server and network hardware. However, due to existing large investments in on-premises hardware and software, there was still a requirement to maintain non-cloud *legacy applications*. This new company *ecosystem* created challenges for companies. Usernames and passwords were now being managed in multiple places to support application access. The user experience became more challenging with the need to *authenticate* to applications differently depending upon whether they were on-premises or in the cloud. New *threats* emerged, targeting identities through *phishing* and *dictionary attacks* to attempt to gain access to critical business data or steal personal information.

To address these challenges, new, more advanced IAM capabilities were required. To bridge the gap between on-premises and cloud authentication, *open source protocols* were established, such as **Security Assertion Markup Language (SAML)** and **OAuth**, to allow for *federation* to on-premises directory services. The federation of these systems created a single sign-on user experience but also created additional security challenges. No longer were our identities located within a company data center's control; they were also located within these new cloud applications, creating a higher level of risk to compromised or stolen identities. In order to protect the identities of users, additional security requirements are needed, such as **mulit-factor authentication** for administrators and *Conditional Access policies* for access to certain applications.

The IAM techniques to federate cloud and on-premises identities provided gated access through conditional policies, and the use of analytics to improve our visibility to potential identity theft are all aspects of advanced forms of IAM and *modern authentication*.

Optimal

Once a company has begun the journey to federate cloud and on-premises infrastructures in a federated manner with modern authentication, they can look to get to the optimal level of IAM. To perform at the optimal level of IAM, a company must embrace the modern authentication capabilities that are available through Microsoft and other providers. They should review the recommendations that are found through the advanced analytics regarding user and device behavior, *security best practices* and *baselines*, and security and *compliance* levels for the various cloud applications that they are utilizing. From this information, they can justify the requirements and enforce *multi-factor authentication* for all users, not just administrators, and require dynamic Conditional Access policies based on real-time user behavior and device compliance. As companies move to this optimal level of IAM, **password-less authentication** becomes more accessible and usable throughout the organization.

Performing at the optimal level of IAM does not happen quickly and easily, especially if the company is utilizing legacy applications and devices with older operating systems. Companies must embrace modern authentication through their app development, and update and upgrade applications and operating systems that do not currently support it.

The following table summarizes the key points in the evolution of IAM:

Traditional	Advanced	Optimal
On-premises identity No SSO is present between cloud and on-premises apps Visibility into identity risk is very limited	Cloud identity federates with on-premises systems Conditional Access policies gate access and provide remediation actions Analytics improve visibility	Password-less authentication is enabled User, device, location, and behavior are analyzed in real time to determine risk and deliver ongoing protection MFA is enforced

Table 2.1 – Levels of IAM

These advanced and optimal concepts will be described in detail in later sections of this book. As you continue the journey through this book, it will guide you through the services and solutions that can move an organization to the optimal levels of IAM.

Summary

In this chapter, we covered the foundational understanding of IAM. We defined what identity and access are as they pertain to how you would authenticate to applications and be authorized to view information. In addition, we discussed the evolution of IAM as companies begin to adopt a hybrid infrastructure of on-premises and cloud technologies. This evolution has led to modern authentication solutions that further protect identities and our vulnerabilities from threats. These modern authentication solutions will be the focus of many of the topics as you continue through this book and prepare to take the Identity and Access Administrator exam.

The next chapter will begin to discuss *Azure Active Directory* and the role that it plays in cloud IAM. We will explore the configuration and setup of Azure Active Directory for IAM roles, custom domains, and tenant settings.

Section 2 - Implementing an Identity Management Solution

This section will focus on the planning and execution of an identity management solution. This will include planning for identities in Microsoft 365, Azure Active Directory, and hybrid infrastructures.

This section of the book comprises the following chapters:

- *Chapter 3, Implementing and Configuring Azure Active Directory*
- *Chapter 4, Creating, Configuring, and Managing Identities*
- *Chapter 5, Implementing and Managing External Identities and Guests*
- *Chapter 6, Implementing and Managing Hybrid Identities*

3
Implementing and Configuring Azure Active Directory

Now that you understand **identity and access management** and how it has evolved with the use and adoption of cloud technologies, this chapter will focus on how to implement Microsoft's cloud identity service, **Azure Active Directory** (**AAD**). This chapter will explain the base levels of implementing and configuring the tenant, domain, users, and devices. Later chapters will go deeper into some of these topics.

In this chapter, we're going to cover the following main topics:

- Configuring and managing AAD roles
- Configuring and managing custom domains
- Configuring and managing device registration options
- Configuring tenant-wide settings

Technical requirements

In this chapter, we will begin to explore configuring a tenant for the use of **Microsoft 365** and **AAD**. There will be exercises that will require access to AAD If you have not yet created the trial licenses for Microsoft 365, please follow the directions provided within *Chapter 1, Preparing for Your Microsoft Exam*.

Configuring and managing AAD roles

This section will get us started with the various roles that are required to complete configuration tasks and manage the Azure Active Directory tenant. Azure Active Directory is the cloud identity service within Microsoft that handles all user, device, and service identity and access management for Microsoft 365, Azure, **Dynamics 365**, and **Power Platform**. When you create an account or *tenant* within Microsoft, you are creating an Azure Active Directory account. This section will focus on the planning, configuring, and managing of various role assignments that are required to support the **Azure Active Directory tenant**.

Azure Active Directory tenant

When signing up for services within Microsoft 365 and/or Azure, you are required to create a unique tenant. The tenant serves as your company identity within Azure Active Directory. It is important to note that when you sign up and create the name of your tenant, this name cannot be changed. After the name of the tenant has been selected, Azure Active Directory provides a *domain name* that includes that tenant. This domain name will be `tenantname.onmicrosoft.com`. This is a **fully qualified domain name** (**FQDN**) that can be used externally for email and website addresses.

Most companies have their own registered FQDN that they would like to use, such as `companyname.com`. The process for configuring and registering these domain names in Azure Active Directory will be discussed later in this chapter. Until this custom domain has been verified within the Azure Active Directory tenant, users and resources will use `tenantname.onmicrosoft.com` as their domain identity. Now that we understand what makes up the tenant, let's discuss **Azure Active Directory roles**.

Azure Active Directory roles

In the previous chapter, the process of authentication and authorization was discussed within **IAM**. A key component of the authorization of a user, group, or resource is the role that is assigned. The IAM role defines what that identity is authorized to access and the level at which it can interact with resources within the scope of the role. Let's break down the components of a role within Azure Active Directory.

As previously stated, the role determines the level of authorization a user, group, or resource has within Azure Active Directory. When an employee is added to Azure Active Directory, by default, they are given the *role* of user if they are part of the company tenant or guest if they are invited from an external tenant. If that employee requires some level of management or administration within the tenant, then an additional role or roles may be required to authorize them to perform these tasks.

The following screenshot shows the list of built-in roles that are available within **Azure Active Directory**:

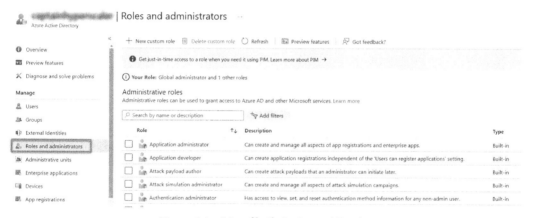

Figure 3.1 – List of built-in Azure AD roles

Within each built-in role, there is a pre-defined set of *permissions*, as shown in the following screenshot:

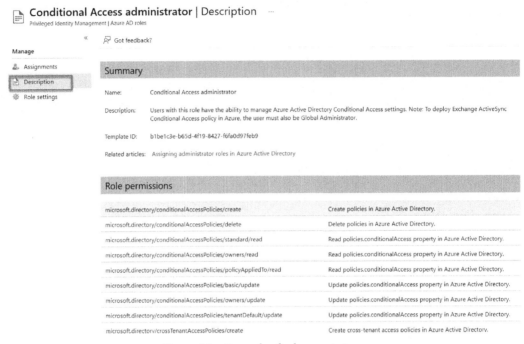

Figure 3.2 – Example of role permissions

A user, group, or resource may be assigned more than one built-in role as their access permissions within the tenant. If you require a more restrictive role than what is provided within the built-in roles, then you can create a **custom role**. For custom roles, as shown in *Figure 3.3*, the permissions are set based on the requirements that you, as the identity and access administrator, have determined are necessary:

New custom role   ...

All roles

 Got feedback?

Basics   **Permissions**   Review + create

Add permissions for this custom role. Currently, permissions for Application registrations and Enterprise applications are supported in custom roles. Learn more

Search by permission name or description	

Permission	↑↓	Description
microsoft.directory/applicationPolicies/allProperties/read		Read all properties of application policies.
microsoft.directory/applicationPolicies/allProperties/update		Update all properties of application policies.
microsoft.directory/applicationPolicies/basic/update		Update standard properties of application policies.
microsoft.directory/applicationPolicies/create		Create application policies.
microsoft.directory/applicationPolicies/createAsOwner		Create application policies. Creator is added as first owner.
microsoft.directory/applicationPolicies/delete		Delete application policies.
microsoft.directory/applicationPolicies/owners/read		Read owners on application policies.
microsoft.directory/applicationPolicies/owners/update		Update the owner property of application policies.
microsoft.directory/applicationPolicies/policyAppliedTo/read		Read application policies applied to objects list.
microsoft.directory/applicationPolicies/standard/read		Read standard properties of application policies.
microsoft.directory/applications.myOrganization/allProperties/read		Read all properties of single-directory applications.

Previous   Next

Figure 3.3 – Permission settings for a custom role

When creating a custom role, it is important to understand the required tasks that a user, group, or resource needs to be able to execute. Knowing this information and planning the role assignments properly will decrease the number of potential support requests from users that cannot access resources that they need to complete daily tasks. The next section will provide some guidance for *planning* and *assigning* roles.

Planning and assigning roles

In the previous chapter, the principle of *least privilege* was discussed. When planning and assigning roles to users, groups, and resources, utilizing the principle of least privilege should be the baseline for determining permissions. The primary goal within our planning process is to limit the number of administrators in order to decrease the attack surface in the case of an identity breach. The **identity and access administrator** should identify those users, groups, and resources that require permanent administrator roles and verify this requirement with stakeholders. These requirements should be reviewed regularly to verify that they are still relevant. If certain users or groups only require administrative permissions on a temporary basis, then they should be assigned an administrator role on a just-in-time basis. The concept of just-in-time administrator roles will be discussed in *Chapter 13, Planning and Implementing Privileged Access and Access Reviews*.

Azure Active Directory roles are governed by the overall tenant in which they are assigned. If you have multiple subscriptions or domains within the tenant, the assigned Azure Active Directory roles will be inherited. Some of the more widely used roles include *Global Administrator, Billing Administrator, Helpdesk Administrator, Security Administrator, Compliance Administrator*, and *User Administrator*. The Global Administrator has full administrative control over the tenant. A best practice is that there is redundancy in this role assignment while also avoiding misuse of this role. The recommendation is that you have more than two but less than five Global Administrators within your tenant. Other users that require administrator-level access can be given more direct roles based on the principle of least privilege. To find out more about built-in roles and their capabilities, please review the Microsoft Docs page: `https://docs.microsoft.com/en-us/azure/active-directory/roles/permissions-reference`.

This page provides the full list of built-in roles within Azure Active Directory and includes a link for each of the roles to show the full set of permissions that role provides to the user. When planning and assigning roles, or preparing for the exam, it is important to understand where the common roles listed previously are required and what permissions they have for services.

For example, the Billing Administrator, User Administrator, and Helpdesk Administrator have similar capabilities when it comes to licenses, user management, and support tickets. However, only the Billing Administrator can add licenses to the tenant, and the User Administrator is the only role in this example that can create users and groups. Each of these roles can assign licenses to users and groups, review service health, and create a support ticket with Microsoft. When planning a role for a user or group, it is important to understand the differences and map the role assignment based on the tasks that user or group will be required to complete.

> **Note: Azure Active Directory and role-based access control (RBAC)**
>
> The scope of the Identity and Access Administrator exam focuses on roles and permissions within Azure Active Directory. However, as an identity and access administrator that works with Azure resources, you should be familiar with **role-based access control**, or **RBAC**. RBAC provides resource-level permissions that are assigned within the resources rather than at the Azure Active Directory level. The terminology changes from the use of Administrator to Owner, Contributor, and Reader. Azure Active Directory roles and RBAC will co-exist within the Microsoft cloud. If you have Azure resources, you will want to plan and determine whether to utilize Azure AD or RBAC for access and permission to subscriptions, resource groups, or individual resources. RBAC roles for managing IAM provide a resource-focused approach to IAM.

The importance of planning cannot be stressed enough when determining role assignments within your organization. As an identity and access administrator, meeting with stakeholders and managers to discuss the tasks required by users and groups within the company is the first step in building a tenant that provides a baseline of security and principle of least privilege, while also allowing users and groups to perform the tasks required to execute the job requirements.

When the planning is complete for user and group role assignments, you are ready to assign those roles. This can be completed through the **Roles and administrators** menu in Azure Active Directory, within the user account, by creating a group that is assigned a role or roles, and using the PowerShell command. Each of these options is provided in the following screenshots.

Figure 3.4 demonstrates assigning a role. You would assign a role to a user or users from the list of roles by selecting the role that you want to assign:

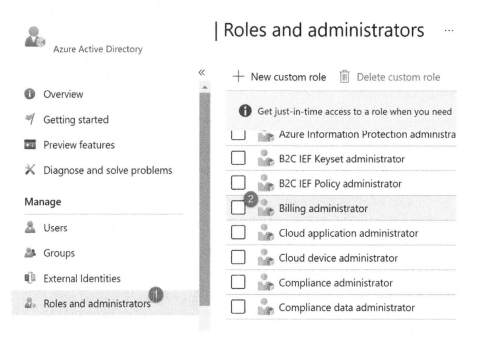

Figure 3.4 – Assigning a role

Next, you would select **+ Add assignments**, as seen in the following screenshot:

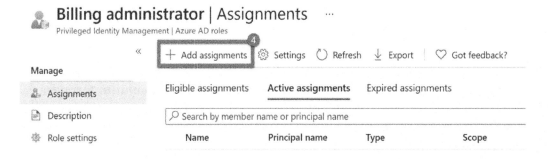

Figure 3.5 – Add assignment from the list of roles

Within the user information in Azure Active Directory, you can also assign a role to that user, as shown in the following screenshot:

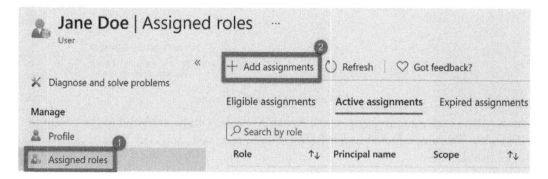

Figure 3.6 – Add an assignment from a user account

If you require the role to be assigned to a group of users, then you can create a group with an Azure Active Directory assigned to that group: `https://docs.microsoft.com/en-us/azure/active-directory/roles/groups-concept`.

To complete this task, within Azure Active Directory, select **Groups**, as shown in the following screenshot:

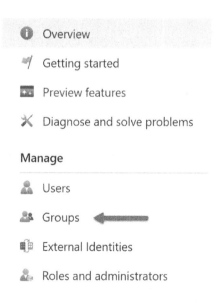

Figure 3.7 – Manage groups in Azure AD

And then you can select **+ New group** as seen here:

Figure 3.8 – Create a new group

In the tile to create a new group, move **Azure AD roles can be assigned to the group** to **Yes**, select **No roles selected** under **Roles**, select a role, save, and click **Create**. All of this is demonstrated here:

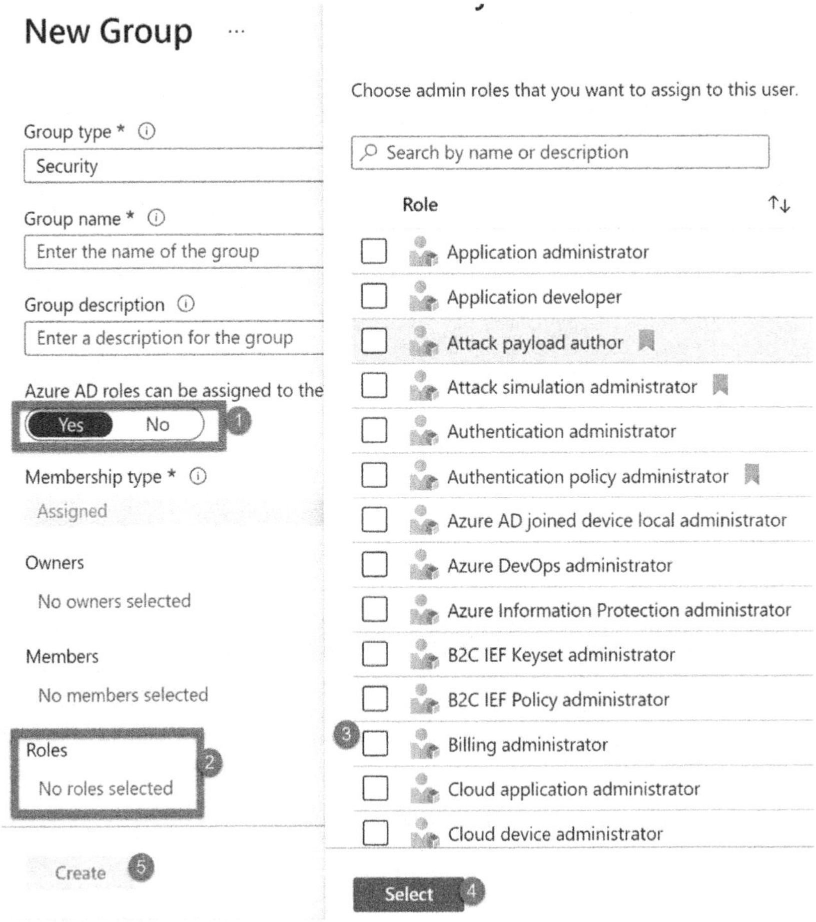

Figure 3.9 – Assign a role to the Azure AD group

In addition to the previous examples of assigning roles within the Azure Active Directory portal, roles can also be assigned using PowerShell with the following commands. These steps can also be found at this link: https://docs.microsoft.com/en-us/powershell/module/msonline/add-msolrolemember?view=azureadps-1:

1. Open PowerShell and install the PowerShell module for Azure AD using the following:

   ```
   Install-module MSOnline
   ```

2. Connect to Azure with your username and password as follows:

   ```
   Connect-MsolService
   ```

3. Next, you will assign that role to a user using the following command:

   ```
   Add-MsolRoleMember -RoleName "[Administrator role name]"
   -RoleMemberEmailAddress "[email address]"
   ```

Once you have established the permissions of users and groups within your tenant based on the tasks that they will need to execute within the tenant, you will want to have a custom domain, most likely for your tenant, that establishes your company brand. The next section will discuss how to **configure**, **validate**, and **manage** a custom domain.

Configuring and managing custom domains

We have planned and assigned our key administrator roles within our organization, now we should determine how we are going to brand our company. When creating a tenant *subscription* within Microsoft 365 or Azure, the domain that is registered is tenantname.onmicrosoft.com. This domain becomes a permanent part of the Azure Active Directory tenant and cannot be removed. The domain is public and can be used for sending and receiving emails, and for users to log in to Microsoft services. However, most companies prefer to have a more recognized naming convention for their company domain. To accomplish this, these custom domains must be registered and verified within Azure Active Directory.

Adding and verifying a custom domain to set as the primary domain

As was stated previously, when you create your Microsoft subscription, you create a name for your tenant that becomes your primary domain for your subscription. This uses onmicrosoft.com as the verified portion of the domain with the name of the tenant in front of it. For example, mycompany.onmicrosoft.com. Once this tenant is created, it cannot be changed. In order to utilize a more recognized branded domain, such as mycompany.com, you will have to go through some steps to verify that domain within Microsoft and with your domain registrar.

If you want this domain to be utilized publicly for email and websites, you must first purchase the domain from a domain registrar. The domain registrar is a broker for checking, validating, and certifying the use of a domain. Microsoft provides the option to buy a domain within the Microsoft 365 admin center, or you can utilize an external domain registrar, such as **GoDaddy.com**. Within the **Microsoft 365 admin center** menu, navigate to the **Settings** drop-down arrow, and then choose **Domains**. The following screenshot shows the **Buy domain** option within the **Domains** settings in the **Microsoft 365 admin center**:

Domains

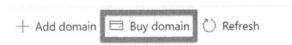

Figure 3.10 – Buy a domain from Microsoft

When you buy your domain directly from Microsoft, this domain will be ready for use without any additional configuration required. The following steps will focus on configuration for an external domain registrar:

1. If you are purchasing, or have purchased, a domain from an external domain registrar, within the same **Domains** settings tile, select **+ Add domain** to add a domain that you own. The following screenshot shows this option in the tile:

Domains

Figure 3.11 – Add a domain that is currently owned

2. From here, the wizard in the admin center will step you through the process of adding the custom domain. Once this custom domain has been added, this domain can be used as the default domain for the company and user email addresses. Next are the steps to complete this verification.

3. Within the **Microsoft 365 admin center** menu, navigate to the **Settings** drop-down arrow and then choose **Domains**.

4. From this tile, select **+ Add domain** to add a domain that you own. *Figure 3.11* illustrates this step.

5. A step-by-step wizard will open. Follow the steps provided. The first of these steps is to enter the domain name that you want to verify and select **Use this domain** as shown in the following screenshot:

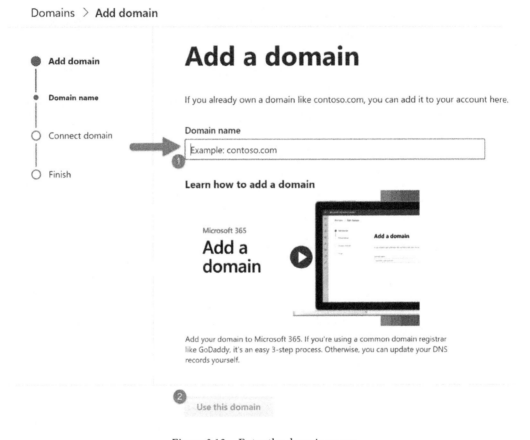

Figure 3.12 – Enter the domain name

6. After identifying the domain to add, you will need to connect the Microsoft account with the domain registrar. To accomplish this, the recommended step is to use the **TXT record** from Microsoft as shown here:

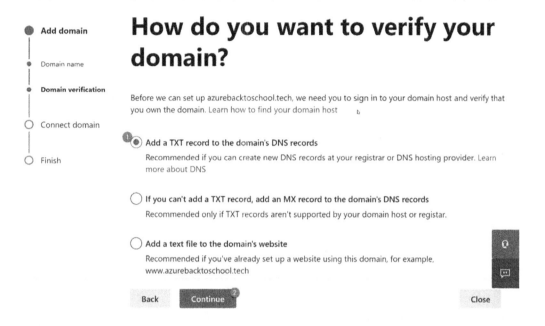

Figure 3.13 – Add a TXT record to the domain registrar

7. After selecting **Continue**, the TXT information will be provided, and you will be instructed to go to your domain registrar and add the provided information shown in *Figure 3.14*. There is also a link on this tile for step-by-step instructions, for additional help. Here is the link to that page in **Microsoft Docs**: `https://docs.microsoft.com/en-us/microsoft-365/admin/get-help-with-domains/create-dns-records-at-any-dns-hosting-provider?view=o365-worldwide#BKMK_verify`:

Figure 3.14 – Information needed for the domain registrar

8. This next step will require you to log in to your *domain registrar* or company that hosts your domain. When you log in to your domain registrar, navigate to your domain, select the option to manage the domain, and then find the TXT records for the domain. From here, you will want to select **Add Record**. The following screenshot illustrates what this looks like on `bluehost.com`:

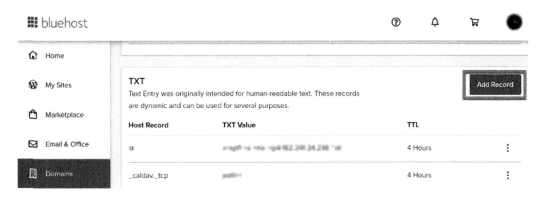

Figure 3.15 – Example of how to add a TXT record to a domain registrar

9. Enter the information provided from *step 7* and select **Save**, as shown in the following screenshot:

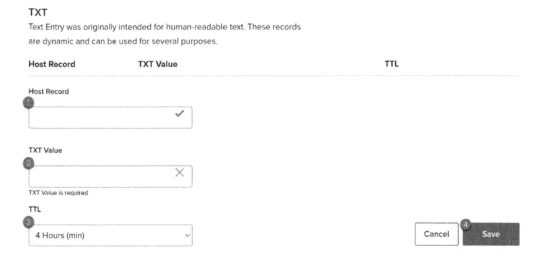

Figure 3.16 – Enter TXT information from Microsoft

10. After you have completed *step 9*, return to the **Microsoft admin center** and select **Verify**. The next tile will provide you with additional information. Simply select **Continue** and you will be directed to the **Add DNS records** tile. This tile allows you to configure the new domain for email protection. Through the verification process, the information needed should be populated as follows:

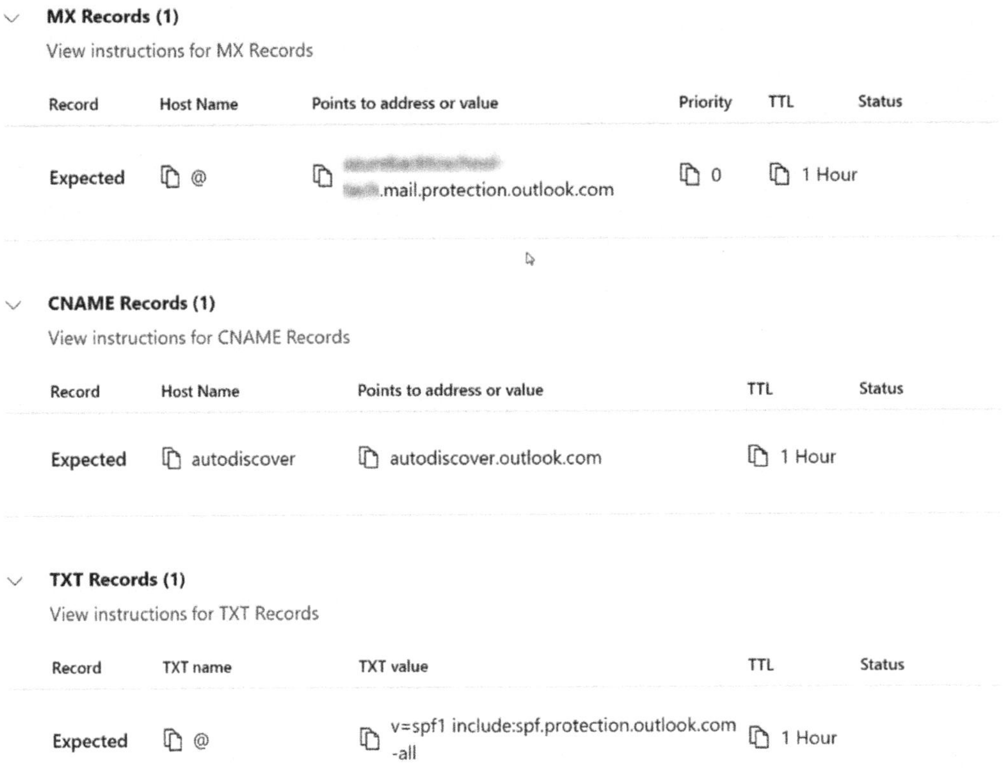

MX Records (1)

View instructions for MX Records

Record	Host Name	Points to address or value	Priority	TTL	Status
Expected	@	.mail.protection.outlook.com	0	1 Hour	

CNAME Records (1)

View instructions for CNAME Records

Record	Host Name	Points to address or value	TTL	Status
Expected	autodiscover	autodiscover.outlook.com	1 Hour	

TXT Records (1)

View instructions for TXT Records

Record	TXT name	TXT value	TTL	Status
Expected	@	v=spf1 include:spf.protection.outlook.com -all	1 Hour	

Figure 3.17 – Exchange Online Protection information

11. Return to the domain registrar and populate the information provided. This is only necessary if you plan on utilizing the **Exchange** or **Exchange Online Protection** services. If this domain is only being used for website addresses and not email, you can uncheck the **Exchange and Exchange Online Protection** box and select **Continue**:

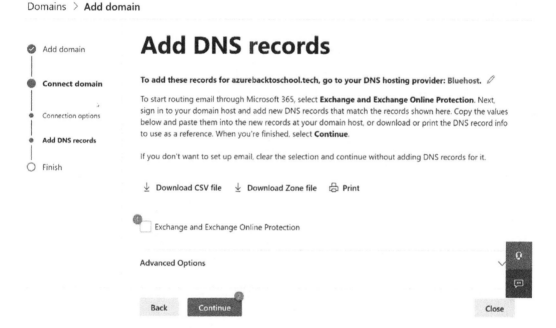

Figure 3.18 – Add domain without Exchange email

> **Note**
>
> If you choose to uncheck this box and continue, your domain will be verified but will not be available through Microsoft for email or other services since DNS will not be configured between Microsoft and the domain registrar. This process can be revisited by going to **Domains**, choosing the domain, selecting **DNS**, and then **Manage DNS**.

12. If you are using this domain for email, return to the domain registrar and enter the information provided in *Figure 3.18* from step *8*. Continue to step *11*.

13. Once you have configured the email protection records, select the checkbox for **Exchange and Exchange Online Protection** and select **Continue** as seen here:

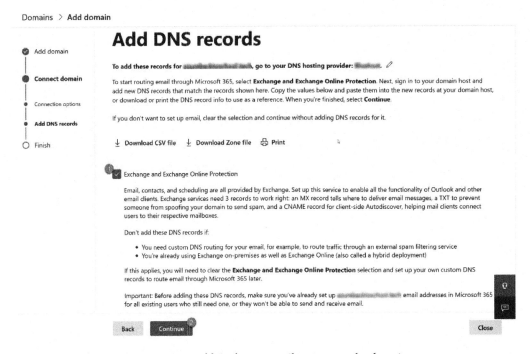

Figure 3.19 – Add Exchange email support to the domain

14. The domain setup is now complete, so select **Done** to exit the wizard, as illustrated here:

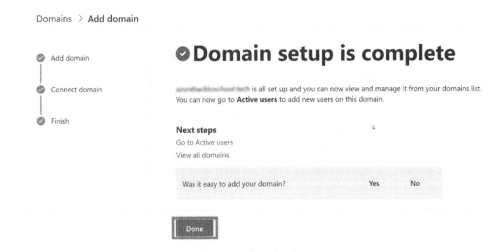

Figure 3.20 – Complete the domain setup

15. You will be directed to your list of domains and will now see your new custom domain in the list. From here, you can choose to make your newly verified domain your default. The following screenshot illustrates how to do this:

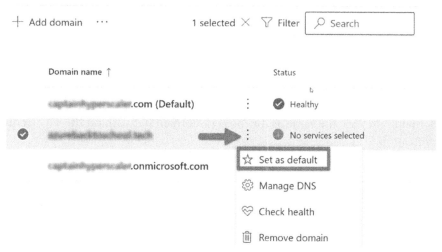

Figure 3.21 – Set the new domain as the default

You have now gone through the steps to add and verify a new custom domain. In the next section, we will discuss how these custom domains can now be used within Microsoft 365, Azure, and Azure Active Directory.

Custom domains and sub-domains

As stated in the previous section, most companies want to have proper branding usage with their domain to provide a professional appearance to visitors of the website and email addresses outside the default `tenantname.onmicrosoft.com` address that is provided upon initial subscription creation. This branded custom domain is usually something that is easy to remember, such as `companyname.com`. For this section, we will refer to this as the **root domain**.

Once we have gone through the steps in the previous section to verify the root domain, we can use that domain within our Azure Active Directory tenant for Microsoft 365 and Azure services. Microsoft can manage up to 900 domain names within Azure Active Directory. If you are federating domains with on-premises Active Directory, this goes down to 450 domains.

Once you verify a root domain, we can add various sub-domains that can be used by department or geography to segment the organization. Examples of department sub-domains may be `sales.mycompany.com` or `support.mycompany.com`. Geographic sub-domain examples could be `us.mycompany.com`, `uk.mycompany.com`, or `au.mycompany.com`. These subdomains can all be used to easily direct to specific internet or intranet sites that are specific to those visitors or users, respectively.

These sub-domains can be created and customized in any manner that the company feels is best to utilize them. If they are strictly for internal use and do not need access across the internet, they can be created and used immediately. In most cases, even for an intranet site, users may require accessing and authenticating them across the public internet. In this use case, the sub-domain DNS will need to be added to the domain registrar for proper access. The following screenshots are the steps to add the DNS for the sub-domain. They are the same as for the root domain but without the TXT requirement for verification:

1. From the **Domains** tile, select **+ Add domain:**

Domains

Figure 3.22 – Add a sub-domain

2. Enter in the sub-domain. This is in the form of `subdomain.mycompany.com`, with `mycompany.com` being a previously verified root domain within Microsoft. After entering the **domain name**, select **Use this domain** as shown here:

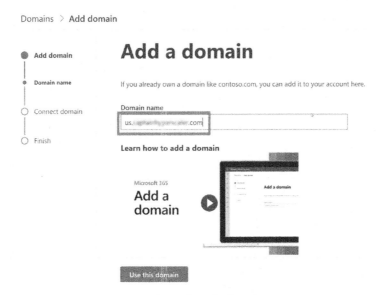

Figure 3.23 – Enter the sub-domain name

3. The next tile will explain the need to configure DNS. Select **Next** and the next tile will provide you with the DNS information that needs to be added to the domain registrar. Note at the top of the tile that this step will automatically prompt you to log in to your domain registrar to add the following information:

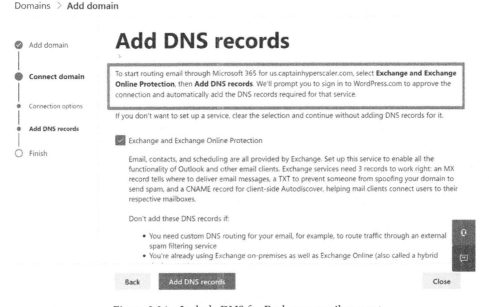

Figure 3.24 – Include DNS for Exchange email support

4. Select **Add DNS records** to continue, as seen in the following screenshot:

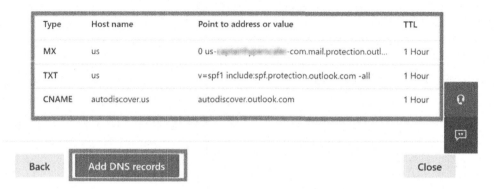

Type	Host name	Point to address or value	TTL
MX	us	0 us-⬛⬛⬛⬛⬛⬛-com.mail.protection.outl...	1 Hour
TXT	us	v=spf1 include:spf.protection.outlook.com -all	1 Hour
CNAME	autodiscover.us	autodiscover.outlook.com	1 Hour

Back   Add DNS records   Close

Figure 3.25 – DNS records to add for the sub-domain

5. Log in to the domain registrar and select **Confirm** to make the required changes to add the sub-domain DNS, as follows:

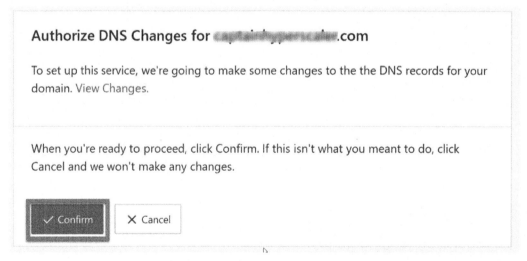

Authorize DNS Changes for ⬛⬛⬛⬛⬛.com

To set up this service, we're going to make some changes to the the DNS records for your domain. View Changes.

When you're ready to proceed, click Confirm. If this isn't what you meant to do, click Cancel and we won't make any changes.

✓ Confirm   ✕ Cancel

Figure 3.26 – Authorize the DNS changes for the domain registrar

6. The final step is to finish the configuration process. You will be returned to the main **Domain** tile and your sub-domain will be available. As you probably noticed, since the root domain was previously verified, the manual process from the previous section to add DNS to the domain registrar was no longer required, making it much easier to add a sub-domain than a new root domain.

The previous sections focused on how to add a custom domain and a sub-domain along with how these may be used within the company. There may be a need to make changes to these domains or remove these domains from your tenant. The next section will provide information on how this can be done.

Managing DNS and deleting a custom domain

In most cases, a company that purchases a primary domain, such as `mycompany.com`, will own that domain for the life of the company. Even though the domain for the company does not change, the domain registrar may change. In this case, the *DNS* will need to be reconfigured for the new domain registrar.

In some cases, a secondary domain may also no longer be needed. For example, the company may be running a sales promotion that has its own verified root domain that was used, or the company may have purchased another company with a brand that no longer exists. In these cases, the domain may need to be deleted from the Microsoft account to avoid use.

Deleting the custom domain can be completed within the Azure Active Directory or Microsoft 365 admin portals. Before deleting the custom domain, it is important to make sure that no users or applications are assigned to that domain. These resources include the following:

- Any user that has a username or email address that uses the custom domain
- Any group that has an email address that uses the custom domain name
- Any application that is registered in Azure AD and is using the custom domain name as its URI

These users, groups, and applications will need to be changed to a different domain name or deleted prior to deleting the custom domain name.

Rather than searching for and finding resources that are utilizing the custom domain name, the `ForceDelete` command can be used in situations where less than 1,000 resources are utilizing the custom domain name. Using `ForceDelete` will remove the custom domain name from resources and reassign the default initial `tenantname.onmicrosoft.com` to those resources.

Now that you have configured your Microsoft 365 and Azure tenant for a company-branded domain, we will discuss in the next section how **Azure AD** can also be used to register devices to Azure AD.

Configuring and managing device registration options

Securing identity and access for users, groups, and resources has become an important aspect of utilizing cloud services. Since organizations that utilize cloud services are no longer the owners of and responsible parties for the physical cloud infrastructure, identity and access have become the perimeter control plane for protection. In the past, we protected device access through the use of VPN connections into the private data center. In hybrid or public architectures, this is no longer the best option. The requirement to register our devices to Azure AD helps to bridge the security control gap. The following sections will discuss more about the process and capabilities that are provided when registering devices to Azure AD.

Azure AD-registered devices

Whether a company has supplied their users with devices, or a device is a personally owned **bring your own device (BYOD)**, a company may require the device to be registered to access company resources. For cloud-only or cloud-first companies, this would require the device to be registered with Azure AD. Registering a device with Azure AD does not require the user account to be used to sign in to the device but will require users to access a company portal to access company apps and resources.

Devices that are registered to Azure AD can be further managed using **mobile device management (MDM)** or **mobile application management (MAM)** to protect sensitive information and applications through **Conditional Access (CA)** policies. MDM, MAM, and CA policies will be further discussed in later chapters.

The important detail to remember is that for Azure AD-registered devices, the user account is not used to access the device, but a company portal for apps and services. This option is best for devices that may be accessed by multiple users for applications in the company portal, or for personal devices where a user has a personal account to log in to the device. This option is also necessary when Azure AD-joined configuration is not an option, such as with **macOS**, **iOS**, **Android**, or **Windows 10 Home** devices. Additional information on Azure AD-registered devices can be found at this link: `https://docs.microsoft.com/en-us/azure/active-directory/devices/concept-azure-ad-register`.

In the next sections, we will discuss scenarios where user accounts are used for device access and authentication.

Azure AD-joined devices

The next option for device configuration in Azure AD is for these devices to be Azure AD joined. In this scenario, a user account on the company Azure AD is used to sign in to the device and that authorizes that user to access the company resources from that device. Azure AD-joined devices are used for cloud-only or cloud-first companies, similar to Azure AD-registered devices, but the company user accounts are set up on these devices and required to unlock the device.

With an Azure AD-joined device, the company can utilize additional login options, such as **Windows Hello for Business** on Windows 10 devices. Like Azure AD-registered devices, Azure AD-joined devices can also be managed through MDM/MAM and CA policies for additional layers of security.

The primary use scenario for a device to be Azure AD joined is when the company needs to secure and encrypt the device when applications and files are native to that device. This option can be used for any **Windows 10** operating system with the exception of Windows 10 Home and is the preferred option when configuring a company-owned device. Additional information on Azure AD-joined devices can be found at this link: `https://docs.microsoft.com/en-us/azure/active-directory/devices/concept-azure-ad-join`.

In the next section, we will discuss how to use devices in a hybrid AD infrastructure.

Hybrid AD-joined devices

Most companies have moved to utilizing cloud services while still maintaining applications in a private data center. Within these hybrid infrastructures, there may be a current **Active Directory Domain Service (AD DS)** in place that is handling identity and access management. In these cases, the AD DS services on-premises need to be synchronized with the cloud identity services of Azure Active Directory in order to provide a seamless authentication experience for users. This synchronization is performed utilizing **Azure AD Connect** on the on-premises domain. The various synchronization and configuration options will be covered in detail in a later chapter.

Hybrid identity infrastructures manage devices differently than cloud-based infrastructures. These devices are generally joined to the on-premises AD DS for management through **Group Policy** or **Endpoint Configuration Manager**, formerly **System Center Configuration Manager**. The devices that can be managed within this on-premises infrastructure are limited to Windows operating systems that include Windows 7, 8.1, and 10.

If your hybrid identity infrastructure requires management of iOS, macOS, and Android devices, then a co-management environment needs to be configured with Endpoint Configuration Manager and **Intune Endpoint Management**. The co-management capabilities provide the flexibility to manage a combination of legacy and modern authentication. Additional information can be found at this link: `https://docs.microsoft.com/en-us/azure/active-directory/devices/concept-azure-ad-join-hybrid`.

In the next section, we will discuss some of the tenant-wide setting options for managing identity and access.

Configuring tenant-wide settings

In this section, we will explore some of the tenant-wide settings within Azure Active Directory. These may be settings that are pre-configured by default when creating your Azure Active Directory tenant, and some may need to be enabled. This section will provide guidance on best practices for these settings.

Member and guest users

In Azure Active Directory, every user falls into one of two categories – they are either a *member* or a *guest*. Depending on which type of user you are, you have certain default permissions within the Azure Active Directory tenant.

Members are those users that are assigned to the tenant directly. They are given a username that is a part of the domain. By default, they have the capability to register applications, invite guest users, manage their user profile, and possibly reset their own password, if this is enabled. To disable or adjust these capabilities, an administrator would need to change the default settings.

Guest users are users that are invited to the tenant by a member. They have limited capabilities by default and by design. Guests are generally from a partner company that may be working on a project with members of the tenant. They may need access to certain applications and need to be a part of an internal distribution group for collaboration and communication. Unlike members, guests can manage their profile and password, but do not have the capability to read directory information and register applications. If enabled, guest users can be given the capability to invite other guests.

External and guest user access will be discussed further in another chapter.

Managing security defaults

If you are just getting started utilizing cloud infrastructure, the *managed security defaults* are helpful to create a baseline security posture for your tenant. Managed security defaults can be enabled through **Properties** on the Azure AD menu tile, as can be seen in *Figure 3.27*. Select **Manage Security defaults**, toggle **Enable Security defaults** to **Yes**, and save:

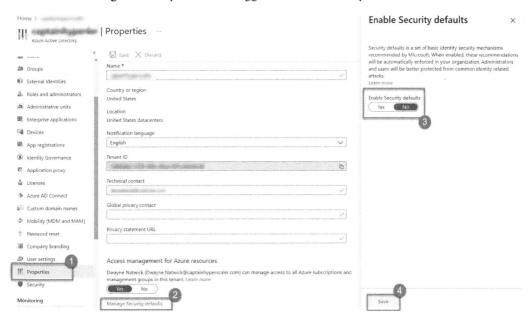

Figure 3.27 – Enable managed security defaults in Azure AD

This enables the defaults for your Azure AD tenant. The defaults that are enabled include the following:

- A requirement for all users to register for Azure AD **Multi-Factor Authentication (MFA)**.

- Enforce and require the use of MFA for all administrators.

- Blocking legacy authentication methods.

- Requiring the use of MFA for all users when necessary for accessing sensitive information.

- Protection of privileged activities such as access to the Azure portal.

> **Note**
> In a later chapter, we will discuss **CA** policies.

When enabling CA policies within Azure AD, it is required to disable **managed security** defaults. Managed security defaults are helpful to enable when you are getting started with your Azure AD tenant to create a protection baseline for your identity and access management. As you progress in your configuration of the Azure AD tenant and services within Microsoft 365 and Azure, you will find additional ways to protect your identities that may provide more flexibility and protection for identity and access.

Summary

In this chapter, we provided the steps to create a brand for your Azure AD tenant by adding a custom domain. We discussed how to add sub-domains and remove domains, as needed. We also provided the different options for connecting and managing devices on your Azure AD or *hybrid identity* infrastructure. Finally, we provided an overview of default user capabilities and how to turn on managed security defaults to protect your Azure AD tenant.

In *Chapter 5, Implementing and Managing External Identities and Guests*, we will further discuss how to create, configure, and manage the identities of users, groups, and applications.

4
Creating, Configuring, and Managing Identities

The previous chapter discussed how to customize the Azure **Active Directory** (**AD**) tenant with a custom domain, and then how to set up users and devices to join to Azure AD and the custom domain. In this chapter, we will go into further detail on how users and groups are created, and how to manage and assign licenses for the various types of users and groups.

In this chapter, we're going to cover the following main topics:

- Creating, configuring, and managing users
- Creating, configuring, and managing groups
- Managing licenses

Technical requirements

In this chapter, we will continue to explore configuring a tenant for the use of **Microsoft 365** and **Azure**. There will be exercises that will require access to Azure AD. If you have not yet created the trial licenses for Microsoft 365, please follow the directions provided within *Chapter 1, Preparing for Your Microsoft Exam*.

Creating, configuring, and managing users

In order to be able to create users in **Azure AD**, you will need to have the *Global Administrator* or the *User Administrator* role. Since the best practice is to adhere to the principle of least privilege, the User Administrator role assignment should be given to anyone who is required to create, configure, and manage users within Azure AD.

Once you are in Azure AD with the proper role, you have the ability to create users. This chapter will focus on member users in detail, with a high-level focus on guest users and hybrid or AD users. External and guest users and hybrid users will be covered in later chapters.

Member users

Member users are those users who are *cloud-native* to the Azure AD tenant. They are the direct users from the company that need access to Microsoft 365 and/or Azure resources. These users are typically the first users that are added to the tenant when it is created and then assigned the various groups and roles that are required for them to interact with the resources within the tenant. When adding these users, they can be assigned the custom domain name that was created in the previous chapter, or the original tenant's name of `tenant.onmicrosoft.com`. Since these users are members of the company and tenant, they are generally assigned the custom domain name for their username and email address.

There are multiple ways for users to be added to Azure AD. They can be added one user at a time through either the **Azure AD portal** or the **Microsoft 365 admin center**. They can be added through a bulk import using a `.csv` file template that can be downloaded from the Azure AD portal. They can also be added using **PowerShell** commands.

We will step through each of these options to help you understand the steps to be able to accomplish this yourself. Let's start by adding a single user through the admin portals.

Adding a single member user in the Azure AD portal

This section will step through adding a member user in the Azure AD portal using the **graphical user interface (GUI)**:

1. Log in to https://portal.azure.com and navigate to **Azure Active Directory**.

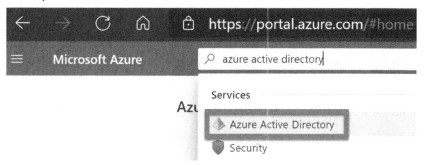

Figure 4.1 – Azure Active Directory in the Azure portal

2. In the menu on the left of the tile, select **Users** under **Manage**.

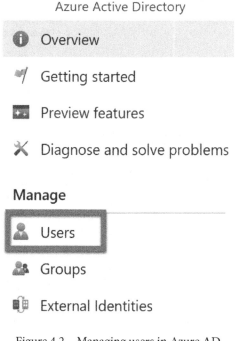

Figure 4.2 – Managing users in Azure AD

3.   Select **+ New user** on the **Users | All users** tile.

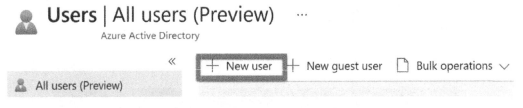

Figure 4.3 – Adding a new user

4.   When the **New user** tile opens, **Create user** will be selected by default. Here, you will add the information for the user. The only required information is the username and display name. Next to the **User name** field, you will see the default domain and a drop-down arrow to select an alternative domain, if necessary.

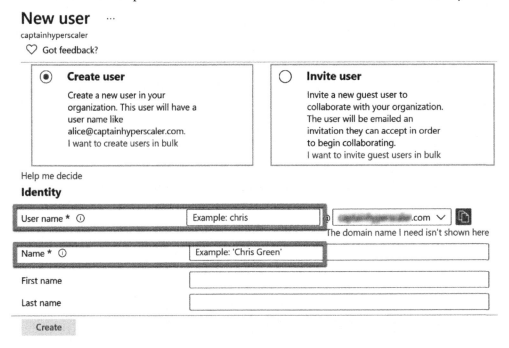

Figure 4.4 – Entering a username and display name

5.   Below the **Identity** fields, you can add the user to a group, assign them a role, and select a usage location. Although the usage location is not a required field when creating a new user, it is required to assign this user any Microsoft 365 licenses. Therefore, it is a best practice to select a usage location at the time that you create the user. Below **Usage location** is also job information, such as **Department** and **Assigned manager**. These fields can be helpful for creating *dynamic groups*, which will be discussed later in this chapter.

Figure 4.5 – Optional selections and usage location

6. After the required information is provided, select **Create** to create the new user. If you choose to autogenerate the password, this password will be sent to the administrators to provide to the user. Selecting an initial password for all new users using **Let me create the password** will allow you to send a standard email to new users with the password to use to log in. In either scenario, the user will be prompted to change their password upon initial login.

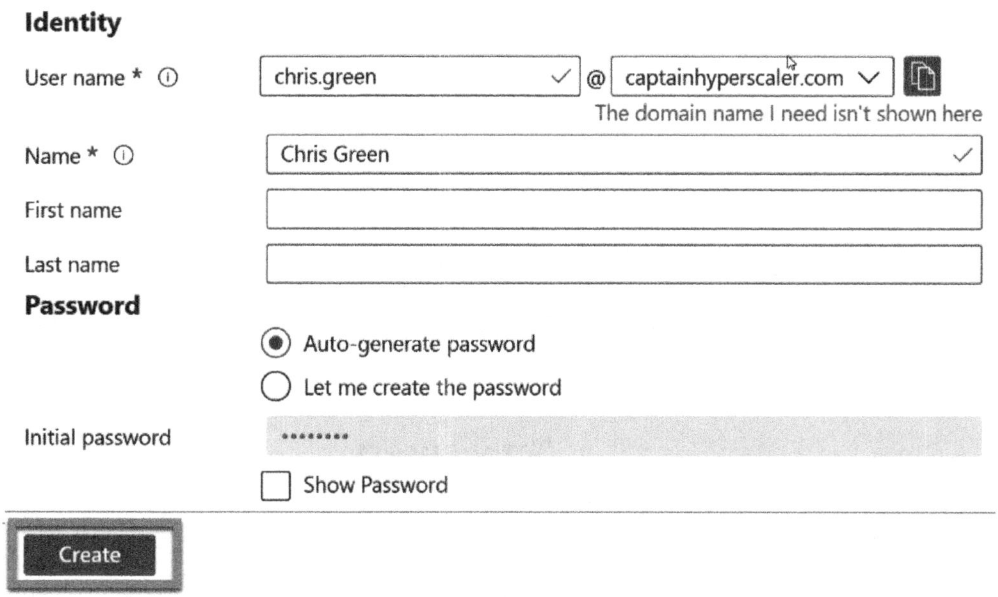

Identity

User name * ⓘ   chris.green ✓ @ captainhyperscaler.com ∨ ⎙

The domain name I need isn't shown here

Name * ⓘ   Chris Green ✓

First name

Last name

Password

⦿ Auto-generate password

◯ Let me create the password

Initial password   ••••••••

☐ Show Password

Create

Figure 4.6 – Entering the required fields and selecting Create

After selecting **Create**, you will return to the **Users | All users** tile and the user that you created will be in your list of users. Next, we will go through the same process in the **Microsoft 365 admin center**.

Creating a new user in the Microsoft 365 admin center

This section will step through adding a member user in the Microsoft 365 admin center using the GUI:

1. Log in to https://admin.microsoft.com and select **Users | Active users** in the left menu using the drop-down arrow.

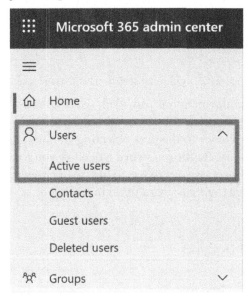

Figure 4.7 – Active users in the Microsoft 365 admin center

2. Select **Add a user** in the **Active users** tile.

Figure 4.8 – Adding a user in the Active users tile

3. This will open up a configuration wizard that will step you through the user creation process. On the first tile, as within Azure AD, you need to create a username and display name as the required fields. You also need to create a password or select to autocreate a password. After this information has been entered, select **Next**.

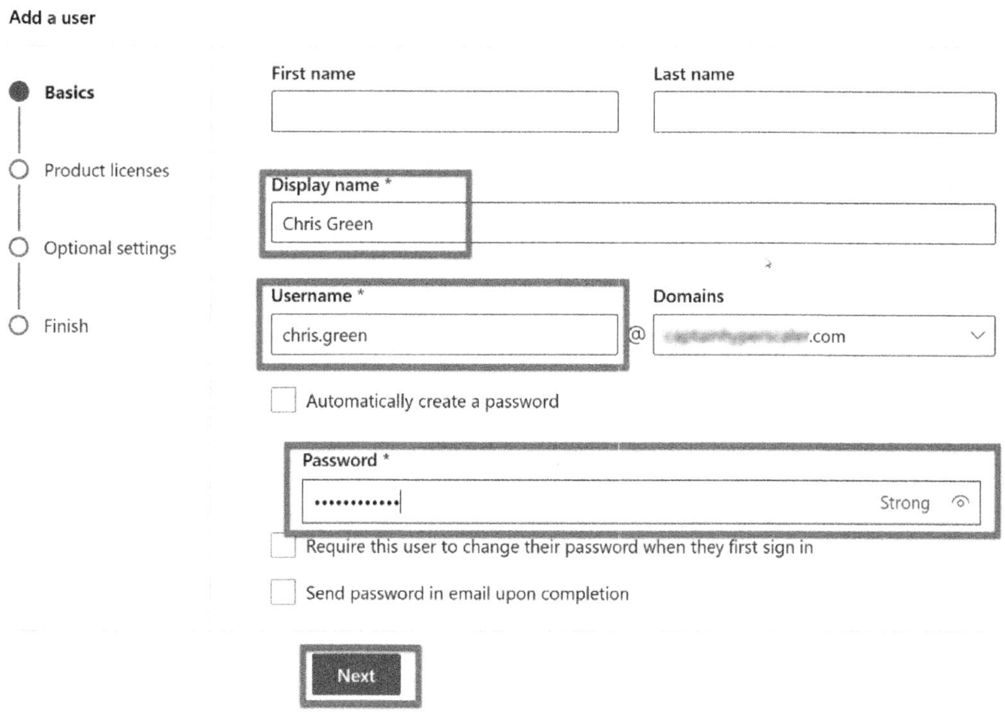

Add a user

● **Basics**	
○ Product licenses	
○ Optional settings	
○ Finish	

First name

Last name

Display name *

Chris Green

Username *

chris.green

Domains

@ ....com ⌄

☐ Automatically create a password

Password *

············| Strong ◉

☐ Require this user to change their password when they first sign in

☐ Send password in email upon completion

Next

Figure 4.9 – Adding basic user information and a password

4. The next tile differs from the Azure AD portal user creation. This tile requires a usage location and license to be selected for the user. Select the correct usage location for the user and the license that they require, and then select **Next**.

Figure 4.10 – Adding a location and licenses

5. The **Optional settings** tile allows you to assign additional roles to this user, if required. Selecting the drop-down arrow for **Profile info** will also provide the option to enter a job title, department, and address information. This can be skipped by selecting **Next**.

Figure 4.11 – Roles and Profile optional settings

6. Review the information that you have entered for the new user and select **Finish adding** to create the user.

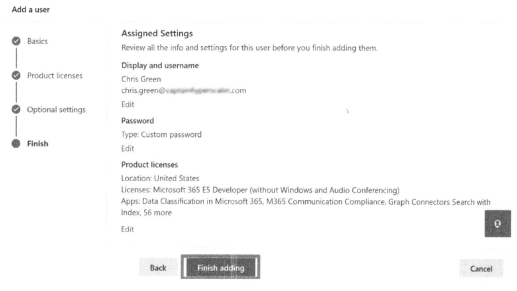

Figure 4.12 – Reviewing and finish adding the new user

After completing these steps, you will return to the **Active users** tile and the user that you added will be in the user list. Next, we will look at how to add multiple users with a `.csv` file bulk import.

Adding users with a bulk import

The previous steps are helpful to use when you have only a few users to add to Azure AD. The next two sections will go through the steps to add a group of users simultaneously to Azure AD. In this first section, we will be using a `.csv` file to bulk import the users:

1. Log in to `https://portal.azure.com` and navigate to **Azure Active Directory**.

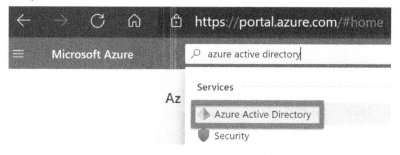

Figure 4.13 – Azure Active Directory in the Azure portal

2. In the menu on the left of the tile, select **Users** under **Manage**.

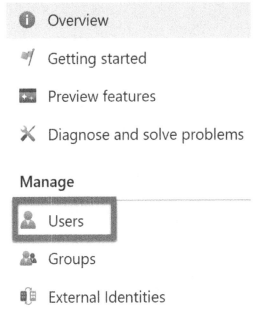

Figure 4.14 – Managing users in Azure AD

3. Select the **Bulk operations** drop-down arrow and then **Bulk create** on the **Users | All users** tile.

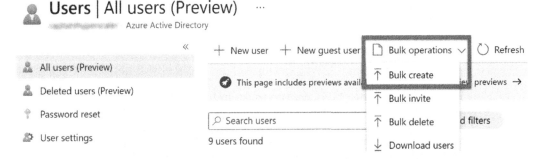

Figure 4.15 – Bulk creating users

4. Selecting **Bulk create** will open a new tile. This tile provides a download link to a template file that you will edit to populate with your user information and upload to add the bulk creation of users.

Figure 4.16 – Bulk create user steps

5. The `.csv` template provides you with the fields included with the user profile. This includes the required username, display name, and initial password. You can also complete optional fields, such as `Department` and `Usage location`, at this time. The following screenshot is an example of how you can complete the `.csv` file:

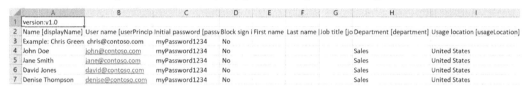

Figure 4.17 – CSV file completion

6. Once populated, save the changes and upload the `csv` file to add the users.

7. You will be notified that the file has been uploaded successfully. Choose **Submit** to add the users as shown in *Figure 4.18*:

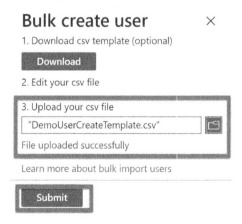

Figure 4.18 – Uploading and submitting the bulk user creation

After the users have been created, you will be prompted that the creation has succeeded. Close the **Bulk create users** tile and the new users will be populated in the list of **Users | All users**. You have now completed a bulk user creation using a CSV template. In the next section, we will add users with PowerShell.

Adding users with PowerShell

This section will step through how to add users with PowerShell. There are some steps to prepare PowerShell to run Azure AD commands. The following steps will get you ready to run the commands to add users to Azure AD:

1. Open PowerShell as an administrator. This can be done by searching for PowerShell in Windows and choosing **Run as administrator**.

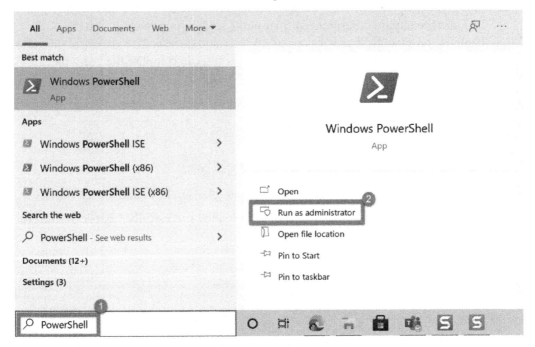

Figure 4.19 – Opening PowerShell as an administrator

2. You will need to add the **Azure AD PowerShell** module if you have not used it before. Run the Install-Module AzureAD command. When prompted, select **Y** to continue.

Figure 4.20 – Installing the AD module

3. Confirm that the module is installed correctly by running the `Get-Module AzureAD` command.

4. Next, you will need to log in to Azure by running `Connect-AzureAD`.

5. The Microsoft login window will appear for you to log in to Azure AD.

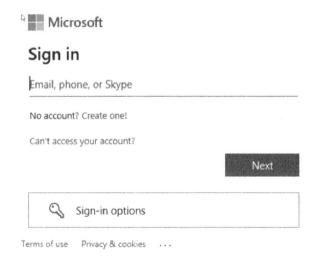

Figure 4.21 – Microsoft login to Azure AD

6. To verify that you are connected and to see existing users, run `Get-AzureADUser`.

7. To assign a common temporary password to all new users, run the following command and replace `TempPW` with the password that you would like to provide to your users:

```
$PasswordProfile = New-Object -TypeName Microsoft.Open.
AzureAD.Model.PasswordProfile
$PasswordProfile.Password = "TempPW"
```

You are ready to create new users. The following command will be populated with the user information and run. If you have more than one user to add, you can use a Notepad .txt file to add the user information and copy and paste it into PowerShell:

```
New-AzureADUser -DisplayName "New User" -PasswordProfile
$PasswordProfile -UserPrincipalName "NewUser@contoso.com"
-AccountEnabled $true -MailNickName "Newuser"
```

Figure 4.22 shows the results after running the PowerShell command to add users. Successful creation of the users will be verified in the table after running the command.

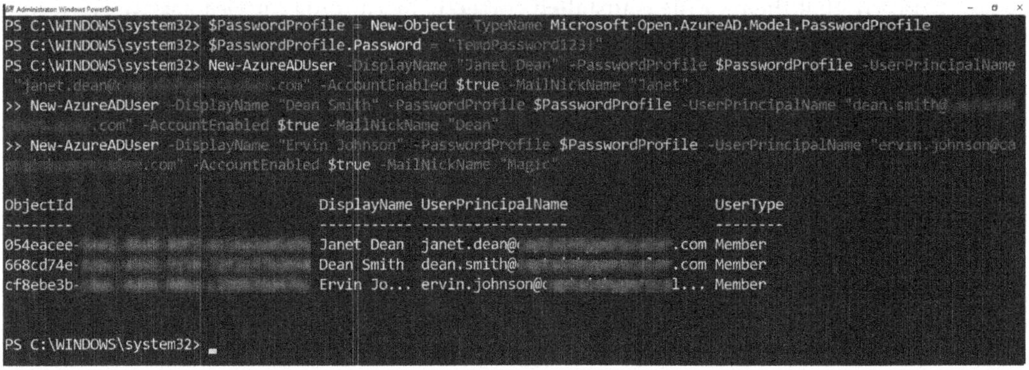

Figure 4.22 – Adding multiple users with PowerShell

You now know how to create users within the Azure AD portal and the Microsoft 365 admin center, carry out bulk creation with a .csv file, and create users with PowerShell commands. Additional information on PowerShell commands for Azure AD users can be found at the following links:

- https://docs.microsoft.com/en-us/powershell/module/
  azuread/new-azureaduser?view=azureadps-2.0

- https://techcommunity.microsoft.com/t5/itops-talk-blog/
  powershell-basics-how-to-add-a-new-azure-active-directory-
  user/ba-p/1189629#:~:text=PowerShell%20Basics%3A%20How%20
  To%20Add%20A%20New%20Azure,%3D%20%22Mike%20Finnegan%22%20
  PasswordProfile%20%3D%20...%20More%20items

In the next section, we will go over guest and external users at a high level. More details on these types of users will be discussed in the next chapter.

Guest and external users

As stated previously, guest and external users will be discussed in further detail in a later chapter, but it is important to understand how they differ from member users. These types of users are invited to the Azure AD tenant and have access to resources that they have been authorized for. This is helpful when someone outside your company needs access to an application to collaborate, or a partner or subsidiary company needs to be given access to resources.

Guests are invited from within the **User** tile by selecting **+ New guest user** and providing their external email address. Once they accept the invitation, they are now added to the Azure AD tenant and can be assigned permissions allowing them access to resources.

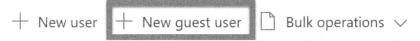

Figure 4.23 – Adding a new guest user

On the next tile, enter the email address for the guest user. You can also add a personal message about why they are being invited, and then select **Invite**:

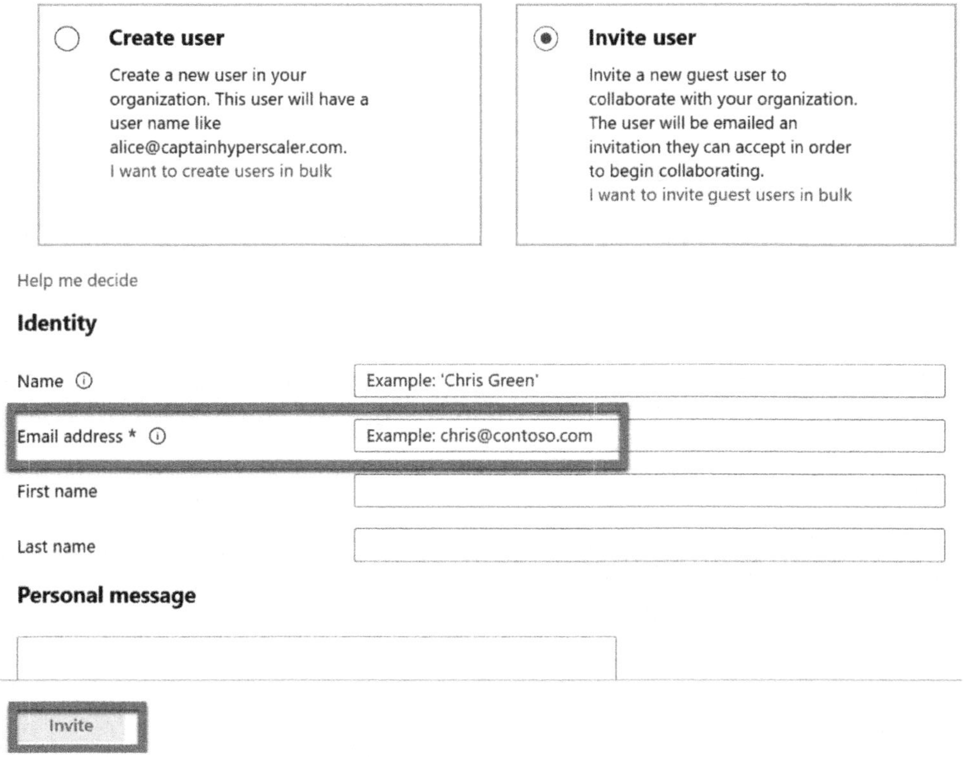

○ **Create user**

Create a new user in your organization. This user will have a user name like alice@captainhyperscaler.com.
I want to create users in bulk

◉ **Invite user**

Invite a new guest user to collaborate with your organization. The user will be emailed an invitation they can accept in order to begin collaborating.
I want to invite guest users in bulk

Help me decide

Identity

Name ⓘ	Example: 'Chris Green'
Email address * ⓘ	Example: chris@contoso.com
First name	
Last name	

Personal message

[Invite]

Figure 4.24 – Guest user invite information

External users are different from guest users; these users are usually from partner companies that have multiple users that require access. They also have their own Azure AD tenant, so they can join and use their existing Microsoft 365 licenses. Connecting these users starts with creating a collaborative trust relationship between the two companies. Then, authorization to resources can be configured. The external collaboration settings are used to set up the restrictions and settings for guest and external users.

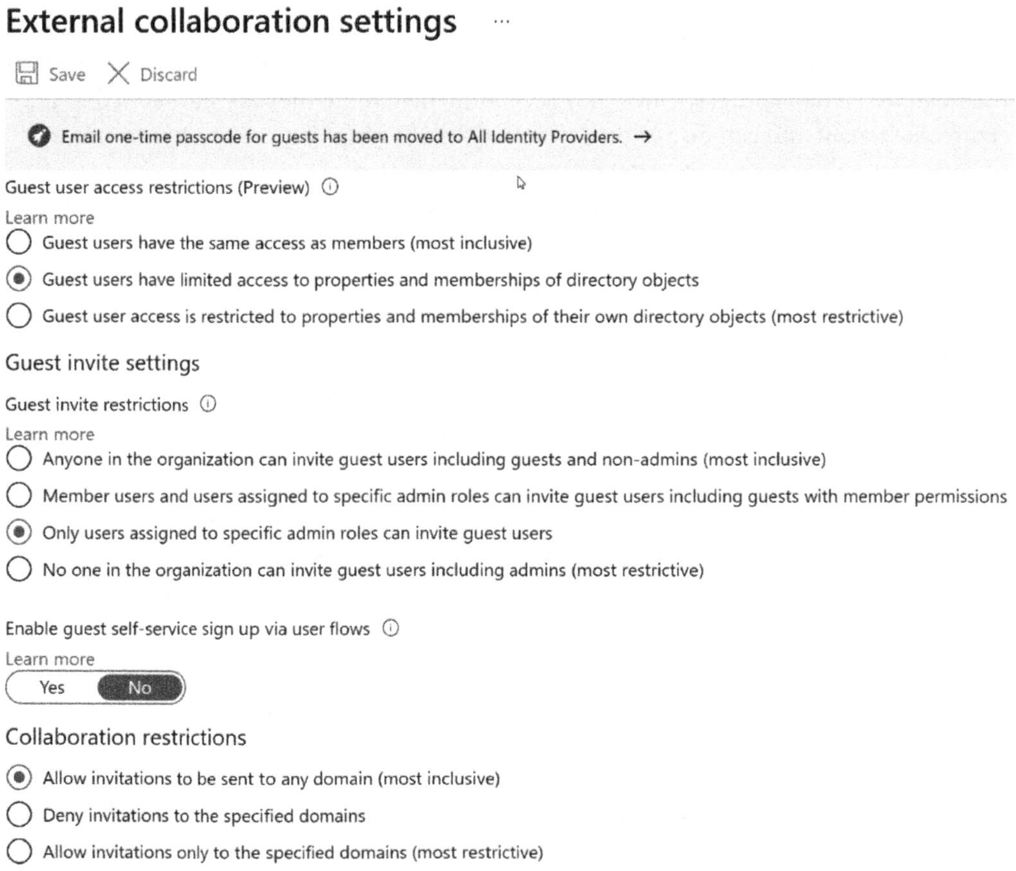

External collaboration settings ⋯

🖫 Save   ✕ Discard

> 🛈 Email one-time passcode for guests has been moved to All Identity Providers. →

Guest user access restrictions (Preview) ⓘ

Learn more
○ Guest users have the same access as members (most inclusive)
◉ Guest users have limited access to properties and memberships of directory objects
○ Guest user access is restricted to properties and memberships of their own directory objects (most restrictive)

Guest invite settings

Guest invite restrictions ⓘ

Learn more
○ Anyone in the organization can invite guest users including guests and non-admins (most inclusive)
○ Member users and users assigned to specific admin roles can invite guest users including guests with member permissions
◉ Only users assigned to specific admin roles can invite guest users
○ No one in the organization can invite guest users including admins (most restrictive)

Enable guest self-service sign up via user flows ⓘ

Learn more
(Yes   **No**)

Collaboration restrictions

◉ Allow invitations to be sent to any domain (most inclusive)
○ Deny invitations to the specified domains
○ Allow invitations only to the specified domains (most restrictive)

Figure 4.25 – Configuring External collaboration settings

The external collaboration settings in Azure AD are used to configure specific domains that can or cannot be invited to your tenant, and who has the authorization to invite guests to the company tenant. Further details on these steps will be provided in the next chapter.

AD (hybrid) users

As companies begin to move resources to Azure and Microsoft 365 cloud services, these companies require the use of Azure AD for managing their cloud identities. However, many of these companies still have resources located in other data centers or on-premises within their building that also has an **AD Domain Services** server managing identities. In this case, creating a hybrid identity management solution to connect these on-premises identities to Azure AD is required. This is accomplished by utilizing Azure AD Connect to act as the synchronization agent between on-premises AD and Azure AD. There are multiple options for synchronizing and managing these identities. These options will be discussed in detail in a later chapter.

Creating, configuring, and managing groups

Now that we understand how to add users in Azure AD, you may want to group these users based on roles, departments, or locations.

Creating groups that users belong to can assist in the management of providing access to licenses, assigning roles, and maintaining compliance and data sovereignty for users located in different countries. Group assignments can be created manually or dynamically based on an attribute. We will step through the creation process of groups later in the chapter. The following sections will explore the different types of groups and the use cases for them to be used.

Microsoft 365 groups

Microsoft 365 groups are the recommended group to create when working only with Microsoft 365 resources. These groups can contain users both inside and outside of the company to allow them to collaborate and be part of Microsoft Teams channels. When these groups are created, a group email address is created to allow users to distribute emails to the group without the requirement to remember everyone who is included in the group. As stated previously, these groups can be created within the Microsoft 365 admin center and the Azure AD portal. Microsoft 365 groups are primarily used for group collaboration rather than access control to resources or device management. For these capabilities, security groups would be required.

Security groups

While Microsoft 365 groups are used for team collaboration, security groups are used for securing and assigning access to resources. Security groups would be used to create access levels for resources with Azure, as well as permissions for OneDrive and SharePoint. When you create a group of user devices to be managed through Intune for endpoint management, they would need to belong to a security group as well. Unlike Microsoft 365 groups, security groups do not have a group email address to communicate with other group members. Since this group type is used specifically for access control permissions, the email group address is not necessary. Security groups can also be created within the Microsoft 365 admin center and the Azure AD portal.

Specialty groups

The majority of the group types that are created on the Microsoft tenant are either Microsoft 365 or security groups. However, there are situations where you may want just an email for a group to communicate, or perhaps need a distribution email address for a security group. For this, there are two special-use groups that can be created within the Microsoft 365 admin center. These groups are the distribution group and the mail-enabled security group.

The distribution group is an email-only group where members are included within a group email address. These groups are helpful for contact lists within the company or for customers to get a response from the company on a web page. Some examples of a distribution group email would be `sales@company.com` or `support@company.com`. These emails would be routed to a group of users to allow the company to respond quickly to customer needs.

The mail-enabled security group provides a distribution email address similar to a Microsoft 365 group, while having the capabilities of a security group. Since an email address is assigned to this type of group, this group cannot contain devices, only users.

Let's step through how to create a Microsoft 365 group within the Microsoft 365 admin center. The Microsoft 365 admin center provides a step-by-step configuration wizard that is easy to follow. Though we are only going through the steps of a Microsoft 365 group, the process would be similar for any of the other group types:

1. In the Microsoft 365 admin center, `https://admin.microsoft.com`, select **Groups** | **Active groups** on the left menu.

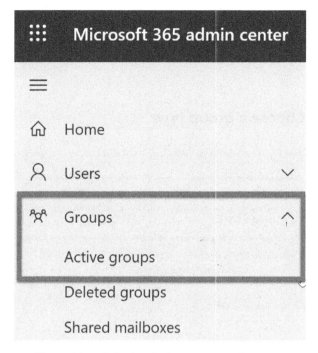

Figure 4.26 – Selecting Active groups on the menu

2.   Next, select **Add a group** on the **Active groups** tile.

Active groups

It can take up to an hour for new distribution groups and mail-enabled security groups to appear in your Active groups list. If you don't see your new group yet, go to the Exchange admin center.

Learn more about group types

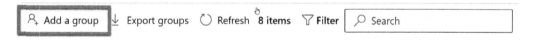

Figure 4.27 – Adding a new group

3. The configuration wizard tile will open and the group types that we previously discussed are listed. For this exercise, we will select **Microsoft 365**, but the process would be the same for any other group type. After selecting the group type, select **Next**.

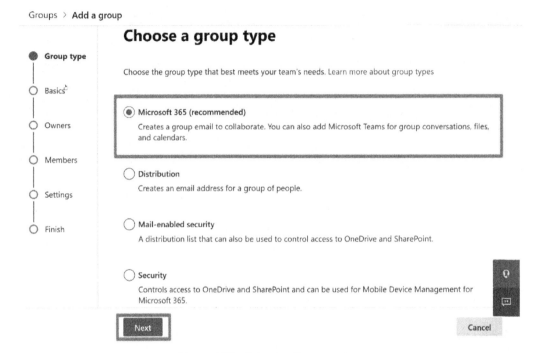

Figure 4.28 – Selecting the group type

4. On the next tile, add a group name and description for the group. Select **Next**.

Groups > **Add a group**

⊘ Group type

● **Basics**

○ Owners

○ Members

○ Settings

○ Finish

Set up the basics

To get started, fill out some basic info about the group you'd like to create.

Name *

sc300demogroup

Description

Test group for SC-300 preparation

Back   **Next**

Figure 4.29 – Adding a group name and description

5.   Assign an owner, or owners, for the group and select **Next**.

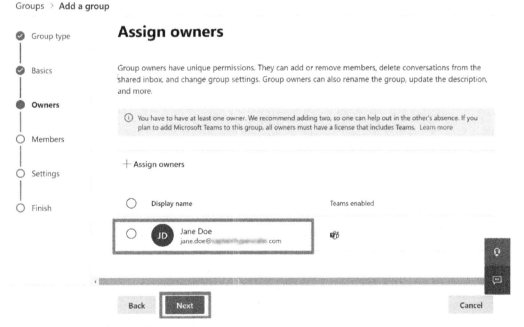

Groups > **Add a group**

⊘ Group type

⊘ Basics

● **Owners**

○ Members

○ Settings

○ Finish

Assign owners

Group owners have unique permissions. They can add or remove members, delete conversations from the shared inbox, and change group settings. Group owners can also rename the group, update the description, and more.

ⓘ You have to have at least one owner. We recommend adding two, so one can help out in the other's absence. If you plan to add Microsoft Teams to this group, all owners must have a license that includes Teams. Learn more

+ Assign owners

○   Display name   Teams enabled

○   JD   Jane Doe
          jane.doe@▓▓▓▓▓▓▓.com

Back   **Next**   Cancel

Figure 4.30 – Assigning an owner(s) to the group

6. Add members to the group and select **Next**.

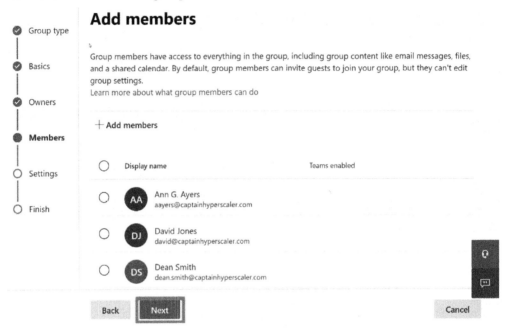

Figure 4.31 – Adding members to the group

7. In the **Edit settings** tile, create an email address for the group and select to create a Teams group, if applicable. Select **Next**.

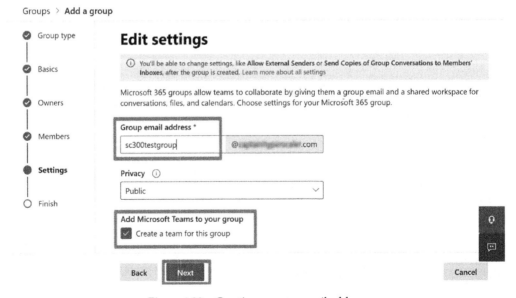

Figure 4.32 – Creating a group email address

8. Review the configuration and select **Create group**.

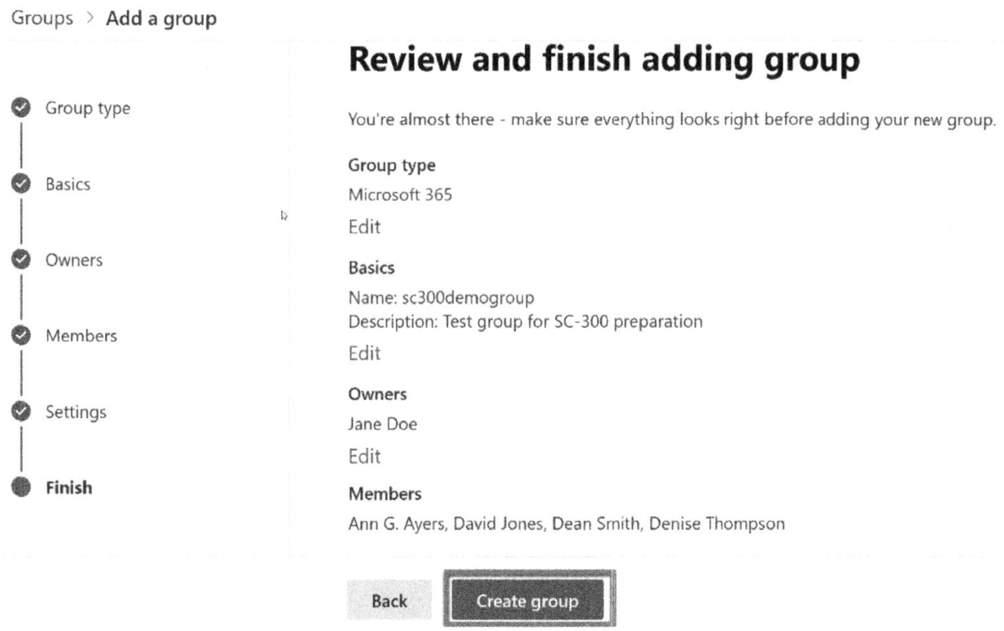

Groups > **Add a group**

Review and finish adding group

You're almost there - make sure everything looks right before adding your new group.

Group type
Microsoft 365

Edit

Basics
Name: sc300demogroup
Description: Test group for SC-300 preparation

Edit

Owners
Jane Doe

Edit

Members
Ann G. Ayers, David Jones, Dean Smith, Denise Thompson

- Group type ✓
- Basics ✓
- Owners ✓
- Members ✓
- Settings ✓
- Finish

Back   Create group

Figure 4.33 – Reviewing and creating a group

Now that you have gone through the steps to create a group manually within the Microsoft 365 admin panel, you can now create other groups for your needs. The steps in the configuration wizard are going to be very similar for security groups, mail-enabled security groups, and distribution groups.

In the next section, we will discuss the types of dynamic groups and go through the steps of creating a group in the Azure AD portal.

Dynamic groups

Dynamic groups are groups that are configured with a particular attribute of a user or device. The attributes of the users or devices determine whether they are a member of the group or not. If that attribute of that user or device changes, the membership of the user or device changes as well. For example, if you have users that have **department of sales** on their profile, and you create a dynamic group that adds members to the attribute of department with the value of sales, users with sales in their **department** field of their profile will be added as members of the group. If one of those users changes departments from sales to marketing, they will be dynamically removed from being a member of the sales group.

Some things to remember about dynamic groups are, firstly, that dynamic user groups are only available with security groups and Microsoft 365 groups, not mail-enabled security groups or distribution groups. Dynamic device groups are only available with security groups. In order to have dynamic groups available, you must have an Azure AD Premium P1 or P2 license.

Additional information on groups can be found at this link: `https://docs.microsoft.com/en-us/microsoft-365/admin/create-groups/compare-groups?view=o365-worldwide`.

The following steps will describe how to configure a dynamic user group within the Azure AD portal. The configuration steps of an assigned group will be similar and you can configure assigned groups here, as you can in the Microsoft 365 admin center:

1. From the **Azure Active Directory** tile, select **Groups**.

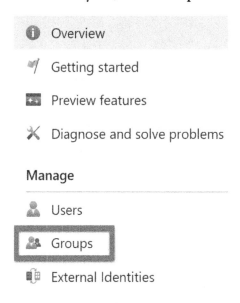

Figure 4.34 – Managing groups

2. In the **Groups | All groups** tile, select **+ New group**:

Figure 4.35 – Adding a new group

3. Select the group type as **Security**, create a group name and group description, and select the drop-down arrow for **Membership type**. Select **Dynamic User**.

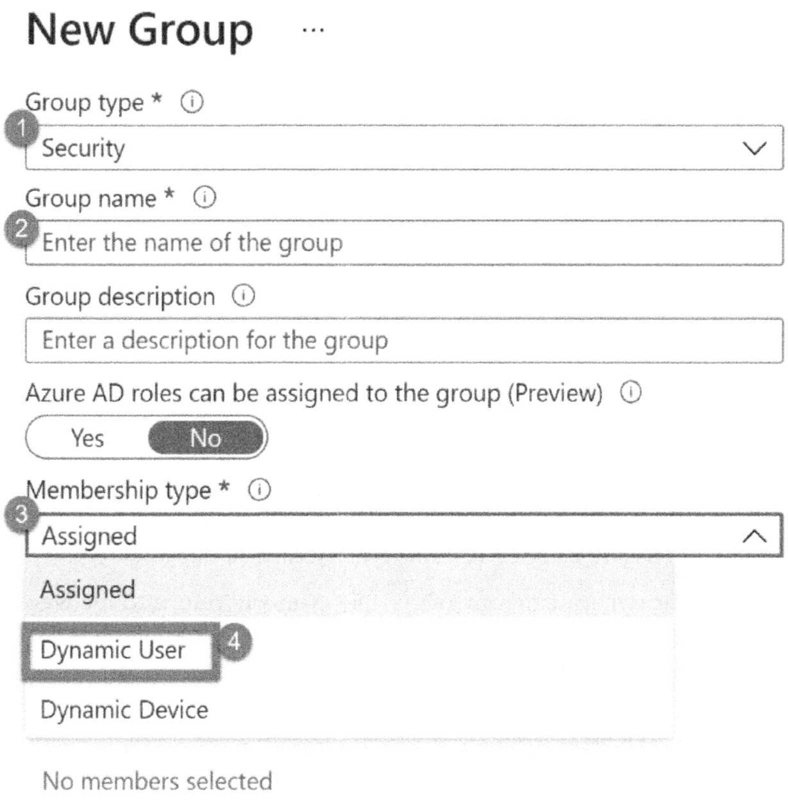

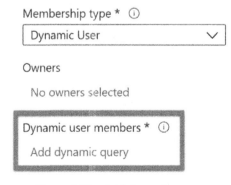

Figure 4.36 – Entering information for the new group

4. After selecting **Dynamic User**, **Dynamic user members** will appear below the membership type. Select **Add dynamic query**.

Figure 4.37 – Add dynamic query

5. On the **Dynamic membership rules** tile, use the drop-down arrows to select **department** for **Property** and **Contains** for **Operator**, and enter `sales` for **Value**. The **Rule syntax** box will appear below when you move out of the **Value** field. Select **Save** to save the dynamic membership rules. If you have additional rules to add to your group, for example, a location property, you can include that in the syntax by selecting **+ Add expression** and filling in the **Property**, **Operator**, and **Value** fields:

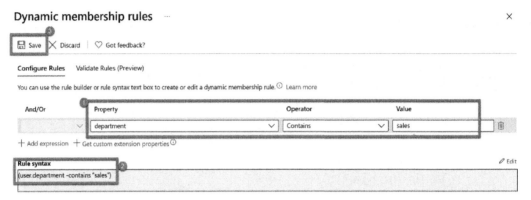

Figure 4.38 – Creating the dynamic membership rules

6. After saving the dynamic membership rules, you will return to the **New Group** tile and select **Create**.

Figure 4.39 – Creating the group

The sales group has now been created. If any users within your Azure AD have the `department` value of `sales`, they will be added to this group. If you completed the exercise to add a user with a CSV bulk import earlier in this chapter, you would have added sales department users that will populate in this group. If you want to see how this group dynamically updates, change the department name in one of the users from `sales` to `marketing` and they will be removed from the group.

The last section of this chapter will talk about licensing in Azure AD and Microsoft 365.

Managing licenses

Licenses are important within Microsoft to be able to use features and capabilities for Microsoft 365 and Azure AD. Without proper licenses assigned, some features may not be available, such as **Exchange Online**, **SharePoint Online**, or **Microsoft Teams**. Users that do not have licenses assigned to them may not be able to be added to groups, have access to resources that they need to work, or allow security features for identity and access management to be configured. The next sections will describe some of these requirements.

License requirements

Some license requirements to enable capabilities have already been discussed in some of the sections already. For example, dynamic groups require an Azure AD Premium P1 or P2 license. These Azure AD Premium licenses are also required for many of the advanced identity and access features that will be discussed in this book. For a full comparison of these features, review the information at this link: `https://azure.microsoft.com/en-us/pricing/details/active-directory/`.

License features

Adding licenses provides features to users to access applications as well as the ability for an administrator to assign security features required for identity and access management. For example, users must be assigned a minimum **Azure AD Premium P1** license to have **multi-factor authentication (MFA)**, **Conditional Access**, or **Intune** assigned. To properly manage and monitor administrator accounts with **Privileged Identity Management (PIM)** or **Azure AD Identity Protection**, users must be assigned an **Azure AD Premium P2** license.

Assigning licenses

Licenses can be assigned from within the Azure AD portal or the Microsoft 365 admin center. Within Azure AD, go to **Licenses** on the **Azure Active Directory** tile under **Manage**. From the **Licenses** tile, you will select **All licenses**, and can then view existing licenses or add licenses. Within the Microsoft 365 admin center, licenses are found under the **Billing** dropdown on the menu. If you remember from earlier in the chapter, when adding users to the Microsoft 365 admin center, one of the requirements is to add licenses to the new user.

Summary

In this chapter, we described how to create users and groups and manage licenses. This included the multiple ways to add member users to Azure AD, adding an assigned and dynamic group, and finally, the use of Azure AD Premium licenses for the advanced identity and access features. In the next chapters, we will go into further detail on how external and hybrid users can be added and used within Azure AD.

5

Implementing and Managing External Identities and Guests

The previous chapter focused primarily on member user accounts, creating groups, and assigning licenses, while also providing a high-level introduction to external users and groups. In this chapter, we will take a closer look at how we can plan, implement, and manage external identities and guests within our **Azure Active Directory (Azure AD)** tenant. The primary focus of the exam is on external identities and guests as they pertain to business partners. **Business-to-customer**, or **B2C**, guest access is not within that scope. Since this is also an important component in managing external access to cloud applications, we will cover this topic at a high level for clarity and understanding when we define external collaboration and discuss configuring identity providers. After completing this chapter, you will understand how to configure, invite, and manage external collaboration and guest user access within Azure AD.

In this chapter, we're going to cover the following topics:

- Managing external collaboration settings in Azure AD
- Inviting guest users
- Managing external users accounts in Azure Active Directory
- Configuring identity providers

Technical requirements

In this chapter, we will continue to explore configuring a tenant so that you can use **Microsoft 365** and **Azure**. There will be exercises that will require access to Azure AD. If you have not created the trial licenses for Microsoft 365 yet, please follow the directions provided within *Chapter 1, Preparing for Your Microsoft Exam*.

Managing external collaboration settings in Azure AD

As stated in *Chapter 4, Creating, Configuring, and Managing Identities*, to be able to create users in Azure Active Directory, you will need to have the *Global Administrator* or the *User Administrator* role. Since the best practice is to adhere to the principle of least privilege, the User Administrator role should be given to anyone that is required to create, configure, and manage users within Azure AD.

Once you are in Azure AD with the proper role, you can create users. This chapter will focus on external and guest users. Different types of external users require separate configuration settings. The primary categories are **business-to-business (B2B)** and **business-to-consumer (B2C)**. The next few sections will define each of these before we discuss external collaboration settings.

B2B

The primary focus of the Identity and Access Administrator exam is based on B2B collaboration and guest users. B2B guests are best described by a partnership relationship between users within two separate companies that need to collaborate on a project. These B2B relationships may be created through business mergers and acquisitions, project needs, or support relationships.

Within these B2B relationships, the external company can bring their own **Azure AD** and **Microsoft 365** licenses for collaboration, though these licenses can be assigned if the external users do not come from an Azure AD tenant with Microsoft 365 licenses. External company collaboration settings provide these users with a single sign-on experience for both business tenants. If an external user does not use these licenses, then the username and password can be used from another identity, and that user can be assigned licenses from within the invited tenant.

B2C

The B2C relationship is an external account that's used for customers that are accessing applications and resources within the tenant. An example of this would be using a LinkedIn, Facebook, or Google username and password to log in and access your account on a shopping site. This is convenient for customers as they don't need to create another username and password. As stated previously, B2C guest users are outside the scope of the **Identity and Access Administrator** exam. We are mentioning this here to provide clarity regarding the different types of external users and to understand that this capability exists. We will discuss this further in the **Configuring identity providers** section, later in this chapter. These identity provider relationships can allow a B2C authentication relationship, but in this book, we will discuss them as they pertain to B2B authentication.

Now that we have defined the different types of external users, let's discuss how external collaboration is configured within Azure AD.

Configuring external collaboration settings

Whether the external users are B2B or B2C, there is a level of collaboration that needs to be planned for and configured within Azure AD to allow these guests access. These settings can be found within the Azure AD portal under **External Identities – External collaboration settings**. The following screenshot shows the settings that are available within **External collaboration settings**:

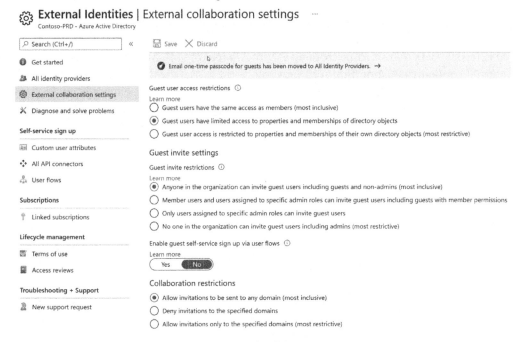

Figure 5.1 – External collaboration settings

Within these collaboration settings, you will define what guest users can access, who is allowed to invite guest users, and the restrictions on collaboration for the tenant. The preceding screenshot shows the default settings for external collaboration. These settings should be discussed with stakeholders to provide a proper plan for external guest access. Let's discuss each of these sections and how they should be utilized.

Guest user access

The first section within external collaboration settings is the overall **Guest user access restrictions**. The default setting is **Guest users have limited access to properties and memberships of directory objects**. Note that within each of these sections, Microsoft provides a level of guidance of what is the most inclusive and the most restrictive within these settings. The following screenshot shows these settings; more information can be found at `https://aka.ms/aadguestpermissions`:

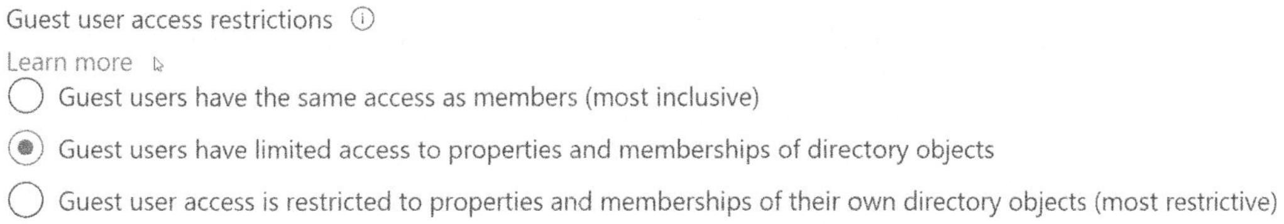

Guest user access restrictions ⓘ

Learn more ⫞

◯ Guest users have the same access as members (most inclusive)

⦿ Guest users have limited access to properties and memberships of directory objects

◯ Guest user access is restricted to properties and memberships of their own directory objects (most restrictive)

Figure 5.2 – Guest user access restrictions

As we can see, the default setting creates a level of inclusion and restriction regarding how guests can interact within the tenant. This may be more restrictive than a member user. Using this setting will allow administrators within applications to determine guest user permissions specifically for those objects.

Guest invite settings

The next section within external collaboration settings is **Guest invite settings**. There are two settings within this section: **Guest invite restrictions** and **Enable guest self-service sign up via user flows**. The default setting for these settings is **Anyone in the organization can invite guest users including guests and non-admins (most inclusive)** for **Guest invite restrictions** and **No** for **Enable guest self-service sign up via user flows**, respectively.

In the following screenshot, the **Guest invite restrictions** options are set to the most inclusive, allowing even guests and non-administrator members to invite guest users to the tenant. Though this option takes some administrative burden off the IT department, it also could be a security risk, especially since this allows guest users from outside the company to invite other guests. Also, selecting the most restrictive option would block guest users from being invited to the tenant completely. If your company is highly regulated and has certain compliance requirements around guest access, then this may be a good option:

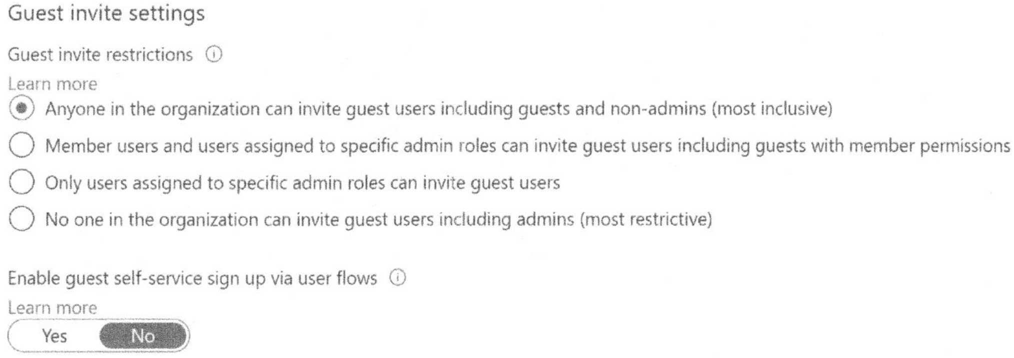

Guest invite settings

Guest invite restrictions ⓘ

Learn more

⦿ Anyone in the organization can invite guest users including guests and non-admins (most inclusive)

◯ Member users and users assigned to specific admin roles can invite guest users including guests with member permissions

◯ Only users assigned to specific admin roles can invite guest users

◯ No one in the organization can invite guest users including admins (most restrictive)

Enable guest self-service sign up via user flows ⓘ

Learn more

(Yes   No)

Figure 5.3 – Guest invite settings

In most cases, a good best practice would be to not allow guests to invite other guests, and to limit the member users that can invite guest users, which is one of the middle options we can see here. More information on these settings can be found here: `https://aka.ms/guestinvitesettings`.

Enable guest self-service sign up via user flows is a setting that is used with external identities, such as personal Microsoft, Facebook, or Google accounts. Before allowing these identity providers to be utilized for B2B or B2C login to the company's Azure AD, this setting will need to be moved to **Yes**. The default is **No**, as shown in the preceding screenshot. More information on guest user flows can be found here: `https://aka.ms/exidenablesssu`.

Collaboration restrictions

The final section within **External collaboration settings** is the **Collaboration restrictions**. Within this section, you have the option to allow invitations to be sent to all domains, deny invitations to specified domains, or allow invitations to only specified domains. As shown in the following screenshot, allowing invitations to only specified domains is the most restrictive option because you are setting a very narrow scope of companies that can be invited to the company tenant:

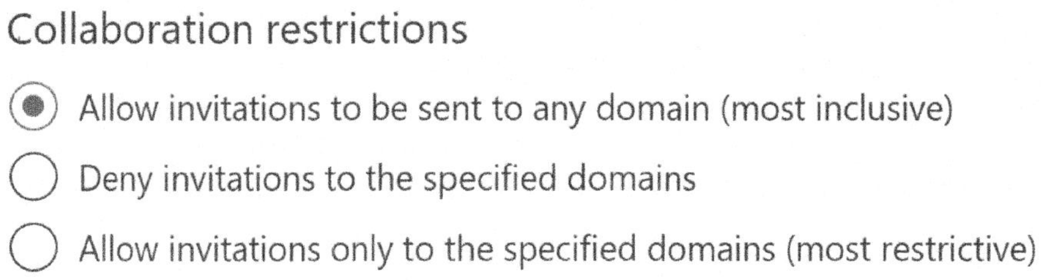

Collaboration restrictions

⦿ Allow invitations to be sent to any domain (most inclusive)

◯ Deny invitations to the specified domains

◯ Allow invitations only to the specified domains (most restrictive)

Figure 5.4 – Collaboration restrictions – Allow invitations

The default setting is to allow invitations to any domain, which has no restrictions and is the most inclusive.

The following screenshot shows that when selecting to deny invitations to specified domains, an entry field appears so that you can enter those blocked domains:

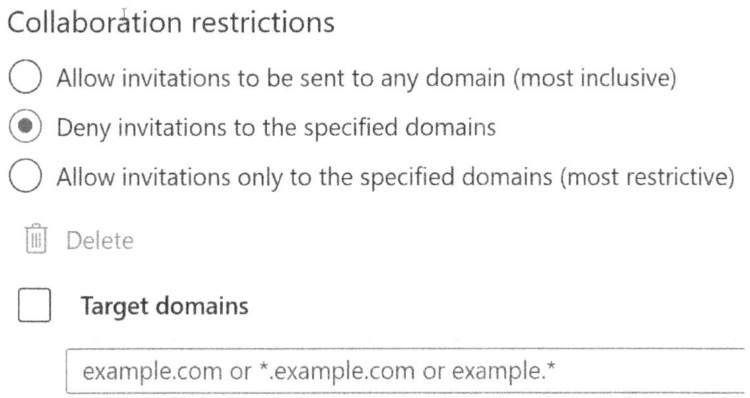

Collaboration restrictions

○ Allow invitations to be sent to any domain (most inclusive)

◉ Deny invitations to the specified domains

○ Allow invitations only to the specified domains (most restrictive)

🗑 Delete

☐ **Target domains**

example.com or *.example.com or example.*

Figure 5.5 – Collaboration restrictions – Deny invitations

Target domains can be used to block competitor companies or companies that would create a conflict of interest if they were allowed to be within your company tenant.

The following screenshot shows that the same field appears when selecting to allow invitations only to specified domains:

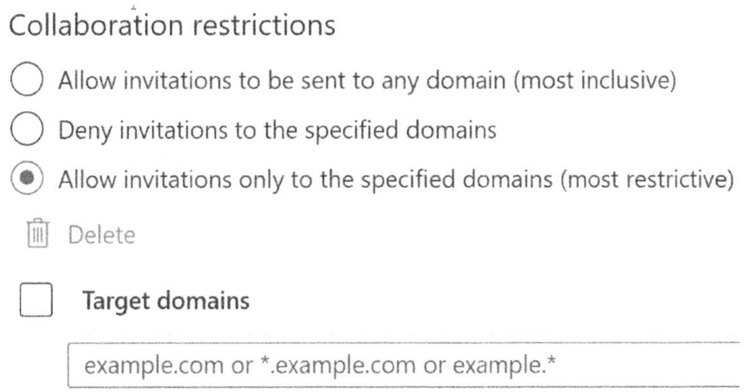

Collaboration restrictions

○ Allow invitations to be sent to any domain (most inclusive)

○ Deny invitations to the specified domains

◉ Allow invitations only to the specified domains (most restrictive)

🗑 Delete

☐ **Target domains**

example.com or *.example.com or example.*

Figure 5.6 – Collaboration restrictions – Allow invitations from specified domains

The difference here is that you are specifying the only domains that are allowed to be invited to the company tenant. Unless the guest user invitation has this domain as their email, they will be blocked from receiving an invitation. In a company that handles sensitive information, this high level of restricting guests may be required. As the identity and access administrator, you will be responsible for identifying what these domains are and should have a process in place for approvals before additional domains are added.

Once these collaboration settings have been planned, approved, and completed, external users can be invited to the company tenant. The next section provides details on how these external guest users can be created in Azure AD.

Inviting external users individually and in bulk

Now that we understand how to configure the external collaboration settings, we are now ready to invite external users to collaborate on our Azure AD tenant.

Once we have set our tenant up to allow external users, the process of adding external users is similar to the process that we discussed in the previous chapter for adding member users, with some minor differences.

The next few sections will explore the different ways to invite external users to the Azure AD tenant.

Inviting guest users

External users within Azure AD are categorized as Guest users. As is the case with Member users, there are multiple ways for these users to be added to Azure AD. They can be added one user at a time through either the **Azure AD portal** or the **Microsoft 365 admin center**. They can also be added through a bulk import using a `.csv` file template that can be downloaded from the Azure AD portal, and they can be added using **PowerShell** commands.

We will step through each of these options to help you understand the steps you must follow to accomplish this yourself. Let's start with adding a single user through the admin portals.

Adding a single guest user in the Azure AD portal

This section will step through adding a guest user in the Azure AD portal using the **graphical user interface (GUI)**.

First, we will use the Azure AD portal:

1. Log into `https://portal.azure.com` and navigate to **Azure Active Directory**:

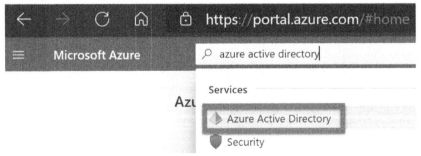

Figure 5.7 – Azure Active Directory in the Azure portal

2. From the menu on the left of the tile, select **Users** under **Manage**:

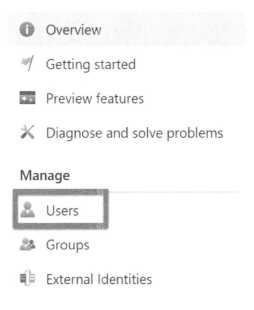

Figure 5.8 – Managing users in Azure AD

3. Select **+ New guest user** on the **Users | All users** tile:

Figure 5.9 – Adding a new user

4. When the **+ New guest user** tile opens, **Invite user** will be selected by default. Here, you will add the information for the user. The only required information is the email address of the guest user. There is an option to also add a **Personal message** to let the user know why they are being invited to collaborate. Once the email address has been added in the required field, select **Invite** to send the invitation:

Figure 5.10 – Entering a guest user email address and an optional message to invite

5. Once the invitation has been sent, the guest user will appear in the Azure AD users list as a **Guest**, with the creation type field showing **Invitation**. The following screenshot shows what this looks like in the list of users in Azure AD. Also note that **User principal name** includes the external email address, with the @ changed to an underscore and a prefix of #EXT#. The user is also not added to the custom domain but the default tenant domain name of tenantname.onmicrosoft.com:

Figure 5.11 – Guest user in the Azure AD user list

6. Selecting the guest user will take you to the profile page for that user. Here, you can view whether the invitation has been accepted in the **Identity** section. Selecting **Manage** will allow you to resend the invitation, if necessary. The following screenshot shows that the guest user has not accepted the invitation:

Figure 5.12 – Guest user invitation status

7. The invited guest user will receive an email to accept the invitation, as shown in the following screenshot. Once they accept the invitation, they will be an active guest user on the Azure AD tenant:

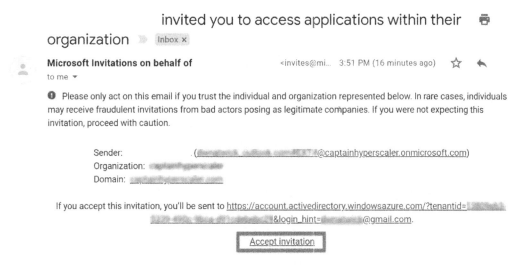

Figure 5.13 – Guest user email to accept the invitation to join

Once the guest user accepts the invitation, they can be assigned Microsoft 365 licenses in the same manner that member users are assigned licenses from their user profile. This process was discussed in the **Assigning licenses** section of *Chapter 4, Creating, Configuring, and Managing Identities*. Next, we will go through the same guest invitation process in the Microsoft 365 admin center.

Creating a new user in Microsoft 365 admin center

This section will step through adding a guest user to **Microsoft 365 admin center** using the GUI:

1. Log into https://admin.microsoft.com and select **Users – Guest Users** from the left menu using the drop-down arrow:

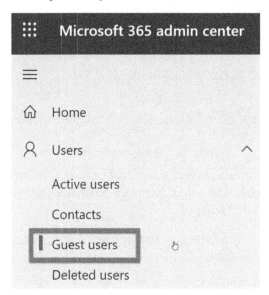

Figure 5.14 – Guest users in Microsoft 365 Admin center

2. Select **Add a guest user** from the **Guest users** tile. Notice that within this tile, we can go to **Manage Teams settings** to adjust guest access to Teams. The following screenshot shows that this tenant has already been configured to allow guest access to Teams. Configuring access to Teams for guests is not within the scope of the *Identity and Access Administrator exam*. However, it is covered in detail within the Teams Administrator course and exam topics:

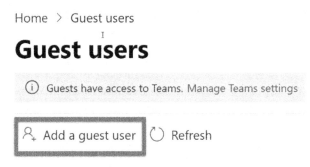

Figure 5.15 – Add a guest user via the Guest users tile

3. Unlike the process of adding an active user, which we discussed in the previous chapter, when adding a guest user from the Microsoft 365 admin center, you are taken directly to Azure AD to create the guest user via the same process we covered in the previous section. This is shown in the following screenshot and is the same as what we saw in *Figure 5.10*:

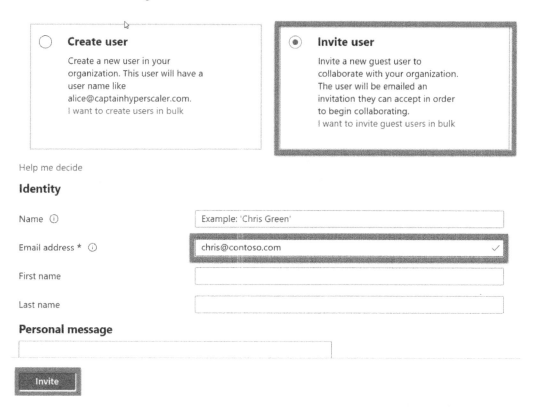

Figure 5.16 – Entering a guest user email address and an optional message to invite

4. Scrolling down below the personal message also shows additional options for assigning the guest user to a group and a manager within the Azure AD tenant. This can be seen in the following screenshot:

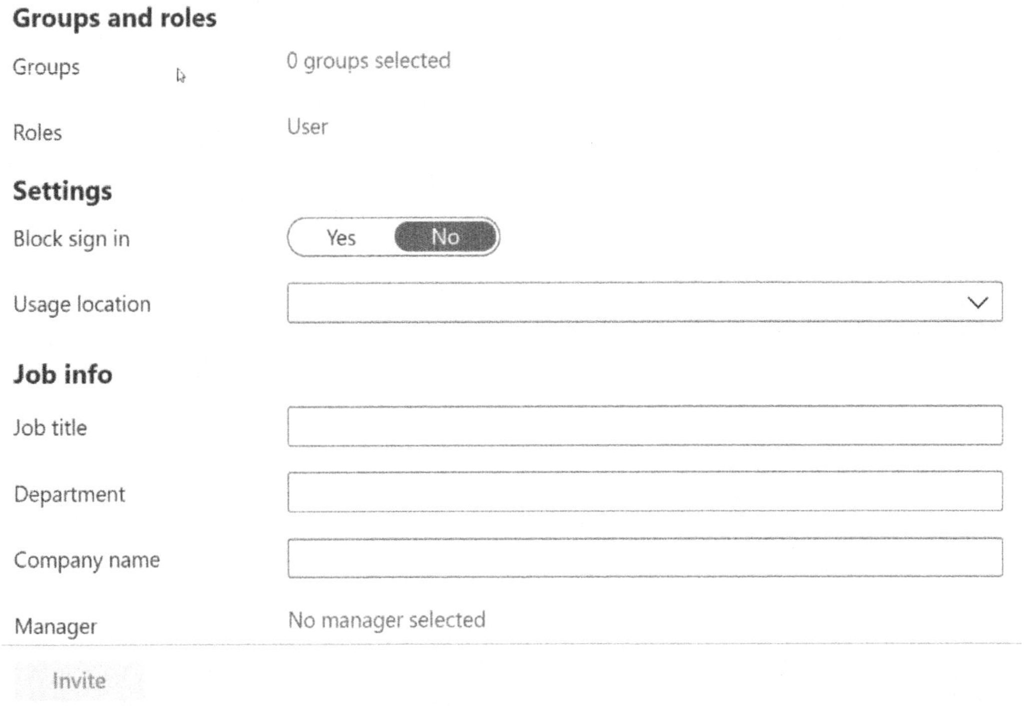

Groups and roles

Groups	0 groups selected
Roles	User

Settings

Block sign in	Yes No
Usage location	⌄

Job info

Job title	
Department	
Company name	
Manager	No manager selected

Invite

Figure 5.17 – Addng a location and licenses

5. The remaining steps for inviting this user can be found in the previous section by following steps 4 through 7.

After completing these steps, you can return to the **Guest users** tile; the user that you added will be in the user list. Next, we will look at how to invite multiple guest users with a `.csv` file bulk import.

Inviting guest users with a bulk import

The previous steps are helpful when you have only a few users to add to Azure AD. The next two sections will go through steps of adding or inviting a group of users simultaneously to Azure AD. The first will be using a `.csv` file to bulk invite guest users. Let's get started:

1. Log into `https://portal.azure.com` and navigate to **Azure Active Directory**:

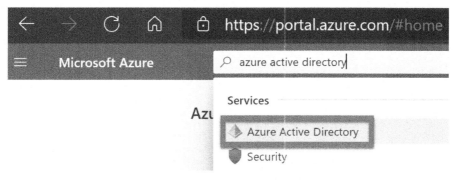

Figure 5.18 – Azure Active Directory in the Azure portal

2. From the menu on the left of the tile, select **Users** under **Manage**:

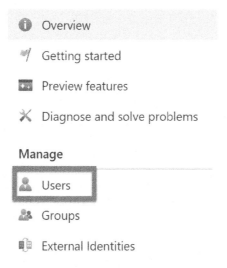

Figure 5.19 – Managing users in Azure AD

3. Select the **Bulk operations** drop-down arrow and select **Bulk invite** for the **Users |
    All Users** tile:

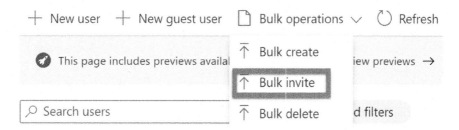

Figure 5.20 – Bulk invite users

4. Selecting **Bulk invite** will open a new tile. This tile provides a download link to a template file that you must edit and populate with your user information. Once you've done this, you can upload it to bulk invite guest users:

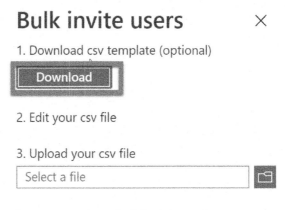

Figure 5.21 – Bulk create user steps

5. The CSV template provides you with the fields included with the user profile. The required fields are the email address of the guest user and the redirection URL. The following screenshot shows how you can complete the .csv file:

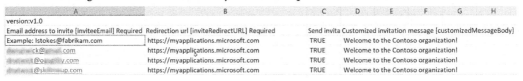

Figure 5.22 – .csv file completion

6. Once populated, save the changes and upload the CSV file to add the users.

7. You will be notified that the file was uploaded successfully. Click **Submit** to add the users, as shown in the following screenshot:

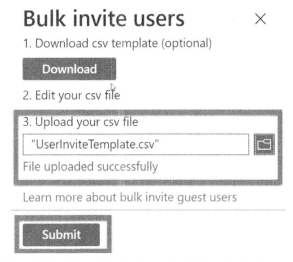

Figure 5.23 – Uploading and submitting the bulk invitation for guest users

8. Once the file has been submitted and uploaded, you will be notified that the file was successfully processed. The following screenshot shows the completion of this process:

Figure 5.24 – Bulk invitation file has been successfully processed

9. You also have the option to download the updated `.csv` file, which contains a field that documents this successful invitation for each of the guest users. The following screenshot shows the new field showing the successful completion in column **E**. If an invitation failed, a failure reason will be provided in column **F**:

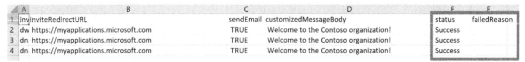

	A	B	C	D	E	F
1	inv	inviteRedirectURL		sendEmail	customizedMessageBody	status	failedReason
2	dw	https://myapplications.microsoft.com		TRUE	Welcome to the Contoso organization!	Success	
3	dn	https://myapplications.microsoft.com		TRUE	Welcome to the Contoso organization!	Success	
4	dn	https://myapplications.microsoft.com		TRUE	Welcome to the Contoso organization!	Success	

Figure 5.25 – Bulk invitation status in the updated CSV file

Once the users have been invited, they will receive an email, stating that they will need to accept the invitation. This process is the same as step 7 in the **Adding a single guest user in the Azure AD portal** section. The added guest users will be populated in **Users | All users**. With that, you have completed a bulk user invitation using the CSV template. In the next section, we will add users with PowerShell.

Adding users with PowerShell

This section will step through how to add users with **PowerShell**. There are some steps you must follow to prepare PowerShell to run Azure AD commands. The following steps will get you ready to run the commands for adding users to Azure AD:

1. Open PowerShell as an administrator. This can be done by searching for PowerShell in Windows and choosing **Run as administrator**:

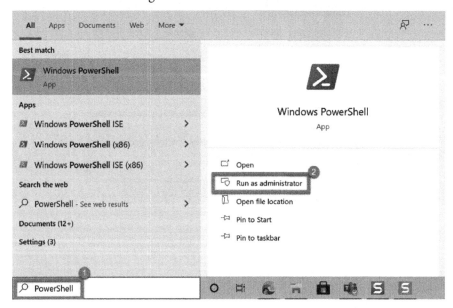

Figure 5.26 – Opening PowerShell as an administrator

2. You will need to add the Azure AD PowerShell module if you have not used it before. Run the `Install-Module AzureAD` command. When prompted, press Y to continue:

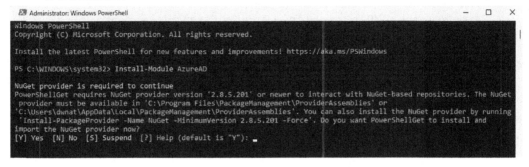

Figure 5.27 – Installing the Active Directory module

3. Confirm that the module has been installed correctly by running the `Get-Module AzureAD` command.

4. Next, you will need to log in to Azure by running `Connect-AzureAD`. The Microsoft login window will appear for you to log into Azure AD:

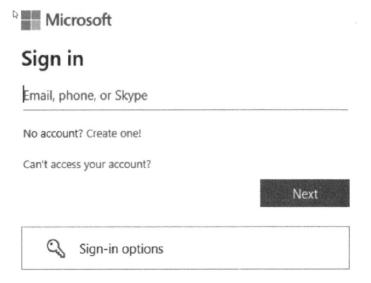

Figure 5.28 – Microsoft – log into Azure AD

5. To verify that you are connected and to see existing users, run `Get-AzureADUser`.

6. You are now ready to invite a guest user. The following command will be populated with the user information and run. If you have more than one user to add, you can use a `.txt` file to add the user information and copy and paste it into PowerShell:

```
New-AzureADMSInvitation -InvitedUserDisplayName
"Display" -InvitedUserEmailAddress name@emaildomain.
com -InviteRedirectURL https://myapps.microsoft.com
-SendInvitationMessage $true
```

7. The following screenshot shows the format of running the invitation command for multiple invitations:

Figure 5.29 – Inviting multiple guest users with PowerShell

8. The following screenshot shows the response that is received for each invitation that was sent after running the invitation command:

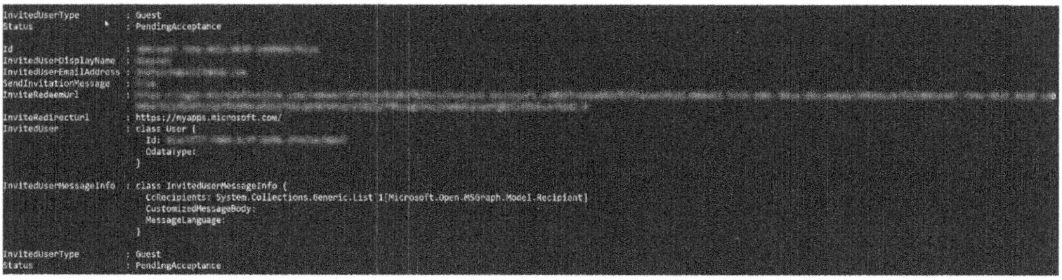

Figure 5.30 – Successful invitation sent response from within PowerShell

You now know how to invite users within the Azure AD portal and Microsoft 365 admin center, how to use bulk invitations with a CSV file, and how to invite users with PowerShell commands. Additional information on `PowerShell` commands for Azure AD guest users can be found at the following link:

```
https://docs.microsoft.com/en-us/azure/active-
directory/external-identities/b2b-quickstart-invite-
powershell#:~:text=%20Quickstart%3A%20Add%20a%20guest%20
user%20with%20PowerShell,the%20email%20address%20specified.%20
%20.%20More%20.
```

In the next section, we will discuss how to manage external accounts within Azure AD.

Managing external user accounts in Azure AD

Now that we understand how to invite guest users in Azure AD, you may want to group these users based on roles, departments, or locations.

Once a guest user accepts the invitation to join the Azure AD tenant, they are now a B2B user. These B2B users can be assigned roles, added to groups, and assigned licenses in the same way as a member user. However, there are some differences that you should know about.

Managing guest user licenses

Regarding licenses, B2B users from partner businesses that currently have a Microsoft 365 license can utilize their licenses to collaborate on documents and join Microsoft Teams meetings on the Azure AD tenant, without the need to assign additional licenses. If the guest users are using a personal email, such as from Microsoft or Gmail, then licenses will need to be assigned to these guest users. For these users, it is the host tenant who has these licenses and assigns them to the guest account.

Password management

Unlike member users on the Azure AD tenant, where administrators assign the initial temporary password to the user and then they create their password, guest user accounts are different. Guest users are invited to the Azure AD tenant and utilize the current password of the email account that was used for the invitation. Any password updates and changes that are made on that email account are maintained by that email account and not on the Azure AD tenant. Therefore, guest user accounts cannot be managed with the same **self-service password reset** (**SSPR**) capabilities as a member account. SSPR will be discussed in more detail in *Chapter 7, Planning and Implementing Azure Multi-Factor Authentication and Self-Service Password Reset*.

Multi-factor authentication

Enabling, enrolling, and enforcing **multi-factor authentication** (**MFA**) will be discussed in detail later in *Chapter 7, Planning and Implementing Azure Multi-Factor Authentication and Self-Service Password Reset*. However, it is necessary to mention that as a host Azure AD tenant, guest users can be enrolled and enforced into MFA to access resources. This also allows *conditional access policies* to be enforced on guest users and groups that contain guest user accounts. The guest accounts for MFA are managed in the same way as member accounts. The following screenshot shows the MFA configuration page with user accounts available to enroll:

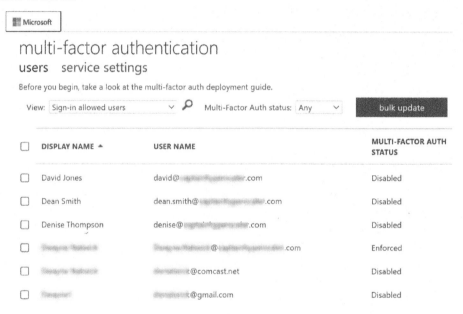

Figure 5.31 – MFA configuration page with guest accounts

With MFA enabled and enforced on the guest user accounts, they will be required to provide the additional verification information that is needed, such as a cell phone number or registering to the authenticator app for the host Azure AD tenant.

When managing an external user account, it is important to know that you cannot manage the original email address that was used to invite the guest user or their password. However, we do have the ability to enter information into their profile, such as their name, display name, usage location, profile picture, and other information that is important to identify the user on our Azure AD tenant. The guest user can also access their user portal to make these customizations. This section discussed how these guest users can be managed from a B2B invitation to allow partner collaboration. The final section of this chapter will discuss how to configure the use of identity providers for use within our Azure AD tenant.

Configuring identity providers

As we have already established, Azure AD is a cloud-based authentication service that is used by Microsoft 365, Azure, and all of Microsoft's cloud services and solutions for identity and authentication management. Some companies may have another IAM solution that they are using. Azure AD allows these companies to utilize these providers as part of the B2B authentication relationship as guests on the Azure AD tenant.

Azure AD is built on open source standards and, therefore, can support **Security Assertion Markup Language** (**SAML**) or *WS-Federation*. Configuring these direct federation relationships allows users to start collaborating while utilizing their existing identity credentials from their existing *identity provider*. These relationships are configured within the Azure AD tenant to create this federated B2B relationship between companies.

The users would then access the Azure AD tenant as a guest through the same portal URL that is used in the guest user invitation, but with the federated tenant ID added to the end to create a customized URL; for example, `https://myapps.microsoft.com/?tenantid=tenant id` or `https://portal.azure.com/tenant id`. The tenant ID will be created as part of the identity provider configuration, which we will discuss in the next section. If the guest is using their own Azure AD tenant, the URL would look like this: `https://myapps.microsoft.com/guesttenantname.onmicrosoft.com`.

When using an identity provider federation for these guest user B2B relationships, there are a few points to note:

- If a guest user has accepted an invitation to be part of the Azure AD tenant before the federation relationship has been created, they will continue to authenticate in the same manner.

- Regarding guest users that have been invited through direct federation as a partner company, and then the partner company moves to Azure AD, those guest users will continue to have access so long as the direct federation relationship between tenants exists.

- Guest users that have been invited through direct federation between partner companies will lose access if that direct federation relationship is removed.

With direct federation, the login experience for the user is the same as if they were logging into their own company resources. This maintains a consistent and unchanged experience for these users when they're collaborating with partner companies.

To create a direct federation relationship, navigate to **External Identities** from the **Manage** section of the **Azure Active Directory** portal, as shown in the following screenshot:

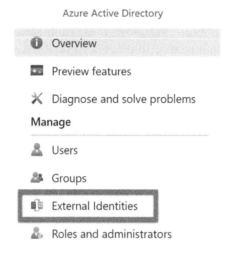

Figure 5.32 – External Identities in Azure AD

From there, you must select **All identity providers**, as shown in the following screenshot:

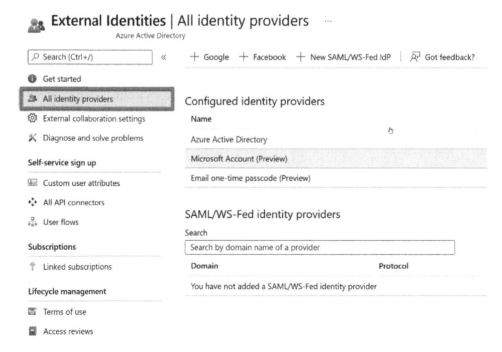

Figure 5.33 – All identity providers within the External Identities blade

For additional information and the steps for configuring direct federation, go to `https://docs.microsoft.com/azure/active-directory/external-identities/direct-federation`.

From within the **External Identities | All identity providers** blade, you will see that **Azure Active Directory**, **Microsoft Account**, and **Email one-time passcode** are the default pre-configured identity providers. You don't need to follow any additional steps to allow direct federation. For **Azure Active Directory** and **Microsoft Account**, the guest user invitation process is used to collaborate. The following screenshot shows what appears when selecting either of these identity provider options:

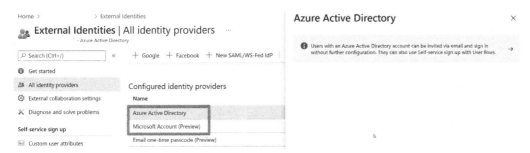

Figure 5.34 – Azure AD and Microsoft Account direct federation configuration

To allow a user to have guest access with a one-time passcode, multiple options can be used for configuration. These are shown in the following screenshot:

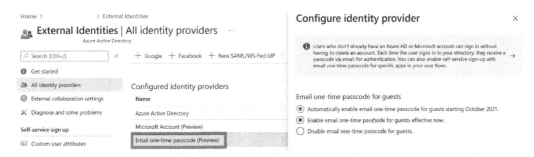

Figure 5.35 – Configuring a one-time passcode for guest user federation

The one-time passcode option is helpful when you have a single guest user that needs to be added rather than multiple guest users from a partner company.

In addition to the default identity providers of **Azure Active Directory, Microsoft Account**, and **Email one-time passcode**, additional *SAML* and *WS-Federation* identity providers can be configured, as well as **Google** and **Facebook**. In the following sections, we will discuss how this configuration is done with these two popular identity providers.

Google configuration

Microsoft provides a direct federation for Google as an identity provider. This can be initiated by selecting **+ Google** from the **External Identities | All identity providers** blade, as shown in the following screenshot:

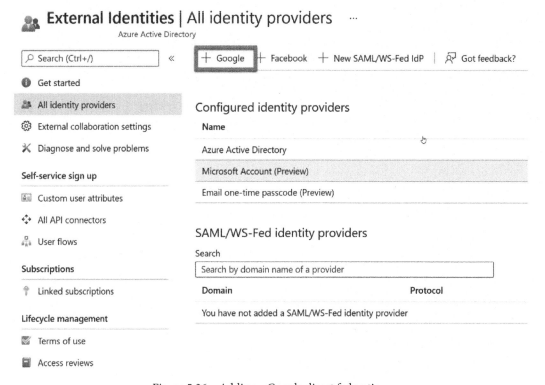

Figure 5.36 – Adding a Google direct federation

After selecting **+ Google**, another blade will open with additional information that is required to configure Google as an identity provider. To obtain this information, the Azure AD account must be configured within Google. There is a link to these directions within the blade that opens, as shown in the following screenshot:

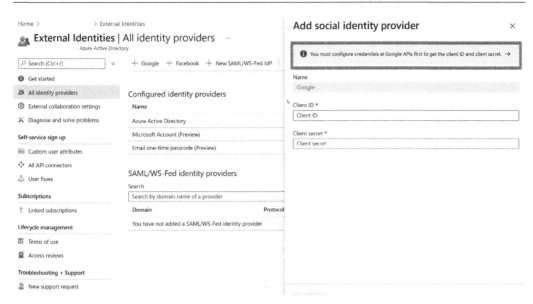

Figure 5.37 – Google identity provider configuration

The link for these directions is also provided here: `https://docs.microsoft.com/azure/active-directory/external-identities/google-federation`.

After going through the steps within Google for federation, a **Client ID** and **Client secret** will be provided. You must copy these values into the fields shown in the preceding screenshot and select **Save** to complete the direct federation.

The next section will show you how to configure Facebook as a direct federation identity provider.

Facebook configuration

Microsoft provides a direct federation for Facebook as an identity provider. This can be initiated by selecting **+ Facebook** from the **External Identities | All identity providers** blade, as shown in the following screenshot:

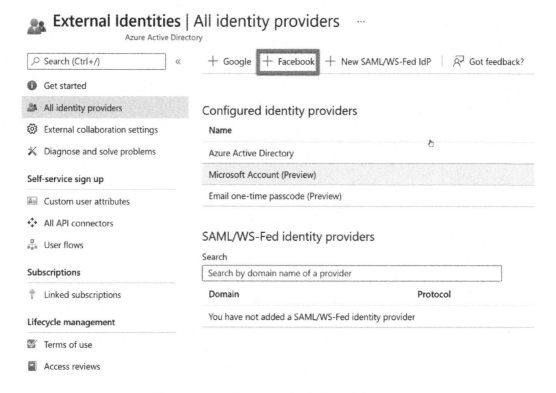

Figure 5.38 – Adding a Facebook direct federation

After selecting **+ Facebook**, another blade will open with additional information that is required to configure Facebook as an identity provider. To obtain this information, the Azure AD account must be configured within Facebook. There is a link to these directions within the blade that opens, as shown in the following screenshot:

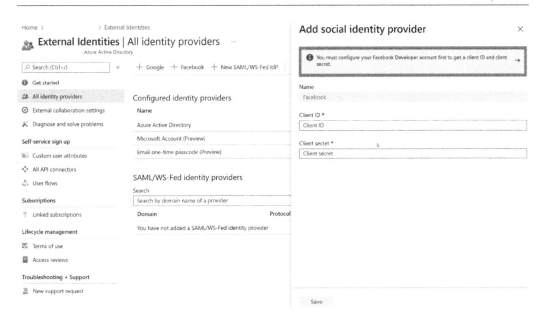

Figure 5.39 – Facebook identity provider configuration

The link for these directions is also provided here: `https://docs.microsoft.com/azure/active-directory/external-identities/facebook-federation`.

After going through the steps within Facebook for federation, a **Client ID** and **Client secret** will be provided. You must copy these values into the fields shown in the preceding screenshot and select **Save** to complete the direct federation.

Summary

In this chapter, we described how to configure external collaboration settings, invite external users, manage these users, and configure external identity providers. External users are important within our Azure AD tenant since they allow partner organizations and individuals to collaborate. In the upcoming chapters, we will discuss the ability to configure a hybrid identity, as well as the authentication infrastructure for users that need access to an on-premises Windows AD and cloud resources within Azure AD

6
Implementing and Managing Hybrid Identities

The previous chapter focused primarily on guest user accounts. We discussed how these guest users would be able to access and collaborate on resources with member users and how we would manage these users. In this chapter, we will bring together on-premises identities and allow them to create a seamless single identity with our **Azure Active Directory** (**Azure AD**) tenant. After completing this chapter, you will understand how to configure, manage, and troubleshoot connections between on-premises and cloud **identity and access management** (**IAM**) solutions.

In this chapter, we're going to cover the following main topics:

- Implementing and managing **Azure AD Connect**
- Implementing and managing seamless **single sign-on** (**SSO**)
- Implementing and managing Azure AD Connect Health
- Troubleshooting sync errors

Technical requirements

In this chapter, we will continue to explore configuring a tenant for use with **Microsoft 365** and **Azure**. There will be exercises that will require access to Azure AD. If you have not yet created trial licenses for Microsoft 365, please follow the directions provided in *Chapter 1, Preparing for your Microsoft Exam*.

Implementing and managing Azure AD Connect

In order to be able to configure hybrid identities and synchronization in Azure AD and on-premises environments, you will need to have the *Global Administrator* or *Hybrid Identity Administrator* role within the Azure AD tenant and the *Domain Enterprise Administrator* role within the on-premises Windows AD tenant. We will explain more about the differences between these two directory services in this section.

Before we discuss the implementation of hybrid identities, it is important to understand what a hybrid identity is and why it is necessary. The following sections will provide this information.

Hybrid identity

The term *hybrid identity* is meant to signify that a company has users that use on-premises resources, and users that use cloud-native resources. Within this hybrid identity infrastructure, there is going to be an on-premises **Windows AD** domain controller that is used to manage the on-premises users, and **Azure AD**, which manages the cloud-native users, both members and guests. This infrastructure coincides with companies that use a *hybrid cloud*. Many companies have this Windows AD domain controller in place today. The next section will provide some understanding of what this means before we discuss how we can connect it to our Azure AD.

Azure AD

To review, Azure AD is Microsoft's cloud-based IAM solution. The role of Azure AD is to manage cloud identities for Microsoft and Azure resources, as well as other third-party cloud applications that utilize open source identity protocols, such as **Security Assertion Markup Language (SAML)** or **Web Services Federation (WS-Federation)**. For users to access these cloud applications and services, they require their identity to be configured and recognized within the Azure AD tenant.

Many companies do not utilize only cloud-native applications and services, therefore they rely on an on-premises Windows AD to manage access to these applications. The next section will explain Windows AD and its role in a hybrid identity infrastructure.

Windows AD

Windows AD is the software that we are referencing. Within an on-premises infrastructure, we also refer to the role of domain controller and the overall solution of **AD Domain Services (AD DS)**. AD DS is the legacy IAM solution for companies with on-premises infrastructure. The focus of the exam is not to have a deep-dive into Windows AD and AD DS, but it is important to understand how it compares to Azure AD as it pertains to users and groups. If you would like to understand more about AD DS, you can read more at this link: https://docs.microsoft.com/en-us/windows-server/identity/ad-ds/get-started/virtual-dc/active-directory-domain-services-overview.

There are similarities and differences between AD DS and Azure AD. They both manage identities and access by assigning roles and authorizing access to users and groups; however, AD DS does this through an object-based structure. Within this object structure, there can be multiple **organizational units (OUs)** to which these objects belong. This creates a more hierarchical structure than the flat structure of Azure AD, but this difference creates challenges when wanting users and groups to access on-premises and cloud resources utilizing the same username and password. Additionally, creating duplicate entries in both AD DS and Azure AD will cause an issue with the management of users and groups.

To address this problem, Microsoft has Azure AD Connect as a solution to bring together AD DS and Azure AD. The next section will discuss how this works.

Azure AD Connect

Since a company that is adopting the use of cloud resources has, in most cases, this on-premises identity infrastructure in place, we need to have a way to synchronize these identities to our cloud-based Azure AD. **Azure AD Connect** is a software solution that is installed within the on-premises infrastructure and configured to synchronize users and groups to Azure AD. Azure AD Connect simplifies the management of these users and groups by providing ways that an identity and access administrator can manage users in one interface and have the changes update in near real time.

Since there are structural differences in how AD DS and Azure AD are built, Azure AD Connect provides a conduit to create a consistent user and administrator experience with IAM.

There are some prerequisites and aspects that are out of scope within Azure AD Connect that you should understand. The installation prerequisites can be found at this link: `https://docs.microsoft.com/en-us/azure/active-directory/hybrid/how-to-connect-install-prerequisites`. When planning to implement Azure AD Connect, the following information should be understood and planned accordingly:

- Azure AD Connect synchronizes users and groups, not devices or applications. There are ways to co-manage devices and support on-premises application access within Azure AD—this will be covered in later chapters.

- Azure AD Connect synchronizes a single AD DS forest per Azure AD tenant. If there are multiple forests, then multiple tenants will be required in Azure AD.

There are additional considerations in planning for AD DS and Azure AD synchronization with Azure AD Connect, but these will be covered within the use cases for each synchronization type.

There are three options when configuring Azure AD Connect for synchronization, outlined as follows:

- **Password hash synchronization (PHS)**
- **Pass-through authentication (PTA)**
- **AD Federation Services (AD FS)** synchronization

Before we move into how to configure Azure AD Connect, let's take a closer look at each of these synchronization types and how they are used.

PHS

PHS is the easiest option to configure and is the default option that is within the **Express** setup. PHS maintains both the on-premises and cloud identities of users. This takes place through providing on-premises user identities to Azure AD, along with an encrypted hash of their passwords. This allows users to sign in to on-premises and cloud applications with the same authentication credentials.

PHS is a good option when a company has a single on-premises domain and is moving quickly to a cloud-native infrastructure. PHS is not for companies with complex authentication and password requirements within on-premises AD.

As previously stated, PHS maintains authentication credentials on-premises and in Azure AD. Therefore, PHS can have users authenticate to cloud applications through Azure AD while passing authentication responsibilities of on-premises applications to on-premises AD. The benefit here is that if a connection fails in Azure AD Connect between the on-premises AD DS and Azure AD, users are still able to authenticate to their cloud applications and remain partially productive. The following diagram provides a visual representation of how this workflow is handled. Additional information can be found at `https://docs.microsoft.com/en-us/azure/active-directory/hybrid/whatis-phs`:

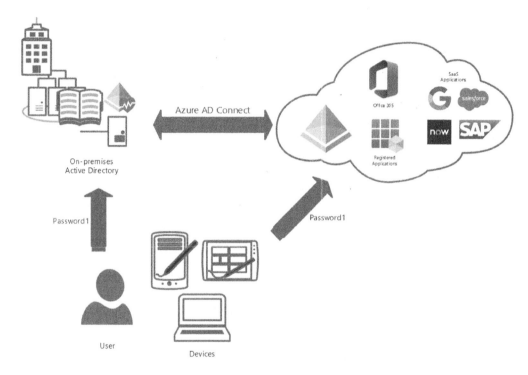

Figure 6.1 – PHS diagram

As the preceding diagram shows, a user can go to either Azure AD or on-premises AD to authenticate. Therefore, if the Azure AD Connect connection is down, users still have access to their cloud resources. This allows them to continue to work until the synchronization connection is restored. Now, let's look at PTA.

PTA

The next hybrid identity synchronization option that we will discuss is PTA. Unlike PHS, which allows user identities to be authenticated in either the on-premises AD or Azure AD, PTA requires all users to authenticate to the on-premises AD.

In this configuration, if the Azure AD Connect connection between Azure AD and the on-premises AD were to become disconnected, no users would be able to authenticate to on-premises or cloud resources. Therefore, it is important to actively monitor this connection and build resiliency in the architecture. The following diagram shows how PTA functions and how you can architect resiliency with redundancy in **PTA agents** and a backup domain controller:

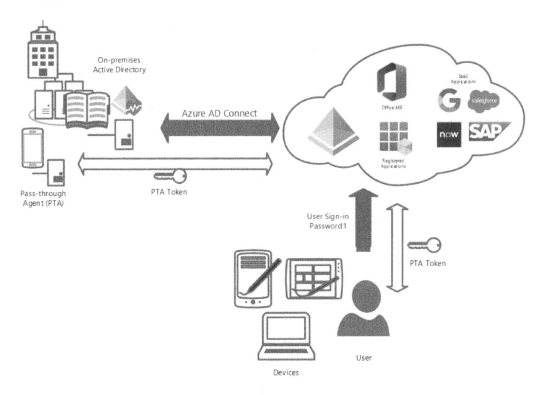

Figure 6.2 – PTA diagram

There are some good reasons to utilize PTA. If a company requires authentication parameters and limits that only allow users to access resources during certain times, these rules can only be configured currently on an AD domain controller. With PTA, you can utilize modern authentication features with Azure AD, such as **multi-factor authentication (MFA)** and **self-service password reset (SSPR)**. However, for SSPR, you will need to enable the **Password writeback** feature within Azure AD Connect. Additional information on PTA can be found at this link: `https://docs.microsoft.com/en-us/azure/active-directory/hybrid/how-to-connect-pta`.

AD FS synchronization

AD FS synchronization is the most complex of the three Azure AD Connect synchronization types. Unlike PHS and PTA, which can be installed directly on the on-premises domain controller in many cases, AD FS requires additional infrastructure in place to support the authentication process. Here is a diagram that shows the complexity of the infrastructure and the necessary components:

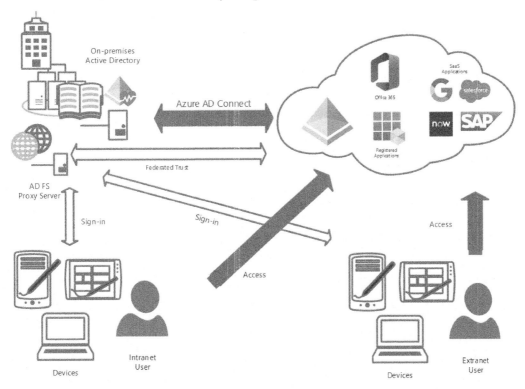

Figure 6.3 – AD FS synchronization diagram

AD FS synchronization is utilized in complex AD infrastructures where there are multiple domains, and third-party MFA solutions or smart cards are utilized. For additional information on the configuration of AD FS synchronization, you can use this link: `https://docs.microsoft.com/en-us/azure/active-directory/hybrid/how-to-connect-fed-management`.

PHS and PTA are the more widely discussed of the three Azure AD Connect options. It is important to understand when each should be used within a hybrid identity architecture, as discussed in each of the corresponding sections.

Now, let's go through the initial steps of installing Azure AD Connect and connecting to Azure AD.

Configuring Azure AD Connect

The first steps are to download and install Azure AD Connect in the on-premises infrastructure. This can be done on the on-premises AD domain controller server or on another member server that is joined to the domain. For our example, we will use the on-premises domain controller server to install Azure AD Connect. Follow these next steps:

1. If you are not already logged in to the AD domain controller, access it through **Remote Desktop Protocol (RDP)** with domain administrator credentials. This is important because, as stated previously, you need to have this level of administrator privileges to configure Azure AD Connect. Once logged in, you should see a screen like this:

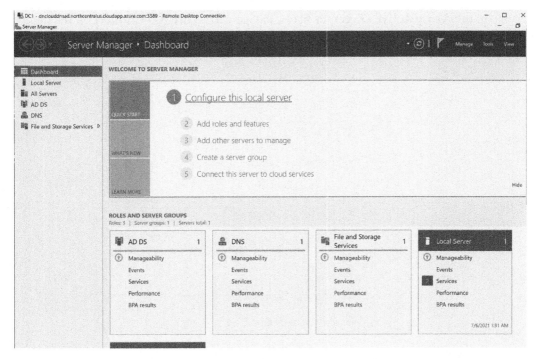

Figure 6.4 – RDP login to the AD domain controller

2. From the AD domain controller, use the web browser to navigate and log in to Azure AD at `https://portal.azure.com`. Once logged in, you should see a screen like this:

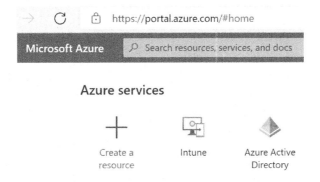

Figure 6.5 – Azure AD in Azure portal

3. In the **Azure Active Directory** blade, navigate to **Azure AD Connect** on the menu under **Manage**, as illustrated in the following screenshot:

Azure Active Directory

Administrative units

Enterprise applications

Devices

App registrations

Identity Governance

Application proxy

Licenses

Azure AD Connect

Custom domain names

Figure 6.6 – Azure AD Connect on Azure AD menu

4. Within the **Azure AD Connect** blade, find **Download Azure AD Connect** under **PROVISION FROM ACTIVE DIRECTORY**, as illustrated in the following screenshot:

PROVISION FROM ACTIVE DIRECTORY

 Azure AD cloud sync

This feature allows you to manage sync configurations from the cloud, in addition to syncing Active Directory users and groups from disconnected forests.

Manage Azure AD cloud sync

Azure AD Connect sync

Not Installed	Download Azure AD Connect
Last Sync	Sync has never run
Password Hash Sync	Enabled

Figure 6.7 – Download Azure AD Connect link

5. The **Microsoft Azure Active Directory Connect** download page will open. Select **Download** to download Azure AD Connect, as illustrated in the following screenshot:

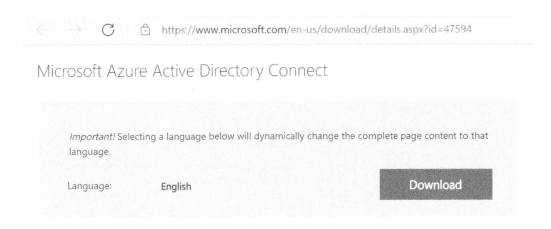

Figure 6.8 – Azure AD Connect at Microsoft download page

6. After the download completes, navigate to the Downloads folder and install the application, as illustrated in the following screenshot:

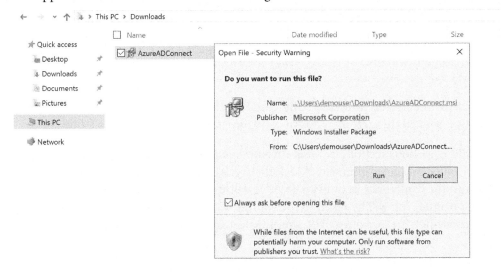

Figure 6.9 – Installation of Azure AD Connect

7. When the installation is complete, you will begin the configuration wizard for Azure AD Connect. Agree to the licensing terms and click **Continue**, as illustrated in the following screenshot. Additional configuration steps will be covered in the following sections based on the synchronization that your company will use:

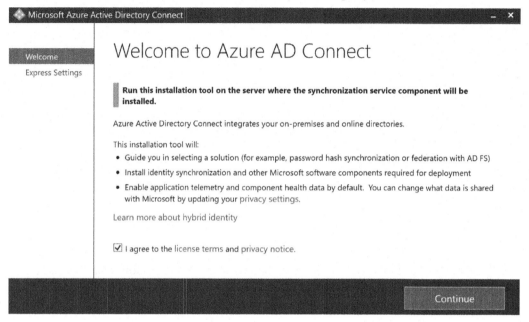

Figure 6.10 – Azure AD Connect configuration wizard

The next sections will discuss the use cases for each and how to configure them with Azure AD and AD DS.

Now that we understand how PHS handles authentication and where we would use it, the next action is to go through the steps to configure it. Let's do this now, as follows:

1. In the previous section, we went through the process to get Azure AD Connect installed on the on-premises AD domain controller. We will pick up from *step 7* with the configuration of PHS. After accepting the licensing terms and selecting **Continue**, you will be taken to the express settings, as shown in the following screenshot. To configure PHS, simply select **Use express settings**:

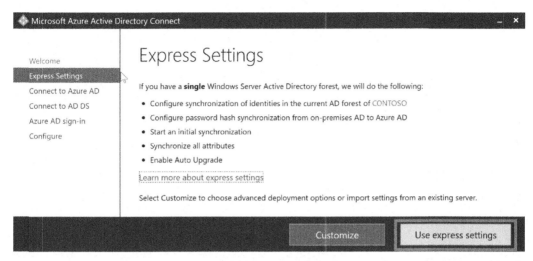

Figure 6.11 – Express settings wizard

2. Next, you will be prompted to enter the global administrator or hybrid identity administrator credentials for the Azure AD account, as illustrated in the following screenshot:

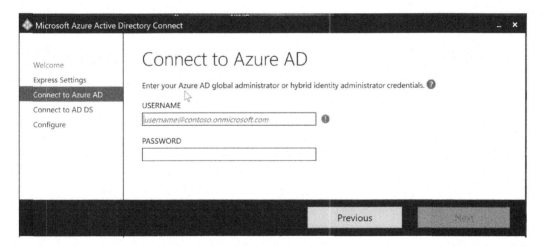

Figure 6.12 – Entering Azure AD global administrator or hybrid identity administrator credentials

3. After the Azure AD credentials have been verified, you will be prompted to enter the domain enterprise administrator credentials for the on-premises AD DS, as illustrated in the following screenshot:

Figure 6.13 – Entering AD DS enterprise administrator credentials

4. The next step verifies that the on-premises domain is an active domain registered in Azure AD. If it is not, you have an option to select to continue without matching the **User Principal Name (UPN)** suffixes, as shown in the following screenshot:

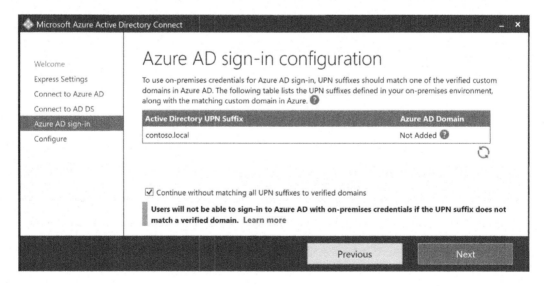

Figure 6.14 – AD UPN suffix and Azure AD domain

5. Selecting **Next** will verify the configuration and provide a summary of the settings for Azure AD Connect. You have an option to start synchronizing users immediately after the configuration is complete. Select **Install** to complete the Azure AD Connect installation, as illustrated in the following screenshot:

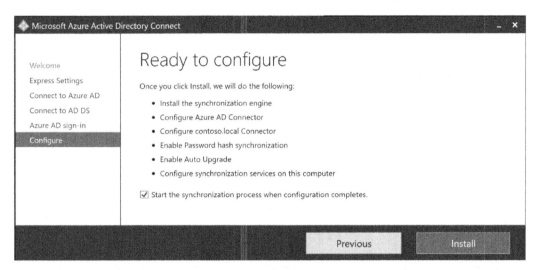

Figure 6.15 – Ready to configure and install Azure AD Connect

After the installation completes, Azure AD Connect will be configured to synchronize users from on-premises AD to Azure AD, utilizing PHS. This configuration for Azure AD Connect is the least complex of the three options. The next sections will provide information about PTA and AD FS synchronization.

Configuring PTA

We will now go through the steps to configure PTA within Azure AD Connect, as follows:

1. Follow *Figure 6.4* through *Figure 6.10* to get started. After accepting the licensing agreement, instead of selecting **Use express settings** as we did for PHS, you will select **Customize**, as shown in the following screenshot:

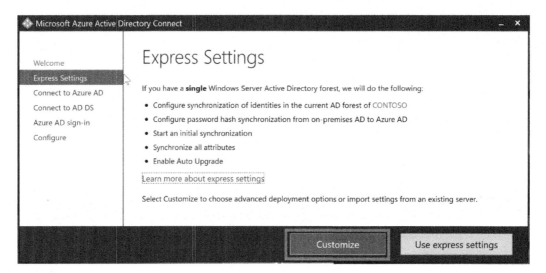

Figure 6.16 – Customize settings wizard

2. In the next section of the wizard, there are some options to use existing setup options. If this is a new installation, no additional boxes need to be checked; just select **Install**, as illustrated in the following screenshot:

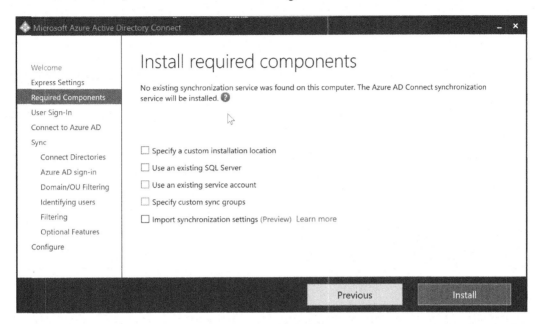

Figure 6.17 – Installation of Azure AD Connect Structured Query Language (SQL) and synchronization services

3. This will begin the local SQL Server express and synchronization installation.

4. When the database and synchronization components complete installation, you can then customize the synchronization options. **Pass-through authentication** will be chosen for this exercise; then, select **Next**. The following screenshot shows this selection. Later in this chapter, we will discuss the implementation of SSO within hybrid identities. The following screenshot also shows that there is a checkbox to enable this during this step, but it can also be configured later:

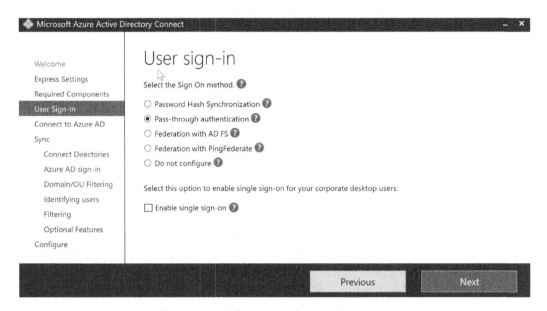

Figure 6.18 – Selecting synchronization option

> **Note**
>
> All of the synchronization types are available in this blade, including PHS. These steps would only be used with PHS if certain OUs were going to be synchronized with Azure AD.

5. Next, you will enter the global administrator credentials to **Connect to Azure AD** and select **Next**, as illustrated in the following screenshot:

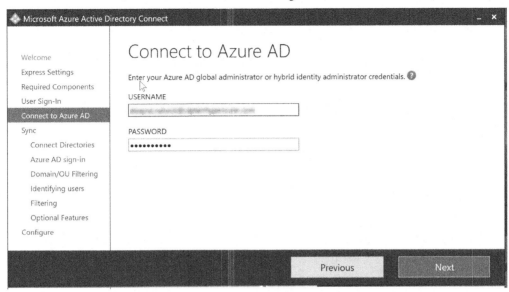

Figure 6.19 – Entering Azure AD global administrator credentials

6. In the next step, locate the AD forest that you will be synchronizing with Azure AD Connect and select **Add Directory**, as illustrated in the following screenshot:

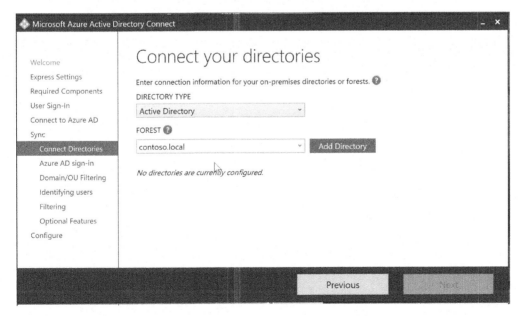

Figure 6.20 – Adding directory forest to synchronize

7. The tile will open to create a new AD account, or you can use an existing AD account. This is not the enterprise domain administrator account. If this is a new Azure AD Connect installation, select **Create new AD account** for the AD forest synchronization and select **OK**, as illustrated in the following screenshot:

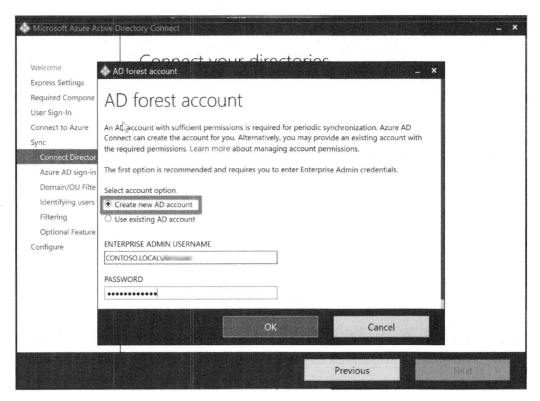

Figure 6.21 – Creating a new AD account for synchronization

8. The directory is now configured, and you can select **Next** to continue the configuration, as illustrated in the following screenshot:

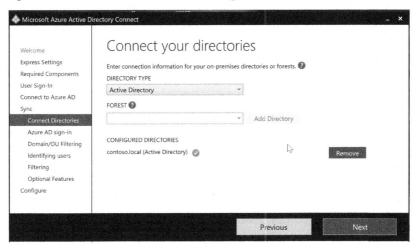

Figure 6.22 – Configured directories are complete

9. The connection between Azure AD and the AD domain is initiated and checked. Azure AD Connect is now signed in to both Azure AD and the on-premises AD, and they are almost ready to synchronize. The following screenshot shows the configuration—this should be similar to yours. Since authentication is handled within the on-premises AD domain controller, the domain selected does not need to be a publicly verified domain. You can select the box to continue without matching and then select **Next**, as illustrated here:

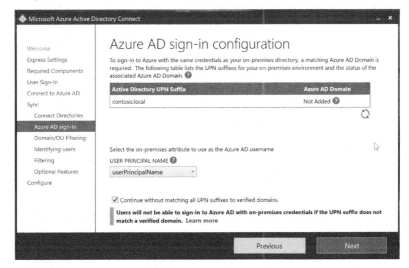

Figure 6.23 – Azure AD sign-in configuration

10. The next few blades allow for the customizing of selected domains, object units, or users to be synchronized. The first blade is the **Domain/OU Filtering** blade. If you select **Sync selected domains and OUs**, you can select and deselect the checklist options for a more targeted synchronization. This is shown in the following screenshot:

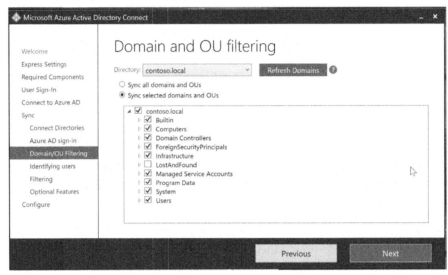

Figure 6.24 – Syncing selected domains and OUs

11. For our example, we are going to select all domains and OUs, as shown in the following screenshot, and then select **Next**:

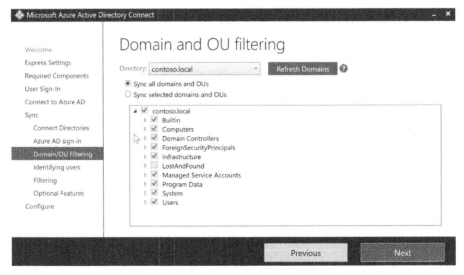

Figure 6.25 – Syncing all domains and OUs

12. The next blade allows us to identify users to synchronize. In this example, we are going to leave this as **All** and select **Next**. One point to note in the following screenshot is that **Azure** is selected as the source anchor. You can select different attributes within the on-premises AD domain to be a source anchor, if necessary. The source anchor is a unique attribute for the user and it cannot be changed once it is chosen:

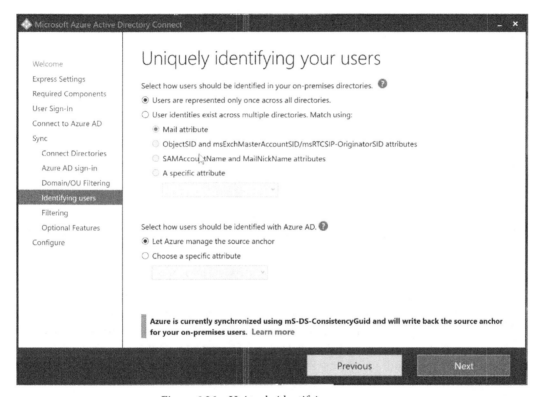

Figure 6.26 – Uniquely identifying your users

13. In the **Filtering** blade, you can select certain users and devices to be synchronized. In the following example, we will select **Synchronize all users and devices** and select **Next**:

Figure 6.27 – Filtering users and devices

14. The final blade in the customization settings is **Optional Features**. Some of the selections here are grayed out during the initial setup, but you do have an option to include **Password hash synchronization**, **Directory extension attribute sync**, **Azure AD app and attribute filtering**, and **Password writeback**. **Password writeback** is required to allow SSPR to be used within Azure AD. These options can be included by going back into Azure AD Connect after installation, so for this exercise, you will leave them unchecked and select **Next**, as illustrated in the following screenshot:

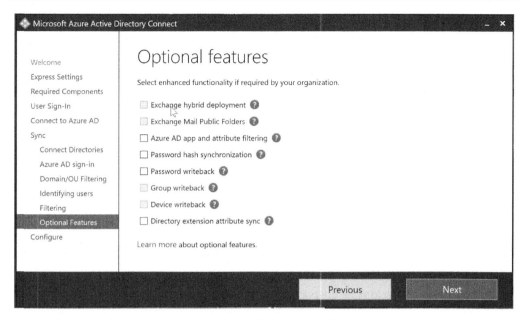

Figure 6.28 – Optional Features configuration

15. The final blade shows the configuration settings that you have completed through this exercise. Select **Install** to complete the installation of Azure AD Connect with PTA, as illustrated in the following screenshot:

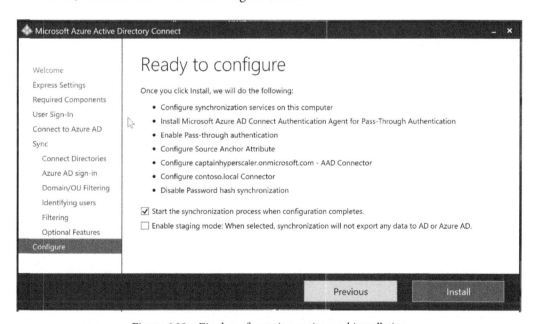

Figure 6.29 – Final configuration review and installation

16. This will complete the installation of Azure AD Connect with PTA. One of the components that are installed on the AD domain controller server is a **PTA agent**. In order to have a resilient architecture, it is recommended that at least two of these PTA agents are installed on member servers in the on-premises infrastructure.

The third and final synchronization type within hybrid identity infrastructures is AD FS. The customization of Azure AD Connect would be initiated within the customized fields within the Azure AD Connect wizard. However, AD FS requires additional federated proxy servers, as shown in *Figure 6.3* earlier in this chapter.

The next section will discuss how to implement and manage SSO within a hybrid identity infrastructure.

Implementing and managing seamless SSO

Seamless SSO provides users with a consistent sign-on experience, whether they are accessing cloud applications or on-premises applications. Within a hybrid identity through Azure AD Connect, this is configured based on the synchronization settings. PHS provides this experience when the users are synchronized since the passwords from on-premises environment are synchronized as a hash to Azure AD. PTA requires **Password writeback** to be enabled in the **Optional Features** blade. For additional security, **Password hash synchronization** can also be enabled with PTA. Once these configurations are in place, users can authenticate to their applications on-premises and within Azure AD with the same username and password.

In addition, many third-party cloud applications are registered and available within the Azure AD application marketplace. These applications can also be configured to use Azure AD credentials for SSO. The more applications your company uses that can be configured for Azure AD authentication, the better the experience for users. *Chapter 10, Planning and Implementing Enterprise Apps for Single Sign-On (SSO),* will cover the registration of applications within Azure AD in detail.

The next section will discuss Azure AD Connect Health and how it can be used to monitor the hybrid identity connection created with Azure AD Connect.

Implementing and managing Azure AD Connect Health

Azure AD Connect Health is used as a monitoring and management tool for Azure AD Connect. Azure AD Connect Health provides a heartbeat from the on-premises installation of Azure AD Connect to Azure AD. The information that is reported in Azure AD Connect Health includes successful and unsuccessful synchronizations and can also alert you as the identity and access administrator of a lost connection between Azure AD Connect and Azure AD. Azure AD Connect Health is not installed by default when installing Azure AD Connect, so you will need to install this application. The following steps will take you through the process and will show you where to access Azure AD Connect Health:

1. Log in to the Azure AD portal and navigate to **Azure AD Connect** under **Manage** in Azure AD. Scroll down to see **HEALTH AND ANALYTICS**. Select the **Azure AD Connect Health** link in blue, as shown in the following screenshot:

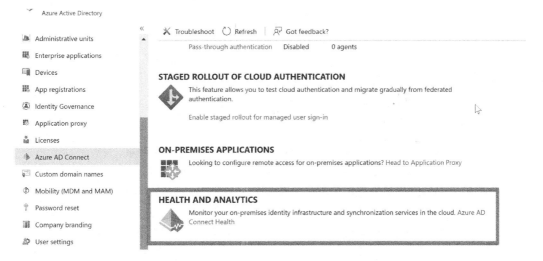

Figure 6.30 – Azure AD Connect Health link

2. The **Azure Active Directory Connect Health** blade will open to the **Quick start** section. If you have used PHS or PTA, you will choose **Download Azure AD Connect Health Agent for AD DS**, as shown in the following screenshot. Note that there is a separate download for AD FS infrastructures:

Figure 6.31 – Azure AD Connect Health Agent download

3. After the file downloads, navigate to the folder and select the file to install the agent, as illustrated in the following screenshot:

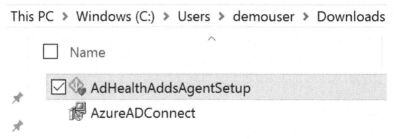

Figure 6.32 – Azure AD Connect Health Agent install file

4. When the installation runs, you will be prompted for some prerequisites. Select **Next** and the agent will install. The installation will prompt a configuration that will run a PowerShell script and ask you to log in to the Azure AD account with the global administrator credentials. Within the PowerShell window, you will be provided with notification of a successful agent installation, as illustrated in the following screenshot:

```
Administrator: Windows PowerShell
2021-07-08 03:00:57.732 Current Monitoring Level in Registry is not set

2021-07-08 03:00:57.732 Updated Monitoring Level in Registry to Full

2021-07-08 03:00:57.732 ProductName: Microsoft Azure AD Connect Health agent for AD DS, FileVersion: 3.1.77.0,
TC Time: 2021-07-08 03:00:57Z

2021-07-08 03:00:57.732 AHealthServiceUri (ARM): https://management.azure.com/providers/Microsoft.ADHybridHeal

2021-07-08 03:00:57.747 AdHybridHealthServiceUri: https://adds.aadconnecthealth.azure.com/

2021-07-08 03:00:57.857 AHealthServiceUri (ARM): https://management.azure.com/providers/Microsoft.ADHybridHeal

2021-07-08 03:00:57.857 AdHybridHealthServiceUri: https://adds.aadconnecthealth.azure.com/

2021-07-08 03:00:58.7 AHealthServiceApiVersion: 2014-01-01

2021-07-08 03:03:09.92 Detecting AdDomainService roles...

2021-07-08 03:03:10.17 Detected the following role(s) for contoso.local:

2021-07-08 03:03:10.186          Active Directory Domain Services

2021-07-08 03:03:18.174 Acquiring Monitoring Service certificate using tenant.cert

2021-07-08 03:03:22.518 Successfully acquired and stored Monitoring Service certificate: Subject=CN=DC1, CN=13
9-490c-9bca-d91cdebebc29, OU=Microsoft ADFS Agent, Issuer=CN=Microsoft PolicyKeyService Certificate Authority,
t=6CE535BD203FF35B3C6F2BFE84C6DF0574791337

2021-07-08 03:03:22.534 Fetched and stored agent credentials successfully...

2021-07-08 03:03:22.534 Starting agent services...

2021-07-08 03:03:40.253 Started agent services successfully...

2021-07-08 03:03:45.393 Agent registration completed successfully.

Detailed log file created in temporary directory:
C:\Users\demouser\AppData\Local\Temp\2\AdHealthAddsAgentConfiguration.2021-07-08_03-00-57.log
```

Figure 6.33 – Azure AD Connect Health Agent installation complete and registered

5. After the agent has been installed and registered, you can view the status of the sync services in **Azure Active Directory Connect Health**, as shown in the following screenshot:

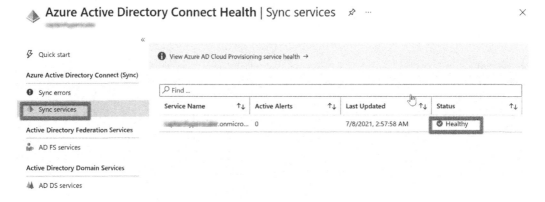

Figure 6.34 – Azure AD Connect Health Agent sync services' status

6. You can also see the status of the on-premises AD DS services, as shown in the following screenshot:

Figure 6.35 – Azure AD Connect Health Agent AD DS services' status

Azure AD Connect Health is now connected and registered within Azure AD. You can now view the health status of the services and determine if any synchronization errors are taking place with the Azure AD Connect services configured in the infrastructure. The final section of this chapter will discuss how to find and troubleshoot errors with Azure AD Connect Health.

Troubleshooting sync errors

The final part of the implementation and management of a hybrid identity infrastructure is how to identify and troubleshoot errors. Azure AD Connect Health provides the platform and heartbeat that is used by Azure AD Connect to verify that the connection and synchronization between the on-premises AD and Azure AD are completing successfully. However, connections are lost and errors happen within every network infrastructure. Azure AD Connect Health can help provide information to troubleshoot and diagnose these synchronization errors.

In the previous section, *Figure 6.34* and *Figure 6.35* showed how to view the health of the sync services and AD DS. Above the sync services' health on the menu is where you can view sync service errors. Further down the menu, you will find the **Troubleshoot** section, as shown in the following screenshot:

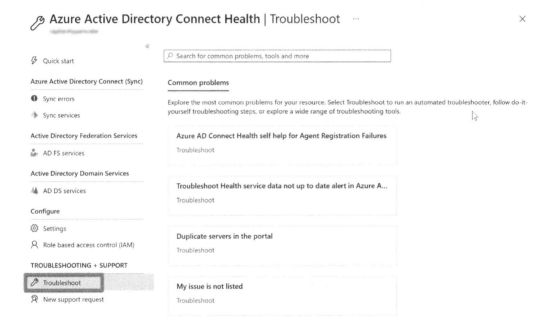

Figure 6.36 – Troubleshooting common problems

Within the **TROUBLESHOOTING + SUPPORT** menu, the **Troubleshoot** blade provides some common problems that might arise and documentation on how to correct the issue. If this documentation does not help, you can use the **New support request** blade to open a support ticket with Microsoft.

Synchronization status can also be viewed on the Azure AD Connect installed on-premises server, which is the AD domain controller, as installed during the chapter exercise, by going to **Synchronization Services Manager**. This is shown in the following screenshot:

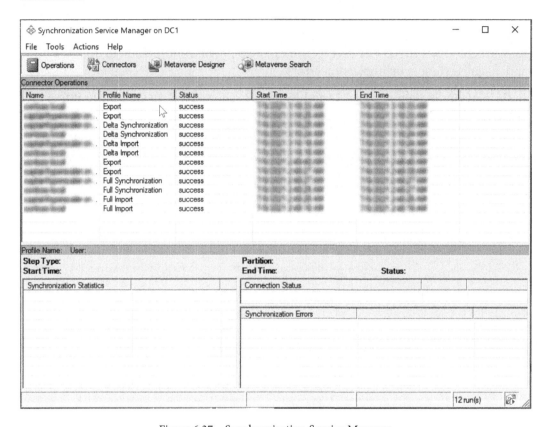

Figure 6.37 – Synchronization Service Manager

This section has shown you how to view and find steps to troubleshoot synchronization issues with Azure AD Connect.

Summary

In this chapter, we described how to configure, manage, and monitor hybrid identities utilizing Azure AD and on-premises AD DS. This included how to configure Azure AD Connect synchronization types, set up SSO, install Azure AD Connect Health, and monitor and troubleshoot synchronization status. The next chapter will discuss securing identities with MFA and providing SSPR for users and groups.

Section 3 – Implementing an Authentication and Access Management Solution

This section will focus on how to plan and implement authentication and access management solutions.

This section of the book comprises the following chapters:

- *Chapter 7, Planning and Implementing Azure Multi-Factor Authentication and Self-Service Password Reset*

- *Chapter 8, Planning and Managing Password-Less Authentication Methods*

- *Chapter 9, Planning, Implementing, and Administering Conditional Access and Azure Identity Protection*

7
Planning and Implementing Azure Multi-Factor Authentication (MFA) and Self-Service Password Reset (SSPR)

The previous chapter covered the various ways to implement hybrid identity synchronization between Azure Active Directory and Windows Active Directory, and how to implement seamless single sign-on. In this chapter, we will discuss the planning and implementation of Azure MFA and SSPR for users and groups. This will include deploying, managing, and configuring MFA for users and groups. This chapter will also cover the differences between verifying identity with MFA and SSPR.

In this chapter, we're going to cover the following main topics:

- Planning Azure MFA deployment (excluding MFA Server)
- Implementing and managing Azure MFA settings
- Configuring and deploying SSPR
- Deploying and managing password protection
- Planning and implementing security defaults

Technical requirements

In this chapter, we will continue to explore configuring a tenant for the use of **Microsoft 365** and **Azure**. There will be exercises that will require access to Azure Active Directory. If you have not yet created the trial licenses for Microsoft 365, please follow the directions provided within *Chapter 1*, *Preparing for Your Microsoft Exam*.

Planning an Azure MFA deployment

As more companies move to cloud technologies and having identities within the cloud, the ability to protect those identities become paramount to avoiding security breaches. Microsoft and Azure Active Directory provide many ways to protect these identities and mitigate risks. Some examples of these solutions include the following:

- **Password complexity rules** are used to protect against users utilizing common terms and easy-to-guess passwords. Enforcing certain lengths and complexities, such as the use of alphanumeric and special characters, along with a minimum length, can deter attackers from their ability to utilize password dictionary attacks or identify dates and information from social media accounts that could be used as a password.

- **Password expiration rules** are utilized to avoid a password remaining the same for an extended period of time. The longer that a password is used by a user, the more likely that it is to eventually be exposed. Having a password expire can enforce that users change their passwords, and blocking the use of previously used passwords assists in disrupting an attacker's ability to gain access to systems through exposed passwords.

- **SSPR** allows users to perform their own password changes when they forget their password or if they feel that their password has been compromised. We will discuss this in detail later in this chapter in the *Configuring and deploying SSPR* section.

- **Azure AD Identity Protection** is a solution within Azure AD that provides additional capabilities for monitoring and managing user identities and determining whether an identity has been compromised. Azure Identity Protection will be discussed further in *Chapter 9, Planning, Implementing, and Administering Conditional Access and Azure Identity Protection*.

- **Azure AD Password Protection** works together with Azure AD Identity Protection to enforce password complexity rules and expiration rules, and also to block common passwords from being utilized. Azure AD Password Protection will also be discussed in *Chapter 9, Planning, Implementing, and Administering Conditional Access and Azure Identity Protection*.

- **Azure AD smart lockout** is part of Azure AD Identity Protection and will be discussed further in *Chapter 9, Planning, Implementing, and Administering Conditional Access and Azure Identity Protection*.

- **Azure AD Application Proxy** allows Azure AD identity and access management to be utilized for enterprise applications that may remain in on-premises infrastructures in a hybrid cloud architecture. Enterprise application **Identity and Access Management (IAM)** will be further discussed in *Chapter 10, Planning and Implementing Enterprise Apps for Single Sign-On (SSO)*.

- **Single sign-on (SSO)** was discussed in *Chapter 6, Implementing and Managing Hybrid Identities*, when configuring hybrid identities and users' abilities to access resources in the cloud and on-premises utilizing the same username and password. SSO utilization will be expanded to other cloud applications and on-premises enterprise applications in *Chapter 10, Planning and Implementing Enterprise Apps for Single Sign-On (SSO)*.

- **Azure AD Connect** provides the synchronization between on-premises Windows Active Directory and cloud Azure AD for a single identity management platform in a hybrid architecture. This allows password requirements and rules to be utilized across the hybrid architecture. Azure AD Connect was discussed in *Chapter 6, Implementing and Managing Hybrid Identities*.

These solutions assist in protection against certain attacks, such as brute force and password dictionary attacks, by making it more difficult to guess passwords. However, passwords are still a vulnerability and stolen passwords are the primary cause of security breaches. To protect user access to company assets and technologies, additional identity verification should be utilized. This can be accomplished utilizing Azure AD MFA.

What is MFA?

In the previous section, we discussed some of the requirements and solutions that can be put in place to protect and manage our identities and avoid exposure of user passwords. Unfortunately, there is nothing that can completely avoid a user password from being stolen and the majority of security breaches are caused by passwords that have been compromised.

If passwords are so insecure, then why do we continue to use them? The foundation of authentication and authorization has been built on the username and password concept. This means that applications that have been developed for years and years have utilized this concept, so rewriting these applications now is not an option.

How can we protect our users and make sure that a user is who they say they are when authenticating? Since username and password authentication is not going away anytime soon, additional solutions should be utilized to protect identities and verify that a username and password being entered is from the person to whom it has been assigned. This can be done utilizing MFA.

MFA addresses the potential of a password to be compromised by requiring the user requesting access to provide an additional form of identification before they are authenticated and authorized access. There are three forms, or factors, of identification that are used for MFA, and MFA is configured to require any two of these three factors to verify a user's identity. The three forms are as follows:

- Something you know

- Something you have

- Something you are

Let's look at each of these in more detail by defining each and giving some examples of how they are used.

Something you know

Something you know is a form of identification that you provide from your memory. This is in many cases your password. It could also be a **personal identification number (PIN)** or the answer to a security question. In most systems for verification, this is usually the factor for verification and then the second form is one of the next two options.

Something you have

Something you have is probably the most difficult to comprehend at times. This factor requires something physically in your possession to verify your identity. In most cases, this generally is a cell phone that you have identified when enrolling into the MFA service. On that cell phone, you can then be provided with ways to verify your identity through a code being sent via text message, a phone call to that cell phone number, a code within an authenticator app on the phone, or pushing an approval notification through the authenticator app. In addition to a cell phone being something that you have, some companies may provide a separate token-generating device that rotates a code every few minutes.

Something you are

Something you are is when some form of biometrics is used as the second factor for verification. Usually, the most popular use here is fingerprints or facial recognition. To use this factor, the devices being used for this factor must be equipped with the capability to provide and process this information. This is a more complex factor than the other two and may not be technically or financially feasible for a company that has older systems. However, many new systems have these capabilities built in, such as Windows 10, and Apple or Android smartphones.

Figure 7.1 shows how these three factors can work together to provide the verification of user identities for authentication:

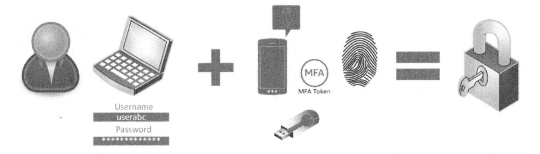

Figure 7.1 – Diagram of MFA

Now that we understand the concept of MFA and what is required to verify a user identity for authentication, let's discuss how MFA can be used within the Azure AD MFA solution. The next sections will go through how Azure AD MFA works, how it is licensed and configured, and how it is enabled and enforced for administrators and users.

How does Azure AD MFA work?

In the previous section, we discussed the overall concept of MFA. Now we will go through how MFA works within the embedded Azure AD MFA solution in Azure AD. Conceptually, it is the same as it requires two factors to authenticate. The important things to note within Azure AD MFA is what you need to license for users, how it is configured and enforced, and the handling of MFA for administrators and standard users.

We will start with the licensing of Azure AD MFA before getting into the technical aspects of configuring, enabling, and enforcing MFA.

What licenses include Azure AD MFA?

Microsoft has made many changes to Azure AD MFA over the past few years as MFA has become more popular for use within companies. Different levels of Azure AD MFA are included with both the Free and Premium Azure AD licenses.

Azure AD Free is standard with any Azure account or standalone Microsoft 365 account. This allows anyone to utilize Azure AD MFA for their personal accounts or users on Azure at no cost. This allows the protection of cloud identities and cloud resources on Azure using MFA. The limitations to the Azure AD Free license is that it does not have the advanced identity protection features for Conditional Access and user risk that are part of an Azure AD Premium license.

Azure AD Premium licenses are recommended for company use. The Premium licenses provide advanced identity and access management security solutions that allow protection of identities. In addition, premium licenses are required to utilize Azure AD for hybrid identity. When subscribing to an Azure AD Premium P1 or P2 license, Azure AD MFA is a fully licensed feature and can be used with Conditional Access policies. Azure AD Premium P2 licenses are required for Azure AD Identity Protection and Privileged Identity Management. Conditional Access policies and Azure AD Identity Protection will be discussed in further detail in *Chapter 9, Planning, Implementing, and Administering Conditional Access and Azure Identity Protection*, and Privileged Identity Management will be discussed in *Chapter 13, Planning and Implementing Privileged Access and Access Reviews*.

Azure AD MFA is available with any Azure subscription to enable, assign, and enforce to Global Administrators. Enforcing Azure AD MFA for all Global Administrators should always be the first step in utilizing MFA within your company.

Now let's discuss the authentication methods that will be used for Azure AD MFA.

Azure authentication methods

As a company, you have the option to determine which authentication methods will be utilized within Azure AD as the factors for MFA. The first factor of a password does not change; the additional Azure authentication method is the second factor that will be used for Azure AD MFA verification.

As an administrator, you need to determine the methods that are going to be used for the second factor. The options are shown in *Figure 7.2* and can be found in the multi-factor authentication service settings. We will go through these steps in further detail in the next section:

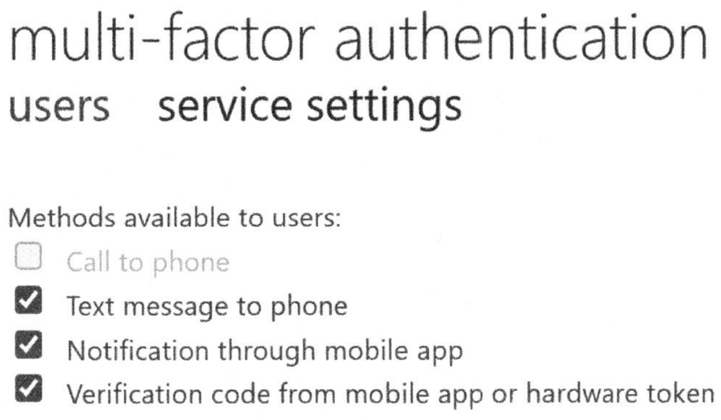

multi-factor authentication
users   service settings

Methods available to users:

☐ Call to phone
☑ Text message to phone
☑ Notification through mobile app
☑ Verification code from mobile app or hardware token

Figure 7.2 – Azure AD MFA authentication methods

The **Call to phone** feature is enabled only if the company administrator has populated a phone number in the global directory for users. Otherwise, this is not available as an option, as seen in *Figure 7.2*. The others mentioned, such as **Text message to phone**, **Notification through mobile app**, and **Verification code from mobile app or hardware token** are available to select. Selecting all of these options will allow users to choose which option would they like as their preferred second factor for Azure AD MFA when they enroll. We will discuss this in further detail later in the *Implementing and managing MFA settings* section.

The next section will go through the exercise of configuring Azure AD MFA and the user enrollment process.

Configuring Azure AD MFA

We have been discussing the ways in which Azure AD MFA can be used for identity verification and protection. This section will step through the configuration of Azure AD MFA. Before implementing and utilizing MFA within your company, it is important to let the users know how the process of authentication will change. Microsoft has provided templates that can be used as a communication plan at `https://www.microsoft.com/en-us/download/details.aspx?id=57600&WT.mc_id=rss_alldownloads_all`.

Configuring for Azure AD MFA is a two-step process: the first step is for the IT administrator to configure and enable users for MFA, and the second step is for the users to complete the enrollment process to enforce Azure AD MFA. Let's go through the steps that administrators will complete to enable users for Azure AD MFA.

Enabling users for Azure AD MFA

After the IT department has communicated with users that MFA is going to be utilized to protect and verify user identities, users need to be configured and enabled to enroll in Azure AD MFA. This starts within Azure AD in the list of users:

1. Navigate to **Azure AD** and select **Users** to display all users, as shown in *Figure 7.3*:

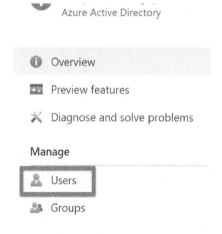

Figure 7.3 – Azure AD manage all users

2. Next, select **Per-user MFA**, as shown in *Figure 7.4*:

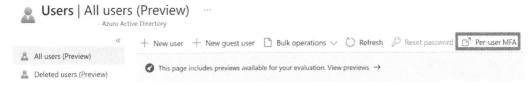

Figure 7.4 – Select Per-user MFA

3. The Azure AD MFA portal opens. Here you can select all users to enable for Azure AD MFA or only select users. *Figure 7.5* shows the list of users and choosing to select all to enable for Azure AD MFA. If there are already users that are utilizing or enabled for MFA, you will need to select **Manage user settings**:

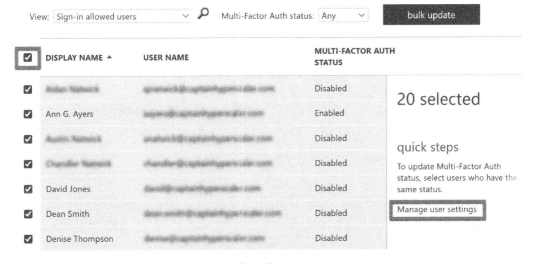

Figure 7.5 – Select all users in Azure AD

4. When selecting **Manage user settings**, a new tile opens where you can require current MFA users to re-enter their information for additional verification. *Figure 7.6* shows selecting for users to provide contact methods again and restore MFA on all remembered devices. Select **save** to continue:

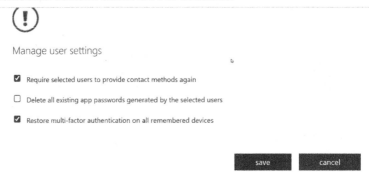

Figure 7.6 – Manage user settings

5. If Azure AD MFA does not have any users currently enrolled, navigating back and selecting all users or only a single user allows us to immediately enable Azure AD MFA to those users, as shown in *Figure 7.7*:

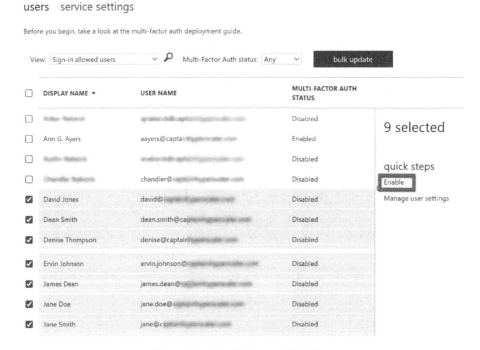

Figure 7.7 – Enable Azure AD MFA

6. Selecting **Enable** will open up a tile that will provide you with a link to the deployment guide, if you have not already reviewed it. This also provides the communication template links discussed earlier in this section. Once you are ready, select **enable multi-factor auth** to enable MFA for the selected users, as shown in *Figure 7.8*:

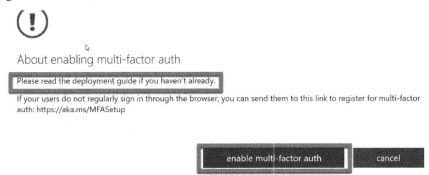

Figure 7.8 – Enable multi-factor authentication

7. *Figure 7.9* shows the confirmation that the selected users had MFA enabled:

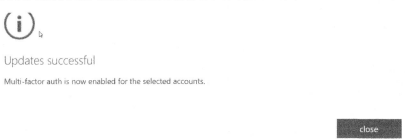

Figure 7.9 – Users enabled successfully

8. These users have been enabled, which means that they have been provided with the ability to use MFA and they will be prompted for the information necessary for a second factor. However, for MFA to be utilized for these users, they must be selected again and enforced for MFA, as shown in *Figure 7.10*:

Figure 7.10 – Select users to enforce MFA

9. *Figure 7.11* shows the final step to enforcing MFA for selected users:

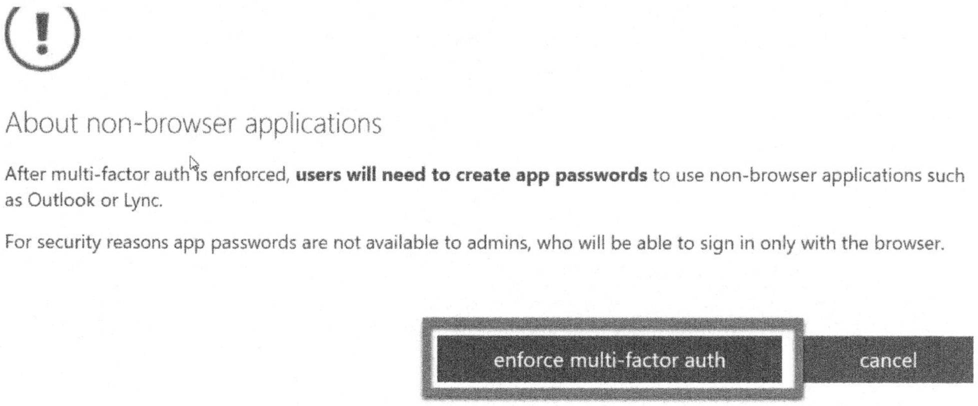

About non-browser applications
After multi-factor auth is enforced, users will need to create app passwords to use non-browser applications such as Outlook or Lync.
For security reasons app passwords are not available to admins, who will be able to sign in only with the browser.
enforce multi-factor auth
cancel

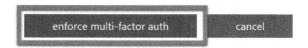

Figure 7.11 – Enforce multi-factor authentication

10. MFA has now been enforced successfully to the selected users. Confirmation of success should be the same as shown in *Figure 7.12*:

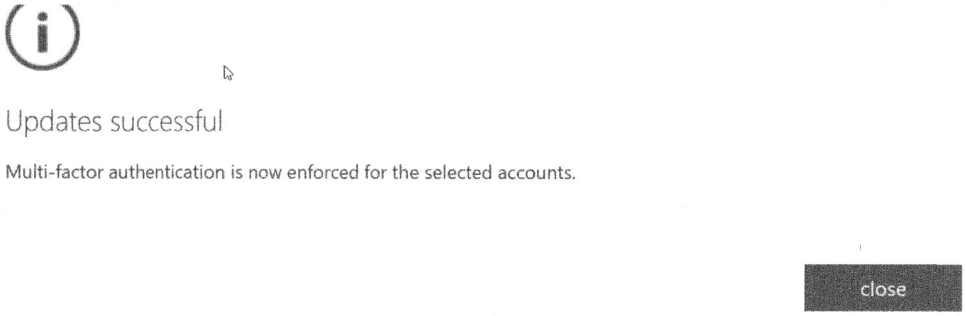

Updates successful
Multi-factor authentication is now enforced for the selected accounts.
close

Figure 7.12 – Successful enforcement of MFA for selected users

11. You should now have a list of users that are both enabled and enforced in the MFA status column, similar to *Figure 7.13*:

	DISPLAY NAME ▲	USER NAME	MULTI-FACTOR AUTH STATUS
☐	Ann G. Ayers	aayers@	Enabled
☐	David Jones	david@	Enforced
☐	Dean Smith	dean.smith@	Enforced
☐	Denise Thompson	denise@	Enforced
☐	Ervin Johnson	ervin.johnson@	Enabled
☐	James Dean	james.dean@	Enabled
☐	Jane Doe	jane.doe@	Enabled
☐	Jane Smith	jane@	Enabled

Figure 7.13 – User MFA status

As an administrator, you have completed the steps for enabling and enforcing Azure AD MFA. In the next section, we will go through the user steps to complete the process.

User enrollment in Azure AD MFA

Once the company administrators have enabled or enforced MFA for users, the next step is for the process to be completed by the users. This is where the communication plan is very important. The company needs the users in the company to understand the importance of completing these steps to protect their identities, their personal information, and the assets of the company. The process that a user is going to experience whether they were set to enabled or enforced MFA is no different.

Let's look at the steps that a user is going to be asked to take once they have had MFA enabled:

1. Go to `https://office.com` to log in as one of the enabled users in Azure AD. When the user logs in with username and password, they will be prompted for more information. Select **Next** to continue, as shown in *Figure 7.14*:

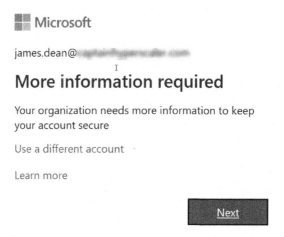

Figure 7.14 – More information required

2. On the next tile, you will be asked to provide a phone number, or you can also select the drop-down menu to use the mobile app for verification. Enter the information and select **Next**:

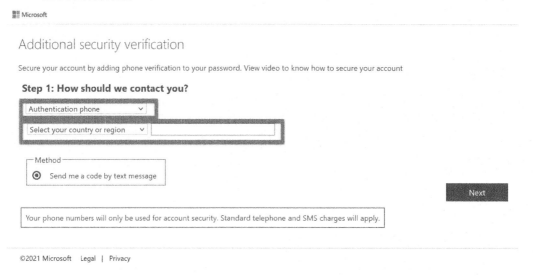

Figure 7.15 – Additional security verification information

3. The next step will allow you to copy an app password that may be necessary to access web apps. Select **Done** to complete the verification process:

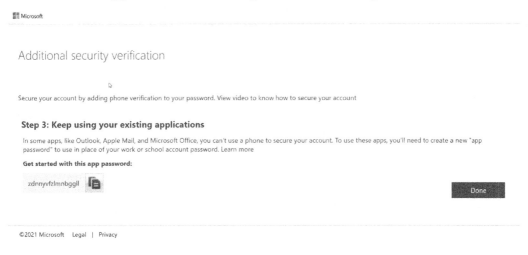

Figure 7.16 – Complete the verification process

4. You will be prompted to log in again and verify the phone number that you entered in the previous steps, as shown in *Figure 7.17*:

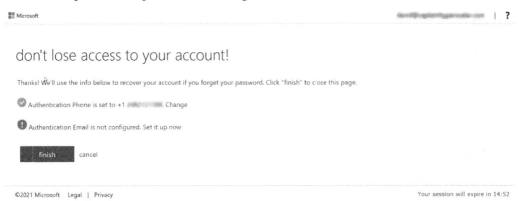

Figure 7.17 – Verify authentication phone

This completes the process of enrolling in Azure AD MFA. As stated previously, there is no difference in the steps that a user completes whether they are set to enrolled or enforced. In addition, *Figure 7.18* shows that once the enabled user completes the process of providing and verifying a second factor, their status changes to **Enforced** within the Azure AD MFA portal:

	DISPLAY NAME ▲	USER NAME	MULTI-FACTOR AUTH STATUS
☐	David Jones	david@	Enforced
☐	Dean Smith	dean.smith@	Enforced
☐	Denise Thompson	denise@	Enforced
☐	Ervin Johnson	ervin.johnson@	Enabled
☐	James Dean	james.dean@	Enforced
☐	Jane Doe	jane.doe@	Enabled

Figure 7.18 – Enabled user status change to enforced

Now that we have enforced Azure AD MFA for users, we should understand the different settings that can be configured for when users are prompted for MFA. The next section will discuss these MFA settings and how they are used.

Implementing and managing MFA settings

When we were planning for Azure AD MFA and the authentication methods that are used, we showed the MFA service settings within the Azure AD MFA portal as the location that you use to define the allowed MFA authentication methods for the second factor. In addition to the authentication methods, MFA service settings have other configuration options to customize the use of MFA within the company. The MFA service settings become the company-wide settings for Azure AD MFA that pertain to all users that are enrolled in Azure AD MFA.

In this section, we will look at each of these settings in detail and how they can be used for the Azure AD MFA enforcement within your company:

1. To access the MFA service settings, access **Azure AD** > **All users** > **Per-user MFA**, as shown in *Figure 7.19*:

Figure 7.19 – Access per-user MFA

2. This will take you to the Azure AD MFA portal site. From this site, select **service settings** as shown in *Figure 7.20*:

Figure 7.20 – MFA service settings

You are now in the service settings for MFA. There are four service setting options that you can configure. We will now discuss each of these and how they would be used.

3. The first option is shown in *Figure 7.21* and is **app passwords**:

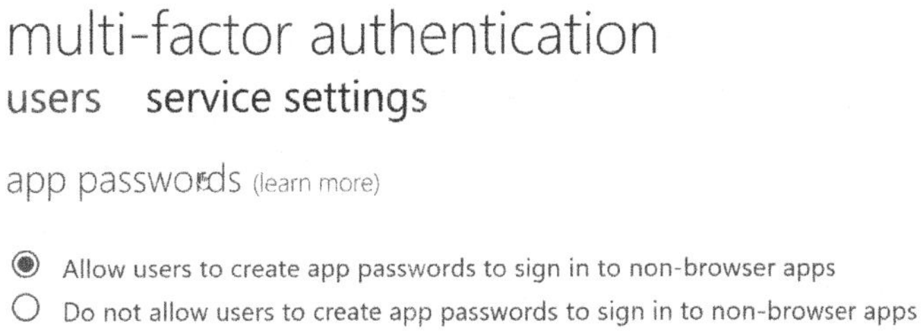

multi-factor authentication
users   service settings

app passwords (learn more)

◉ Allow users to create app passwords to sign in to non-browser apps
◯ Do not allow users to create app passwords to sign in to non-browser apps

Figure 7.21 – App password creation by users

This setting defines whether users are allowed to create app passwords on non-browser apps. This setting is used for hybrid use of Azure AD MFA with on-premises applications.

4. The next option is trusted IP addresses, as shown in *Figure 7.22*:

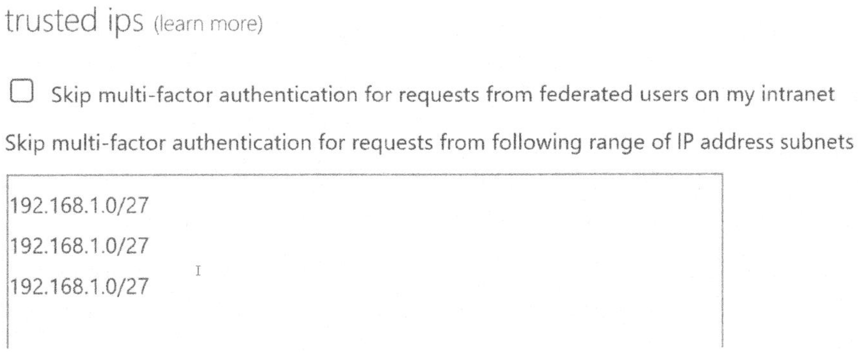

trusted ips (learn more)

☐ Skip multi-factor authentication for requests from federated users on my intranet

Skip multi-factor authentication for requests from following range of IP address subnets

192.168.1.0/27
192.168.1.0/27
192.168.1.0/27

Figure 7.22 – Trusted IPs for MFA

The trusted IP section allows you to configure specific IP addresses that do not require MFA to be enforced. These would usually be IP ranges used by company offices.

5. The next setting is the authentication methods that we discussed previously, as shown in *Figure 7.23:*

verification options (learn more)

Methods available to users:

☐ Call to phone
☑ Text message to phone
☑ Notification through mobile app
☑ Verification code from mobile app or hardware token

Figure 7.23 – Authentication verification options

6. The final option in service setting sets the number of days that MFA will be remembered on a trusted device, as shown in *Figure 7.24:*

remember multi-factor authentication on trusted device (learn more)

☐ Allow users to remember multi-factor authentication on devices they trust (between one to 365 days)
Number of days users can trust devices for [14]
NOTE: For the optimal user experience, we recommend using Conditional Access sign-in frequency to extend session lifetimes on trusted devices, locations, or low-risk sessions as an alternative to 'Remember MFA on a trusted device' settings. If using 'Remember MFA on a trusted device,' be sure to extend the duration to 90 or more days. Learn more about reauthentication prompts.

save

Manage advanced settings and view reports Go to the portal

Figure 7.24 – Remember MFA on trusted devices

This setting allows users to maintain their MFA verification for a determined number of days before re-verifying. This pertains to trusted devices that are joined to Azure AD. Therefore, users who attempt to sign in on other devices will be prompted for MFA.

Additional information on these settings can be found at `https://docs.microsoft.com/en-us/azure/active-directory/authentication/howto-mfa-mfasettings#remember-multi-factor-authentication`.

The next section will discuss how to configure SSPR. We will also discuss how the similarities and differences between the two verification methods of MFA and SSPR..

Configuring and deploying SSPR

SSPR is helpful to both the user and to administrators. SSPR saves time because passwords can be reset without a phone call to a support team. There is the convenience of a user being able to change their password when they forget it. It also helps from a security perspective if a user believes that their password has been compromised.

With this convenience, there is also a level of risk. With SSPR enabled, this allows someone who has obtained user credentials to potentially change a user password and lock them out of their account. Therefore, it is important that the configuration and deployment of SSPR protects against this taking place. This section is going to go through the steps and best practices for configuring SSPR.

To access the configuration for SSPR, navigate to **Azure AD** > **Users**. Within the **Users** tile, select **Password reset**, as shown in *Figure 7.25*:

Figure 7.25 – Password reset

The next steps will go through the configuration of the settings for SSPR:

1. Once you navigate to **Password reset**, you will determine whether to assign to **All** users or only **Selected** users; we will choose **All** users and **Save** as shown in *Figure 7.26*:

Figure 7.26 – SSPR enabled for all users

2.   The next step is to configure the authentication methods. Best practice is to require more than one method to reset the user password. These include the configuration and selection of security questions to use for resetting passwords. The options are shown in *Figure 7.27*. Configure these options and select **Save**:

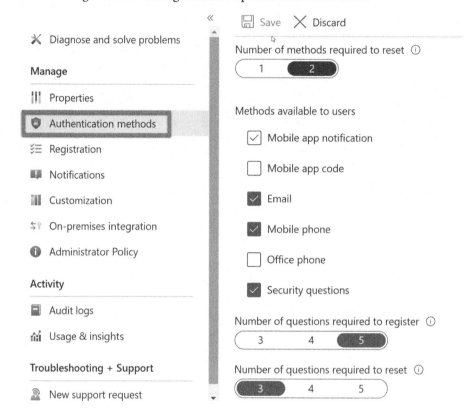

Figure 7.27 – Authentication methods for SSPR

SSPR is now configured for all users. In the same manner as enrolling in Azure AD MFA, users will be required to provide and enter the information required for SSPR before they are able to use this service.

It is important to note that there is similar information that is used for both MFA and SSPR. Both utilize text codes, phone calls, and can utilize the mobile authenticator app. Security questions are only used for SSPR and not for MFA. Email verification codes are used for SSPR and can be used for MFA only in circumstances where security policies prohibit mobile phones within a facility.

Now we know the process for configuring users for Azure AD MFA and SSPR. The next section of this chapter will discuss how to set up password protection.

Deploying and managing password protection

Azure AD Password Protection is used to configure certain parameters to avoid brute force or dictionary attacks on user identities. These attacks are accomplished by an attacker sending multiple requests with a username and multiple passwords to attempt to find the password being used and gain access. Setting up a threshold of how many attempts can be made before lockout and then the lockout duration will stop these attacks. In addition, administrators can identify passwords that are not allowed to be used within the Azure AD tenant. Microsoft also has a list of passwords that they may also block when attempting to use as a password to protect again dictionary attacks.

Once Azure AD Password Protection is configured, it can be set to enforce across the company or simply to audit initially to gauge the effectiveness. *Figure 7.28* shows the Azure AD **Password protection** tile and the fields that can be configured. This can be accessed in the Azure portal by searching Azure AD Password Protection:

Password protection

🖫 Save   ✕ Discard | Got feedback?

Custom smart lockout

Lockout threshold ⓘ

```
10
```

Lockout duration in seconds ⓘ

```
60
```

Custom banned passwords

Enforce custom list ⓘ   Yes   No

Custom banned password list ⓘ

Password protection for Windows Server Active Directory

Enable password protection on Windows   Yes   No
Server Active Directory ⓘ

Mode ⓘ   Enforced   Audit

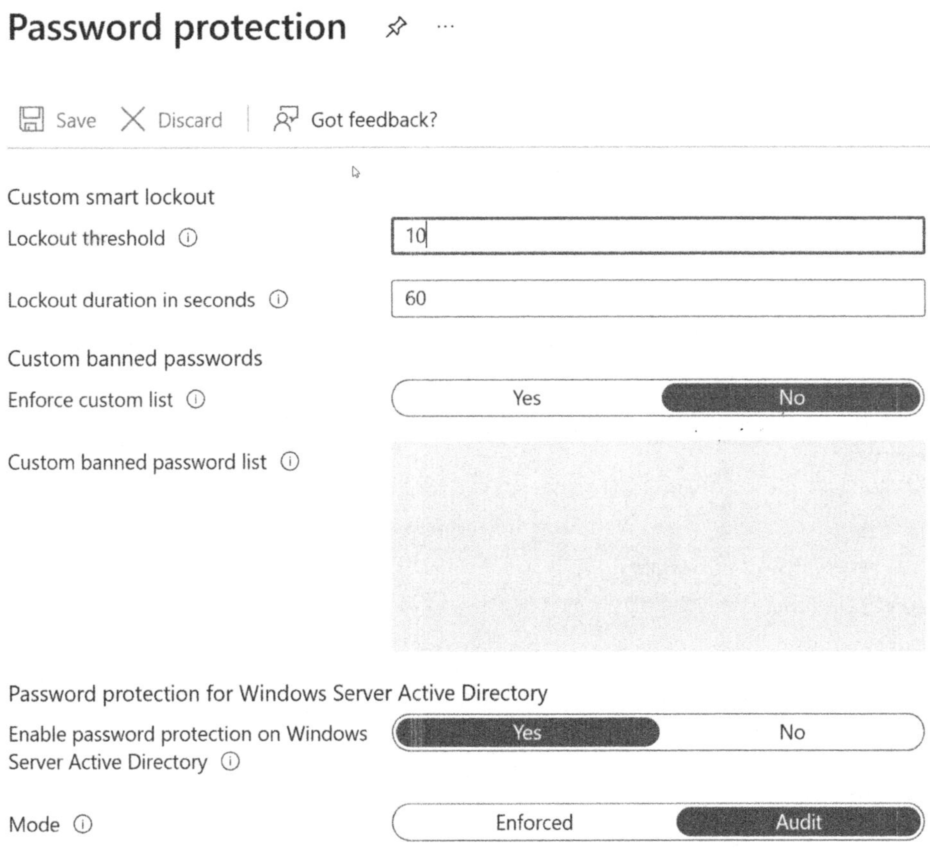

Figure 7.28 – Azure AD Password Protection settings

As stated previously, enforcing Azure AD Password Protection can protect user identities from brute force and dictionary attacks. The final section of this chapter will explore the use of security defaults.

Planning and implementing security defaults

Microsoft provides security defaults within Azure Active Directory to assist companies that are new to Azure AD and Microsoft's cloud in protecting identities. In new tenants, security defaults are already turned on and in place, so there isn't any planning and implementation required. However, there are situations where security defaults will need to be turned off as more advanced identity protection solutions are enabled, such as Conditional Access policies. To access security defaults, navigate to **Azure AD**, scroll down under **Manage** in the left menu to **Properties**, and then scroll down in the **Properties** tile to **Manage Security defaults**, as shown in *Figure 7.29*:

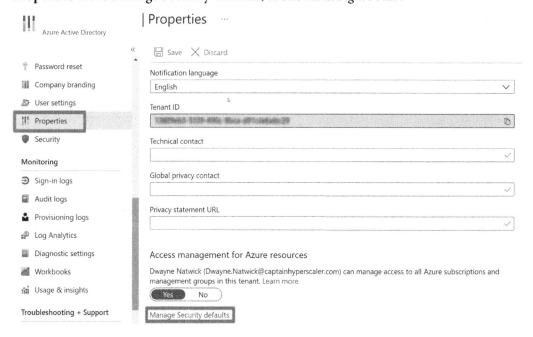

Figure 7.29 – Manage security defaults

Security defaults provide basic identity security settings to the entire tenant and are very helpful in protecting a company. These settings include the following:

- Requiring all users to register for Azure AD MFA
- Requiring administrators to perform MFA
- Blocking legacy authentication protocols
- Requiring users to perform MFA when necessary
- Protecting privileged activities such as access to the Azure portal

Additional information on security defaults can be found at `https://docs.microsoft.com/en-us/azure/active-directory/fundamentals/concept-fundamentals-security-defaults`.

Next, we will provide a summary of what was discussed in this chapter.

Summary

In this chapter, we described how we can protect the identities of our users using Azure AD MFA, how to configure Azure AD MFA, and the settings to provide flexibility to how Azure AD MFA is utilized. We discussed the implementation of SSPR for user and administrator flexibility. We discussed password protection and security defaults for additional protection for identities within the Azure AD tenant.

In the next chapter, we will take identity protection and authentication a step further through the use of passwordless authentication.

8
Planning and Managing Password-Less Authentication Methods

The previous chapter covered protecting and managing our identity and access with multi-factor authentication, password protection, and self-service password resets. In this chapter, we are going to take modern authentication a step further by discussing how we can utilize passwordless authentication methods.

In this chapter, we're going to cover the following main topics:

- Administering authentication methods (FIDO2/passwordless)
- Implementing an authentication solution based on Windows Hello for Business
- Implementing an authentication solution with the Microsoft authenticator app

Technical requirements

In this chapter, we will continue to explore configuring a tenant for use with **Microsoft 365** and **Azure**. There will be exercises where you will require access to Azure Active Directory. If you have not created the trial licenses for Microsoft 365 yet, please follow the instructions provided in *Chapter 1, Preparing for Your Microsoft Exam.*

Administering authentication methods (FIDO2/passwordless)

As we continue through this book, we will expand on the ways that Azure Active Directory provides a modern approach to identity and access management. As we continue to migrate to more cloud applications and hybrid infrastructures, companies can also migrate to these newer modern authentication methods. In *Chapter 7, Planning and Implementing Azure Multi-Factor Authentication and Self-Service Password Reset*, we covered how MFA can provide an additional layer of verification to protect against the inherent insecurity of simply using a password for authentication. As identity and access management continues to evolve, additional solutions have become available to move away from the use of passwords. The following sections will discuss those options and how they can be used within your company's identity and access management infrastructure.

Modern authentication for identity and access management

In *Chapter 2, Defining Identity and Access Management*, we discussed the evolution of identity and access management from the traditional to the advanced and then to the optimal. *Table 2.1* from *Chapter 2, Defining Identity and Access Management*, provided some examples of the solutions within each of these concepts. The goal of a company should be to move further away from the traditional authentication methods, which consists of using passwords, and adopt the modern authentication techniques as they move toward the optimal identity and access management infrastructure. For many companies, *implementing MFA, single sign-on*, and SSPR are the first steps. Microsoft's Azure AD security defaults provide the best practices for modern authentication implementation to get you started. *Chapter 7, Planning and Implementing Azure Multi-Factor Authentication and Self-Service Password Reset*, discussed what is enabled with security defaults.

As we choose authentication methods that our company will utilize in a cloud or hybrid identity infrastructure, we need to understand the capabilities of legacy applications to utilize modern authentication techniques. We will discuss application integration in Azure AD in more detail in *Chapter 10, Planning and Implementing Enterprise Apps for Single Sign-On (SSO)*.

The goal of modern authentication is to decrease the amount that a company relies on passwords as its primary source of authentication. The following diagram shows the different approaches to authentication and how they are viewed on a scale from bad to best:

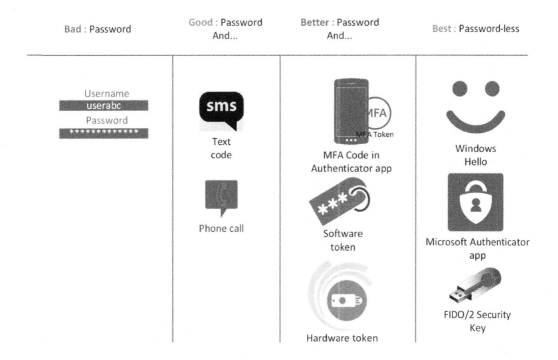

Figure 8.1 – Authentication options

In *Chapter 7, Planning and Implementing Azure Multi-Factor Authentication and Self-Service Password Reset,* we discussed how to implement MFA, which would move our company into the good and/or better category, depending on the configuration options that were put in place. The remainder of this chapter will discuss how to implement the best approaches to passwordless authentication techniques.

Let's look at each of these in more detail by defining each and giving some examples of how they are used.

FIDO/2

Fast Identity Online (FIDO/2) provides passwordless authentication through the use of a security key that the user has in their possession. The FIDO security key is a private key that is used to pass and authenticate the user. The user authenticates the key itself through the use of a PIN that encrypts the key. FIDO is an open source technology, so developers can implement this technology in their authentication configuration. When utilizing Azure AD and Windows 10 version 1903 or higher devices, FIDO/2 authentication can allow users to access cloud applications utilizing the FIDO/2 security key.

One potential deployment issue with this authentication method is that these keys use USB on devices. If USB is disabled by the company in Endpoint Management for security reasons, then this option cannot be utilized.

If you or your company are interested in utilizing FIDO/2 keys for your authentication policy, you can find out more information at `https://docs.microsoft.com/en-us/azure/active-directory/authentication/howto-authentication-passwordless-security-key`.

The next form of passwordless authentication that we will look at is **Windows Hello for Business**.

Windows Hello for Business

Windows Hello for Business is popular for Windows 10 users. Windows Hello is a biometric authentication technique that utilizes facial recognition with the camera of your Windows 10 device. Windows Hello can be enabled on Windows 10 devices for this form of authentication. Windows Hello for Business is used to create groups of users that this type of authentication will be enforced on to join Windows 10 devices in Azure AD.

Windows Hello is considered a passwordless authentication method that utilizes multi-factor authentication. Though you are only using facial recognition as the user to log into your device, when you register your device for Windows Hello, you are required to enter a **personal identification number (PIN)**. This PIN becomes encrypted in the **trusted platform module (TPM)** within the device as part of the overall BitLocker encryption. When a user authenticates with the device camera, it calls that encrypted PIN to verify that it matches the user that registered that device for Windows Hello. Azure AD then authorizes access to the device. The following diagram shows the steps in this process. These steps are transparent to the user when they're accessing their Windows 10 devices:

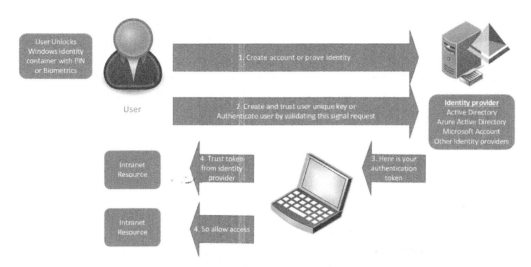

Figure 8.2 – Windows Hello for Business authentication process

We will go through the implementation steps for setting up Windows Hello for Business later in this chapter. Let's discuss using the Windows Authenticator app for passwordless authentication.

Authenticator app

Authenticator apps are becoming a popular technique for users to manage MFA and passwordless authentication to applications. Authenticator apps are applications that are on a user's smartphone. They can provide MFA codes to applications, approval notifications for application MFA, self-service password reset codes, and passwordless authentication. When using an authenticator app for identity and access management, the user's smartphone provides additional layers of verification and protection for a user's identity.

For example, a best practice regarding smartphones is that they should be configured with a PIN or biometric technique, or a fingerprint or facial recognition so that you can access the device. Otherwise, the device remains locked and encrypted. In addition, when accessing some authenticator apps, such as Microsoft Authenticator, you may need to re-authenticate with your PIN or biometrics to open the app to receive the approval notification or access a code. Therefore, leaving a smartphone unlocked does not compromise a user's identity since the authenticator app also requires verification. Using an authenticator app is therefore a very secure authentication method. The following diagram shows how this process works:

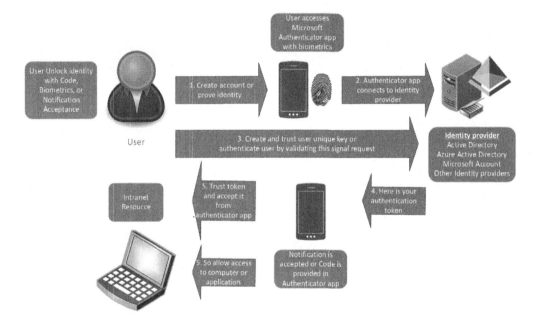

Figure 8.3 – Using an authenticator app

Later in this chapter, we will learn how to implement an authenticator app as the authentication method. This will allow users to verify their identity and authenticate in the authenticator app without the need to enter a password.

The next section will discuss how to implement Windows Hello for Business as an authentication solution.

Implementing an authentication solution based on Windows Hello for Business

In the previous section on passwordless authentication, we discussed how Windows Hello can be used by Windows 10 users for authentication by utilizing facial recognition. Windows Hello for Business allows the company to require users of Windows 10 devices to use this as the required authentication and monitor users. In this section, you will learn how to implement Windows Hello for Business as the authentication solution. Windows Hello for Business is configured within the Windows Active Directory domain controller, not Azure AD.

To implement Windows Hello for Business, multiple security groups are required. These security groups are the KeyCredential Admins security group and the Windows Hello for Business Users security group. If you are in a hybrid architecture with Windows Server 2016 domain controllers, the KeyCredential Admins group is created when you install the domain controller.

If your hybrid domain does not include Windows Server 2016 domain controllers, creating the KeyCredential Admins within the Windows Active Directory domain controllers will synchronize them with Azure Active Directory through Azure AD Connect. This group synchronizes the public key that was created by the user during provisioning for Windows Hello for Business. To create the KeyCredential Admins security group in Azure AD, complete the following steps:

1. Sign into a domain controller with Domain Admin credentials and navigate to **Server Manager**:

Figure 8.4 – Accessing Server Manager

2.   Open **Active Directory Users and Computers** from the **Tools** menu:

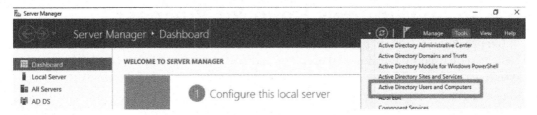

Figure 8.5 – Active Directory Users and Computers

3.   Select **View** and select **Advanced Features**:

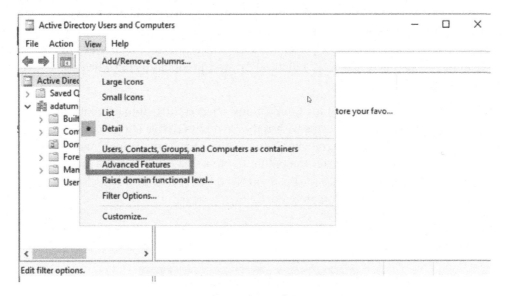

Figure 8.6 – Advanced Features

4. Expand the domain node list from within the navigation pane. Right-click on **Users**, select **New**, and then select **Group**:

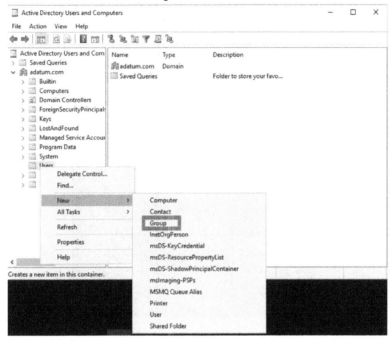

Figure 8.7 – Expanding the domain node list and creating a new group

5. Type **KeyCredential Admins** in the **Group Name** text box. Select **OK** to create the group:

Figure 8.8 – Creating the KeyCredential Admins group

Next, you will create the Windows Hello for Business Users security group on the Windows Active Directory domain controller:

6. Sign into a domain controller with Domain Admin credentials and navigate to **Server Manager**:

Figure 8.9 – Accessing Server Manager

7. Open **Active Directory Users and Computers** from the **Tools** menu:

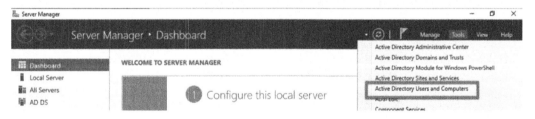

Figure 8.10 – Active Directory Users and Computers

8. Select **View** and select **Advanced Features**:

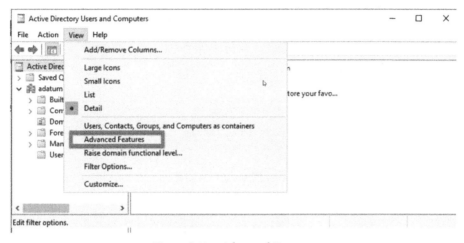

Figure 8.11 – Advanced Features

9. Expand the domain node list from within the navigation pane. Right-click on **Users**, select **New**, and then select **Group**:

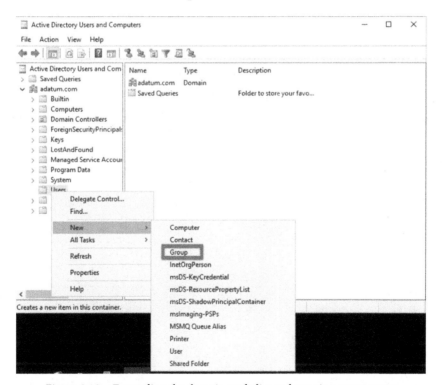

Figure 8.12 – Expanding the domain node list and creating a new group

10. Type **Windows Hello for Business Users** in the **Group Name** text box. Select **OK** to create the group:

Figure 8.13 – Creating the Windows Hello for Business Users group

Now that these groups have been created, users can be assigned to the Windows Hello for Business Users group. Due to this, Windows Hello will become the primary form of authentication for their registered Windows 10 devices.

In the next section, we will look at how to implement the Microsoft Authenticator app as an authentication method.

Implementing an authentication solution with the Microsoft Authenticator app

Where Windows Hello for Business and FIDO/2 are passwordless authentication options for Windows 10, the Microsoft Authenticator app provides more flexibility across all apps and devices. As a recap, Windows Hello for Business utilizes biometric facial recognition as the primary factor for verification, while FIDO/2 utilizes a USB key that the user has in their possession to authenticate with a private encrypted key. The requirement of providing all users or a group of users with a separate FIDO/2 token device adds additional cost to the passwordless implementation. Authenticator app authentication utilizes something that most likely all users have: a smartphone. Let's go through the steps to set up the Microsoft Authenticator app for passwordless authentication:

1. Log into `https://portal.azure.com`.

2. Navigate to **Azure Active Directory** from the search bar:

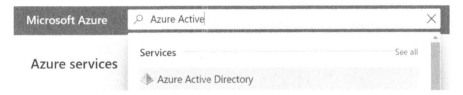

Figure 8.14 – Navigating to Azure Active Directory

3. From the **Azure Active Directory** menu, scroll down and select **Security** under the **Manage** heading:

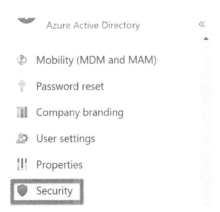

Figure 8.15 – Azure AD – Security

4. From the **Security** tile, select **Authentication methods**:

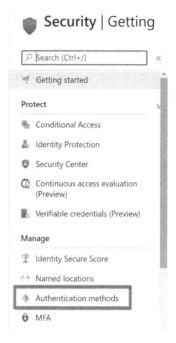

Figure 8.16 – Authentication methods

5. Once you are in the **Authentication methods** tile, select **Policies**. **Policies** is where you configure your passwordless authentication methods. Select **Microsoft Authenticator**:

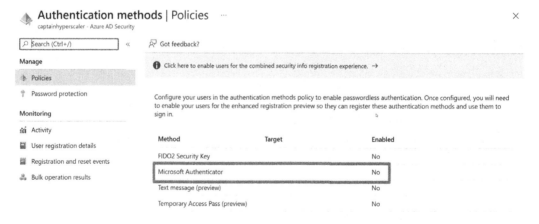

Figure 8.17 – Microsoft Authenticator

6. In the next tile, enable **Microsoft Authenticator** and configure it for all or selected users or groups. Once this has been configured, select **Save**:

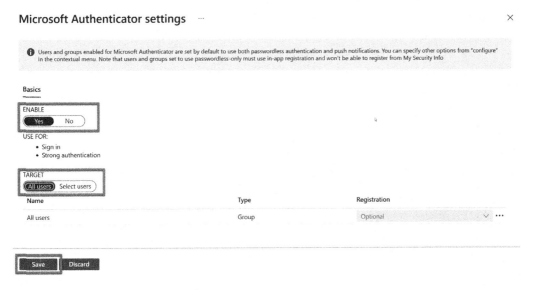

Figure 8.18 – Configuring Microsoft Authenticator settings

7. At the top of the tiles for configuring **Policies** and **Microsoft Authenticator**, there is a blue bar mentioning an additional step to enable users for the combined security info registration experience. Select that blue bar:

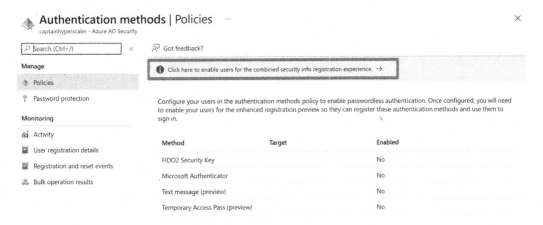

Figure 8.19 – Enabling users for the combined security info registration experience

8. Navigate to the **User features** tile. Select the same users or the selected users and groups that you configured for the Microsoft Authenticator app. Then, select **Save**:

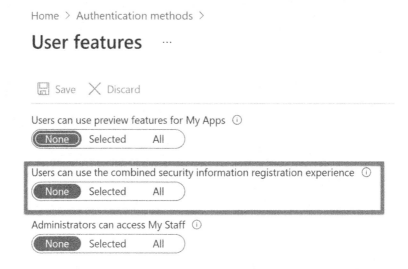

Figure 8.20 – User features configuration

Note

If you are using a combination of Microsoft Authenticator and FIDO/2, this **User features** tile will configure both sets of users.

Once the Microsoft Authenticator app has been installed and connected to the user's smartphone, they can use the Authenticator app as their primary source of verification for Azure AD. The Microsoft Authenticator app helps with passwordless authentication across devices and applications that are registered in Azure AD and can use modern authentication.

Next, we will summarize what was discussed in this chapter.

Summary

In this chapter, we described the next steps in identity protection with passwordless authentication. We discussed the different options that Microsoft provides to allow users to move away from the use of passwords as the primary authentication method. Then, we learned how those options can be configured and utilized within Azure AD and hybrid architectures. In the next chapter, *Chapter 9, Planning, Implementing, and Administering Conditional Access and Azure Identity Protection*, we will discuss advanced solutions that protect a person's identity and enforce the zero trust model with conditional access policies and Azure Identity Protection.

9

Planning, Implementing, and Administering Conditional Access and Azure Identity Protection

The previous chapter covered how to take modern authentication a step further by discussing how we can utilize passwordless authentication methods. This chapter will cover Conditional Access policies. This will include planning for and testing these policies to verify that they are working correctly and providing the proper controls. In addition, we will discuss **Azure Active Directory (AD) Identity Protection** and using sign-in and user risk conditions with policies.

In this chapter, we're going to cover the following main topics:

- Planning and implementing Conditional Access policies and controls
- Configuring Smart Lockout thresholds
- Implementing and managing a user risk policy
- Monitoring, investigating, and remediating elevated risky users

Technical requirements

In this chapter, we will continue to explore configuring a tenant for use of **Microsoft 365** and **Azure**. There will be exercises that will require access to Azure AD. If you have not yet created trial licenses for Microsoft 365, please follow the directions provided within *Chapter 1, Preparing for Your Microsoft Exam*.

Planning and implementing Conditional Access policies and controls

Up to this point, the focus has been on planning, configuration, and implementation of the identities within Azure AD and hybrid identity infrastructures. We have discussed how to use **multi-factor authentication** (**MFA**) to decrease the amount we rely on passwords as a source of authentication. In this chapter, we discuss advanced capabilities to protect our identities and resources. The first of these solutions is the use of Conditional Access policies. Conditional Access policies enforce additional verification actions based on a signal that a user or device may be potentially compromised. The foundation of Conditional Access policies is the zero-trust methodology. So, before we discuss planning and implementing Conditional Access, let's discuss the main points of zero trust.

Zero-trust methodology

As we have moved as companies to using cloud providers such as Microsoft, the responsibility for securing the physical infrastructure for cloud services is provided by these cloud providers. If we are adhering to a **defense-in-depth** (**DiD**) security posture, Microsoft is responsible for the physical first layer of defense, making the first layer that we are responsible for as a company the identity and access layer. Therefore, the statements *identity is the new perimeter* and *identity is the new control plane* have become extremely important in securing cloud infrastructure. Therefore, the concept of a zero-trust methodology becomes the core concept that a company should adhere to when securing identity and access.

A **zero-trust methodology** is a process of continuously requiring someone on the network to verify that they are who they say they are. The concept seems to be straightforward and simple, but if you were to constantly ask users to enter their username and password, they would get frustrated. To avoid this frustration, zero-trust implementation utilizes various signals that alert to potential anomalous behavior, leaked credentials, or insecure devices that trigger the need for a user to reverify their identity. These signals lead to a decision on what is needed to provide access to applications, files, or websites. This workflow is shown in the following diagram:

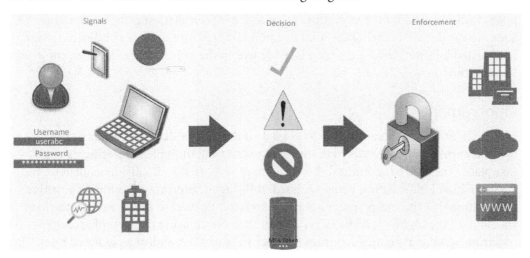

Figure 9.1 – Diagram of the zero-trust model workflow

The next sections will describe each of these components of the workflow in more detail.

Signal

As stated in the previous section, the signal is a state that the user or device is in that triggers a potential need for a user to reverify their identity. This state could be that the user has been identified to be at risk of having a compromised password, that they are at an **Internet Protocol (IP)** address that has been flagged as vulnerable, or that their device is not compliant with current security patches. These are only a few examples of signals that may be reviewed to trigger a decision to request more information. Microsoft utilizes several tools within Azure and Microsoft 365 to identify vulnerabilities and risks of users and devices that create these signals. Once a signal has been identified to require more information to verify a user's identity, a decision is then made as to what happens next.

Decision

As stated in the previous section, when a signal is triggered, a decision is made on what we are going to require or allow to provide access to the resources requested. There are several options here, and this is where a company creates policies on how zero trust is going to be handled, depending on the resource being requested access. This could include a user reverifying that they have not been compromised by requiring MFA before they are given access. The policies may limit or block access to that application entirely until the user or device changes the status or location that they are requesting access to. The least likely policy decision is to allow access if a user or device is seen as having an at-risk status. An allow-access decision is generally used in a policy that identifies a user or device as being in a trusted location. Once a decision is made within the policy, the policy then enforces the workflow.

Enforcement

Enforcement is the action of a decision based on the user or device signal as defined by the company policy. As stated in the previous section, multiple enforcements could take place. The level of access and enforcement of zero trust is usually dependent on the application and information being accessed. If the application contains highly sensitive information that the company cannot have exposed, the level of zero-trust enforcement should be at the highest level by either blocking access, limiting the level of access, or requiring additional verification from the user, such as MFA and/or a password reset. The ability of a company to identify risks and vulnerabilities of users and determine a plan for protecting access to their applications is a critical factor in the success of implementing a zero-trust model for **identity and access management (IAM)**.

As stated previously, the principles of zero trust are an important aspect of protecting access to applications within a cloud and hybrid infrastructure. Decreased access and ability to protect physical access and increased access to applications from various locations across public internet connections require a company to do their due diligence in identifying various scenarios whereby users may request access to company resources and the numerous devices that they may use to access these. Policies that identify potential vulnerabilities and threats that can make a correct decision on how to enforce zero trust will protect the company while maintaining a positive **user experience (UX)**.

Conditional Access policies

The solution within Microsoft that enforces the zero-trust methodology is **Conditional Access**. As you will notice in the following diagram, the flow from signal to decision to enforcement is the same. The policies that we determine for our company is what then enforces these Conditional Access requirements.

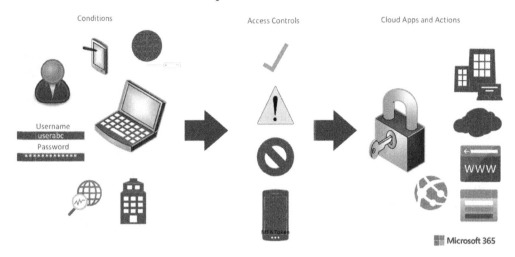

Figure 9.2 – Conditional Access workflow

A key aspect to putting Conditional Access policies in place is to properly plan and understand how they would potentially affect the UX. There is a balance that a company should attempt to maintain between the enforcement of policies to secure and protect data and the ability of a user to have access to applications and data that they need to be effective in their required tasks. The next sections will go through the steps to plan, test, and implement Conditional Access policies in your company.

Preparation and planning

Before we can create a Conditional Access policy, we need to make sure that we are able to do so. There are a couple of areas that we need to address for implementing such a solution: licensing, and security defaults. For licensing, Conditional Access policy features are available with an **Azure AD Premium P1** level license. This level of Azure AD licensing is included with Microsoft 365 Business Premium, Office 365 E3/A3, Microsoft 365 E3/A3, Office 365 E5/A5, and Microsoft 365 E5/A5. These licenses must be assigned to users for whom we are attempting to enforce Conditional Access policies. A full list of licensing requirements can be found at this link: https://docs.microsoft.com/ azure/active-directory/conditional-access/overview.

In addition to having the proper licenses, we will be required to turn off Azure AD Security Defaults. Security Defaults is a feature that is turned on when we create our Azure AD tenant that provides a baseline level of protection to require—for example—users to enroll in MFA, enforce MFA for administrators, and block the use of legacy authentication for applications. Security Defaults was discussed in *Chapter 7, Planning and Implementing Azure Multi-Factor Authentication and Self-Service Password Reset*. In that chapter, we were verifying that this feature was enabled. To be able to implement Conditional Access, navigate back to **Security Defaults** and turn it off. When you do this, there will be reasons that appear, and you will see a selection for using Conditional Access policies. Once **Security Defaults** is no longer active, Conditional Access policies can be created.

Once we have proper licensing assigned and **Security Defaults** turned off, we can begin our planning for Conditional Access policies. Some commonly used Conditional Access policies can be found in the Microsoft documentation at this link: `https://docs.microsoft.com/azure/active-directory/conditional-access/plan-conditional-access`. The key to planning for Conditional Access is to understand the groups of users that are to access company applications and data, the devices that they are using to access that data and those applications, the locations that they may be accessing that data and those applications from, and the applications being used to access the company data.

The next sections will go through the configuration of Conditional Access policies based on this information.

Creating a Conditional Access policy

Once we have gone through the planning process of having the proper licensing and turned off **Security Defaults**, we are now ready to create a policy. Conditional Access policies can be created from an aspect of allowing access based on a condition, denying access, or allowing access after going through additional verification. We will step through the configuration for each of these types of conditions in the next sections.

Conditional Access policy to allow access from a trusted location

This exercise will step through how to create a Conditional Access policy to allow access to cloud apps from a trusted location. Before we can configure this Conditional Access policy, we need to create a trusted location. To do so, follow these steps:

1. In the Microsoft Azure search bar, type `trusted` to find **Azure AD Named locations**, as illustrated in the following screenshot:

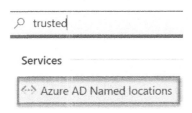

Figure 9.3 – Searching for Azure AD Named locations

2. Select **+ New location** when the **Configure locations** tile opens, as illustrated in the following screenshot:

Configure locations ⭢ ⋯

+ New location   🗗 Configure MFA trusted IPs

🧭 This view will soon be replaced with the 'Named locations (Preview)' view. Try it out. →

Named locations are used by Azure AD security reports to reduce false positives and Azure AD Conditional Access policies. Learn more

🔎 Search locations.

Name	Trusted
No named locations found.	

Figure 9.4 – Adding a new location

3. Name your location—for example, `Company headquarters`. For this exercise, enter your local IP address range by going to `https://www.whatsmyip.org/`, and then select the **Mark as trusted location** checkbox. After this is complete, click **Create**, as illustrated in the following screenshot:

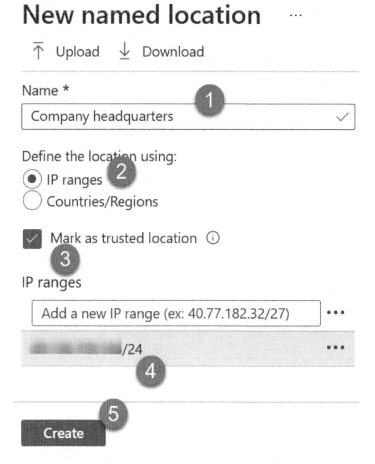

Figure 9.5 – Configuring a named location

Note
You must add a subnet range rather than just the IP address.

---

4. `Company headquarters` is now a trusted location, as we can see in the following screenshot:

Figure 9.6 – Company headquarters as a trusted location

The following steps will go through the configuration of a Conditional Access policy that allows access to cloud apps when accessing from a trusted location:

1. Search for **Azure AD Conditional Access** to access Conditional Access and select this, as illustrated in the following screenshot:

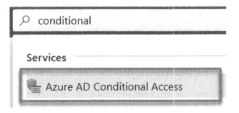

Figure 9.7 – Searching for Azure AD Conditional Access

2. Select **+ New policy** to create a Conditional Access policy, as illustrated in the following screenshot:

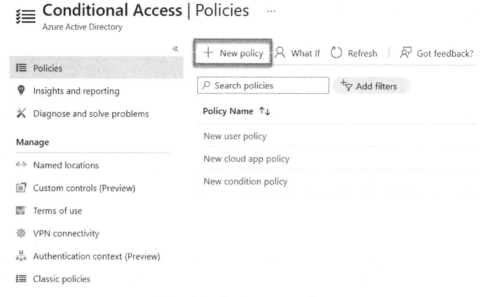

Figure 9.8 – Creating a new policy

3. Enter a name for your policy—for example, `Access from Trusted location`. This is demonstrated in the following screenshot:

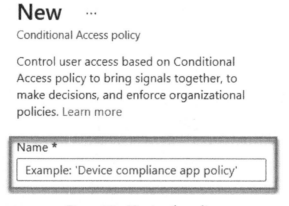

Figure 9.9 – Naming the policy

4. Select **Users and groups** under **Assignments**. Here, you can select everyone in Azure AD by selecting **All users**, or specific users and groups under **Select users and groups**. Options here include **All guest and external users, Directory roles**, and/or **Users and groups**. For this exercise, we will select **Users and groups, Sales group**, and then click **Select**, as illustrated in the following screenshot:

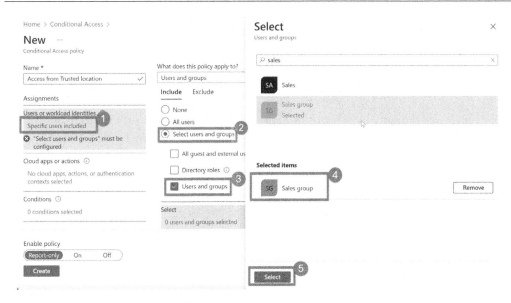

Figure 9.10 – Selecting a group

5. After clicking **Select**, the **Sales group** entry will appear under the included users and groups, as illustrated in the following screenshot:

Figure 9.11 – Including the Sales group and understanding where to exclude groups

> **Note**
> There is also an **Exclude** tab. It is recommended that if the administrator is a part of the included group, they should be added as an excluded assignment to avoid being locked out of resources.

6. Next, we configure cloud apps or actions, which is a similar process to including users and groups. The following screenshot shows **Office 365** being selected as a cloud app:

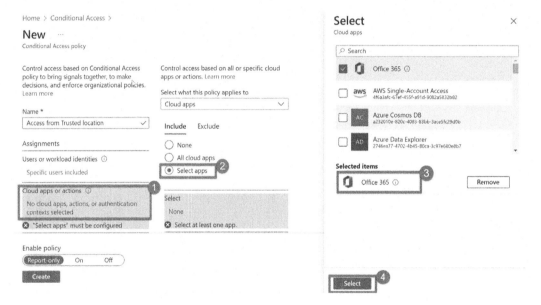

Figure 9.12 – Selecting Office 365 as a cloud app

The following screenshot shows **All cloud apps** being selected. Use this as the preferred setting for this exercise.

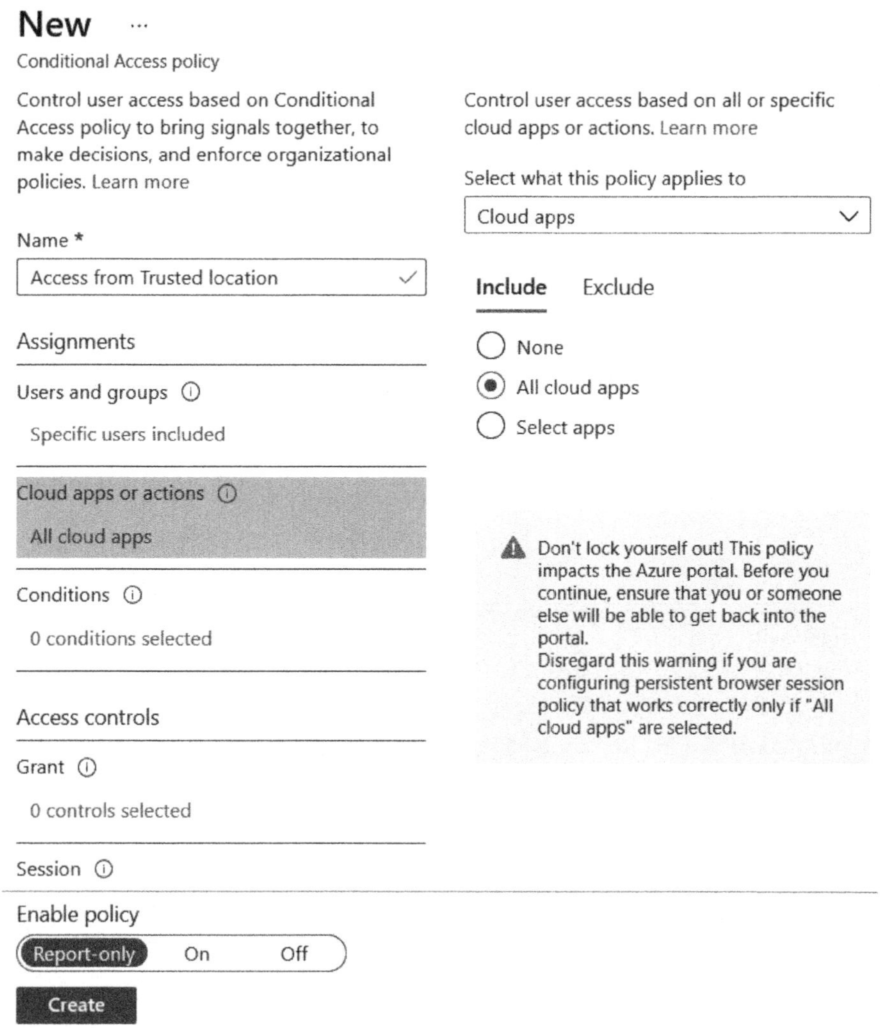

New   ⋯

Conditional Access policy

Control user access based on Conditional Access policy to bring signals together, to make decisions, and enforce organizational policies. Learn more

Control user access based on all or specific cloud apps or actions. Learn more

Select what this policy applies to

Cloud apps   ⌄

Name *

Access from Trusted location   ✓

Include   Exclude

Assignments

○ None

Users and groups ⓘ

◉ All cloud apps

Specific users included

○ Select apps

Cloud apps or actions ⓘ

All cloud apps

⚠ Don't lock yourself out! This policy impacts the Azure portal. Before you continue, ensure that you or someone else will be able to get back into the portal.
Disregard this warning if you are configuring persistent browser session policy that works correctly only if "All cloud apps" are selected.

Conditions ⓘ

0 conditions selected

Access controls

Grant ⓘ

0 controls selected

Session ⓘ

Enable policy

(Report-only)   On   Off

Create

Figure 9.13 – Configuring all cloud apps

7. Next, we will navigate to **Conditions** and select **Locations**, as illustrated in the following screenshot:

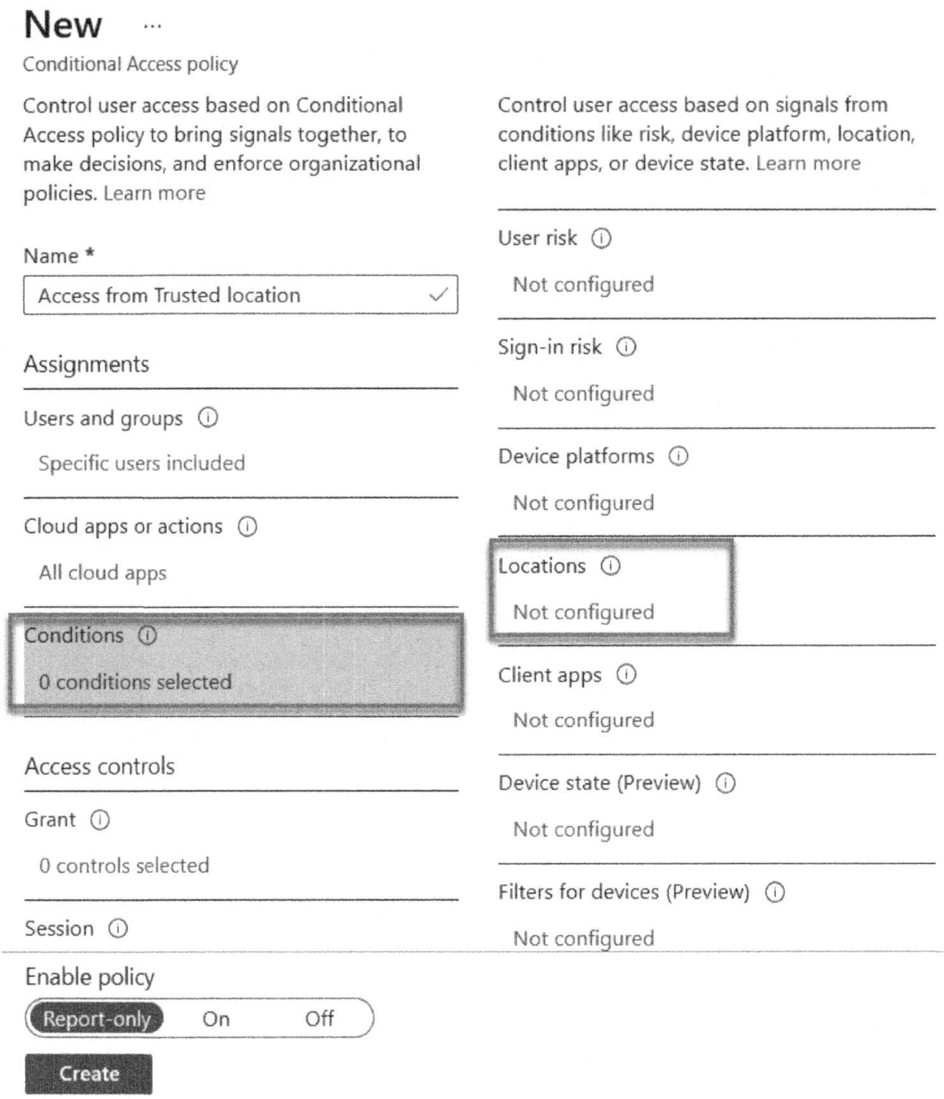

New ...

Conditional Access policy

Control user access based on Conditional Access policy to bring signals together, to make decisions, and enforce organizational policies. Learn more

Control user access based on signals from conditions like risk, device platform, location, client apps, or device state. Learn more

Name *

Access from Trusted location ✓

Assignments

Users and groups ⓘ

Specific users included

Cloud apps or actions ⓘ

All cloud apps

Conditions ⓘ

0 conditions selected

Access controls

Grant ⓘ

0 controls selected

Session ⓘ

User risk ⓘ

Not configured

Sign-in risk ⓘ

Not configured

Device platforms ⓘ

Not configured

Locations ⓘ

Not configured

Client apps ⓘ

Not configured

Device state (Preview) ⓘ

Not configured

Filters for devices (Preview) ⓘ

Not configured

Enable policy

(Report-only) On Off

Create

Figure 9.14 – Configuring the Locations condition

8. Select **Yes** under **Configure** and choose **Selected locations**, as illustrated in the following screenshot:

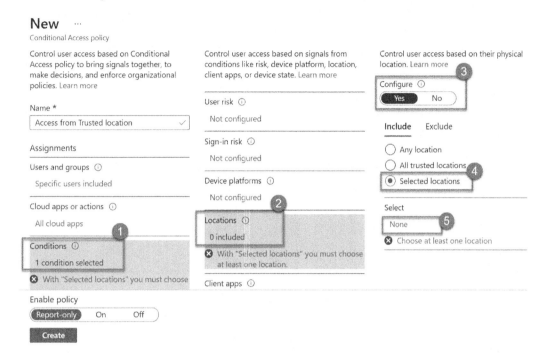

Figure 9.15 – Choosing a selected location

9. In the **Selected locations** tile, choose the trusted location that we created and click **Select**, as illustrated in the following screenshot:

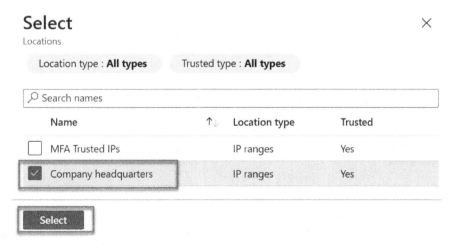

Figure 9.16 – Selecting a location

10. The location has now been selected. Next, we will configure the access controls. Select the link under **Grant**. Select the controls that you will require for access to the cloud apps. For this exercise, we will leave all of these boxes unchecked, choose **Grant access**, and then click **Select**. Since no controls were selected, the `0 controls selected` message will remain, as illustrated in the following screenshot. The next exercises will explore more of these grant access controls:

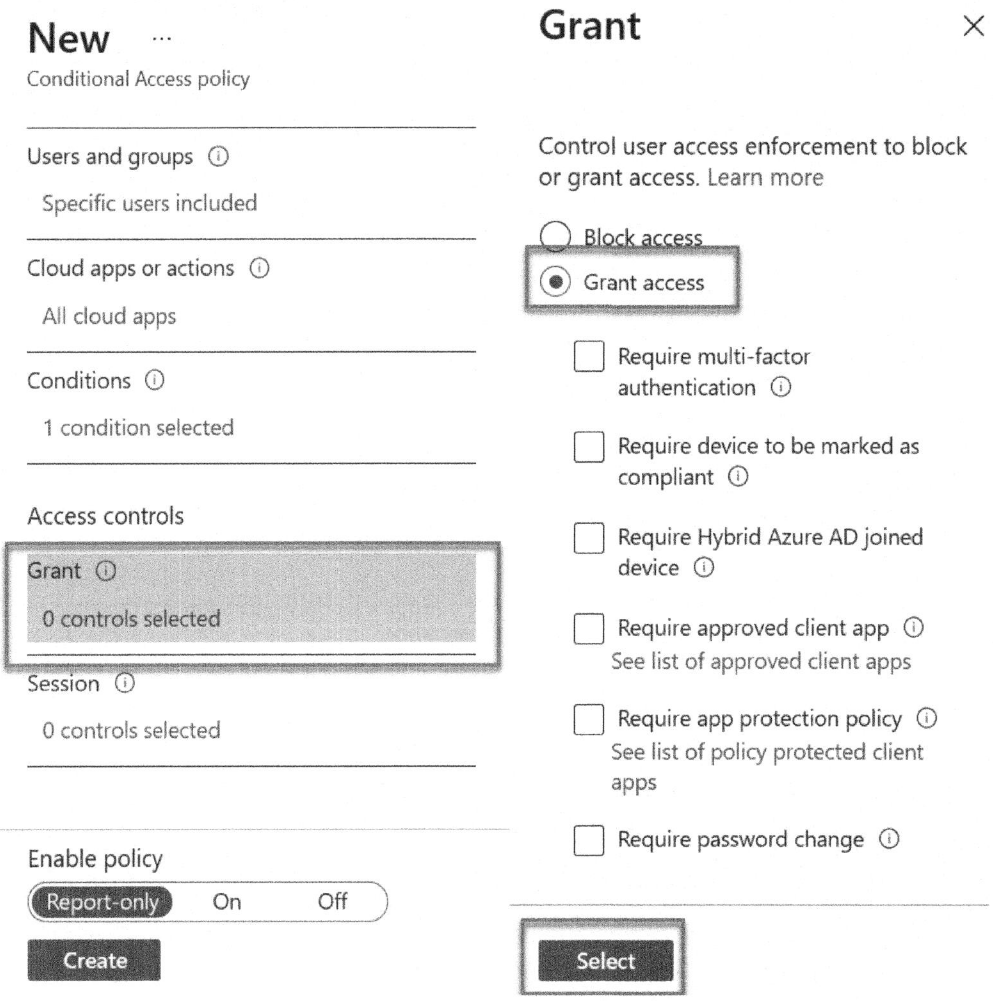

New ⋯

Conditional Access policy

Users and groups ⓘ

  Specific users included

Cloud apps or actions ⓘ

  All cloud apps

Conditions ⓘ

  1 condition selected

Access controls

Grant ⓘ

  0 controls selected

Session ⓘ

  0 controls selected

Enable policy

(Report-only)   On   Off

Create

Grant   ✕

Control user access enforcement to block or grant access. Learn more

◯ Block access

◉ Grant access

☐ Require multi-factor authentication ⓘ

☐ Require device to be marked as compliant ⓘ

☐ Require Hybrid Azure AD joined device ⓘ

☐ Require approved client app ⓘ
  See list of approved client apps

☐ Require app protection policy ⓘ
  See list of policy protected client apps

☐ Require password change ⓘ

Select

Figure 9.17 – Granting access

11. Select **Session controls**. For this control, select **Persistent browser session** and **Always persistent**. Click **Select** to save, as illustrated in the following screenshot:

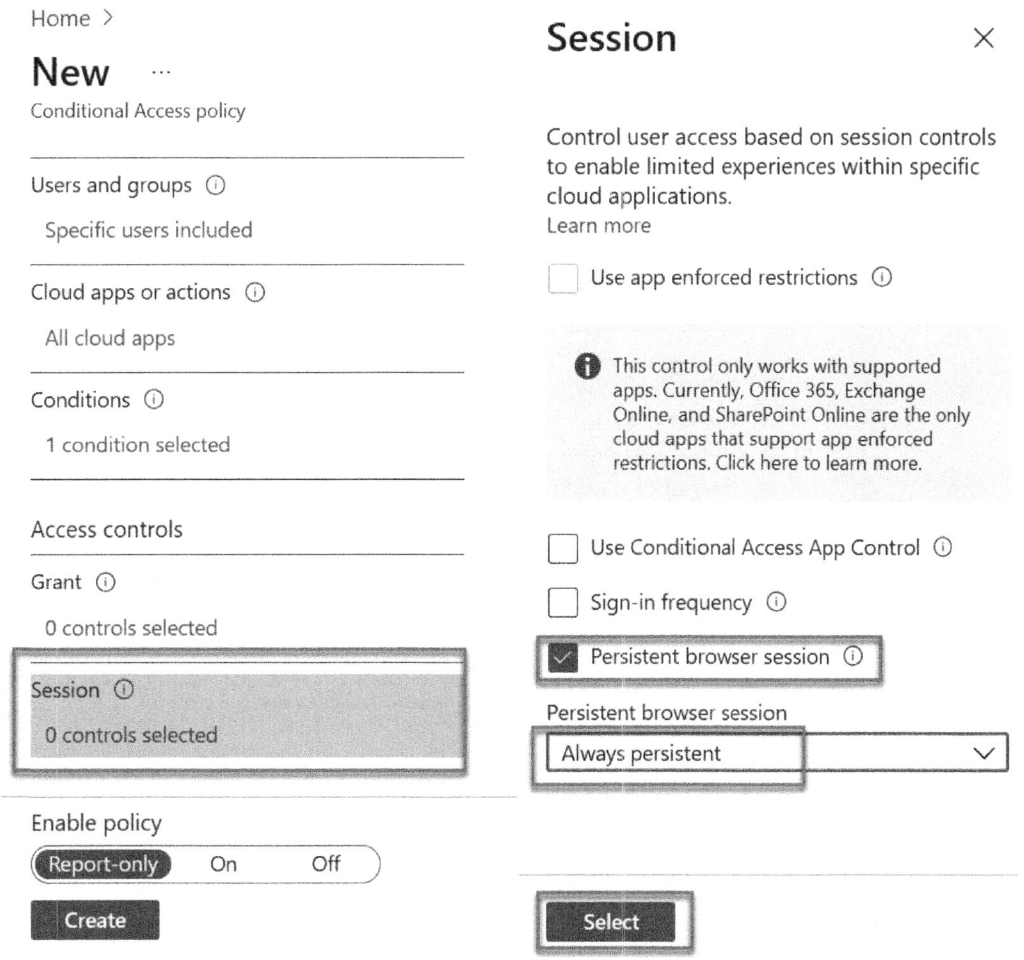

Home >

New ...

Conditional Access policy

Users and groups ⓘ

Specific users included

Cloud apps or actions ⓘ

All cloud apps

Conditions ⓘ

1 condition selected

Access controls

Grant ⓘ

0 controls selected

Session ⓘ

0 controls selected

Enable policy

(Report-only   On   Off)

[Create]

Session   ✕

Control user access based on session controls to enable limited experiences within specific cloud applications.
Learn more

☐ Use app enforced restrictions ⓘ

> ⓘ This control only works with supported apps. Currently, Office 365, Exchange Online, and SharePoint Online are the only cloud apps that support app enforced restrictions. Click here to learn more.

☐ Use Conditional Access App Control ⓘ

☐ Sign-in frequency ⓘ

☑ Persistent browser session ⓘ

Persistent browser session

[Always persistent   ⌄]

[Select]

Figure 9.18 – Configuring Session controls

12. The final settings should match those shown in the following screenshot. Leave **Enable policy** set to **Report-only** for now and click **Create**, as illustrated in the following screenshot:

New   ...

Conditional Access policy

policies. Learn more

Name *

| Access from Trusted location | ✓ |

Assignments

Users and groups ⓘ

  Specific users included

Cloud apps or actions ⓘ

  All cloud apps

Conditions ⓘ

  1 condition selected

Access controls

Grant ⓘ

  0 controls selected

Session ⓘ

  Persistent browser session - Always
  persistent

Enable policy

(Report-only   On   Off)

Create

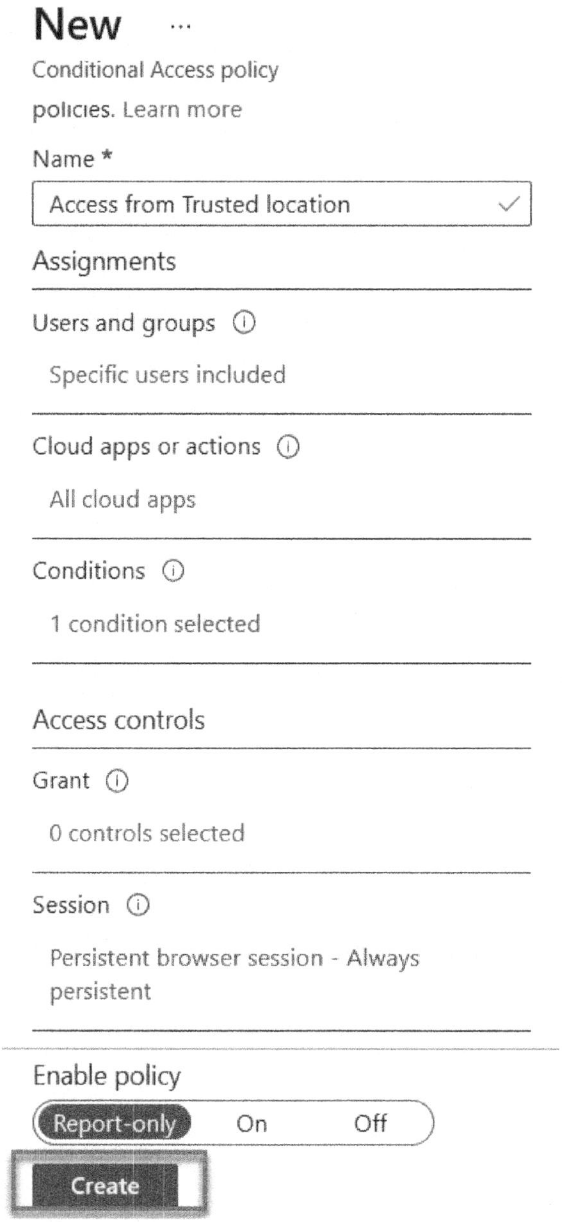

Figure 9.19 – Creating a Conditional Access policy

The following screenshot shows that our Conditional Access policy has been created. This policy will allow access to the trusted location without any additional controls when accessing cloud apps:

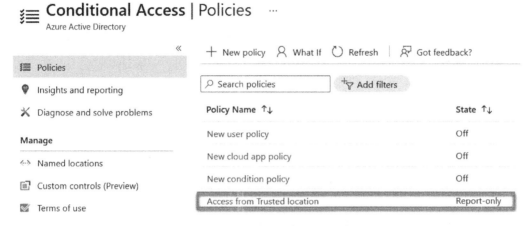

Figure 9.20 – New policy created

Next, we will set up a Conditional Access policy that will deny access when certain devices are used.

Conditional Access policy to deny access from certain devices

The following steps will go through the configuration of a Conditional Access policy that allows access to cloud apps when accessing from a trusted location:

1. Search for **Azure AD Conditional Access** to access Conditional Access and select this, as illustrated in the following screenshot:

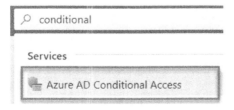

Figure 9.21 – Searching for Azure AD Conditional Access

2. Select **+ New policy** to create a Conditional Access policy, as illustrated in the following screenshot:

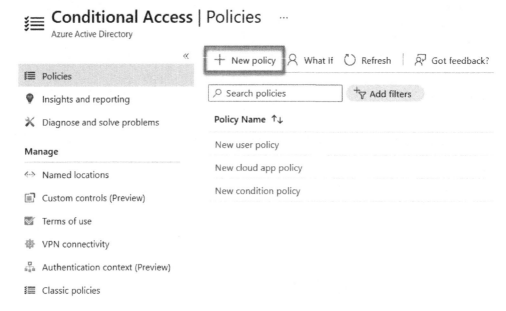

Figure 9.22 – Creating a new policy

3. Enter a name for your policy—for example, `Deny Access from Android devices`. This is demonstrated in the following screenshot:

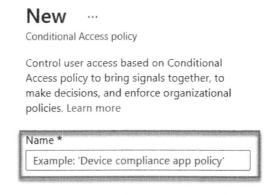

Figure 9.23 – Naming the policy

4. Select **Users and groups** under **Assignments**. Here, you can select everyone in Azure AD by selecting **All users**, or specific users and groups under **Select users and groups**. Options here include **All guest and external users**, **Directory roles**, and/or **Users and groups**. For this exercise, we will select **Users and groups**, **Sales group**, and then click **Select**, as illustrated in the following screenshot:

Figure 9.24 – Selecting a group

5. After clicking **Select**, the **Sales** group will appear under the included users and groups, as illustrated in the following screenshot:

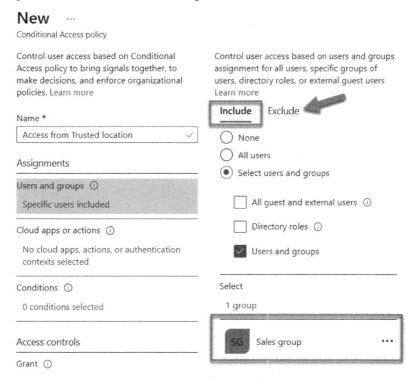

Figure 9.25 – Including the Sales group and understanding where to exclude users and groups

6.   Next, we configure cloud apps or actions. The following screenshot shows **All cloud apps** being selected. Use this as the setting for this exercise:

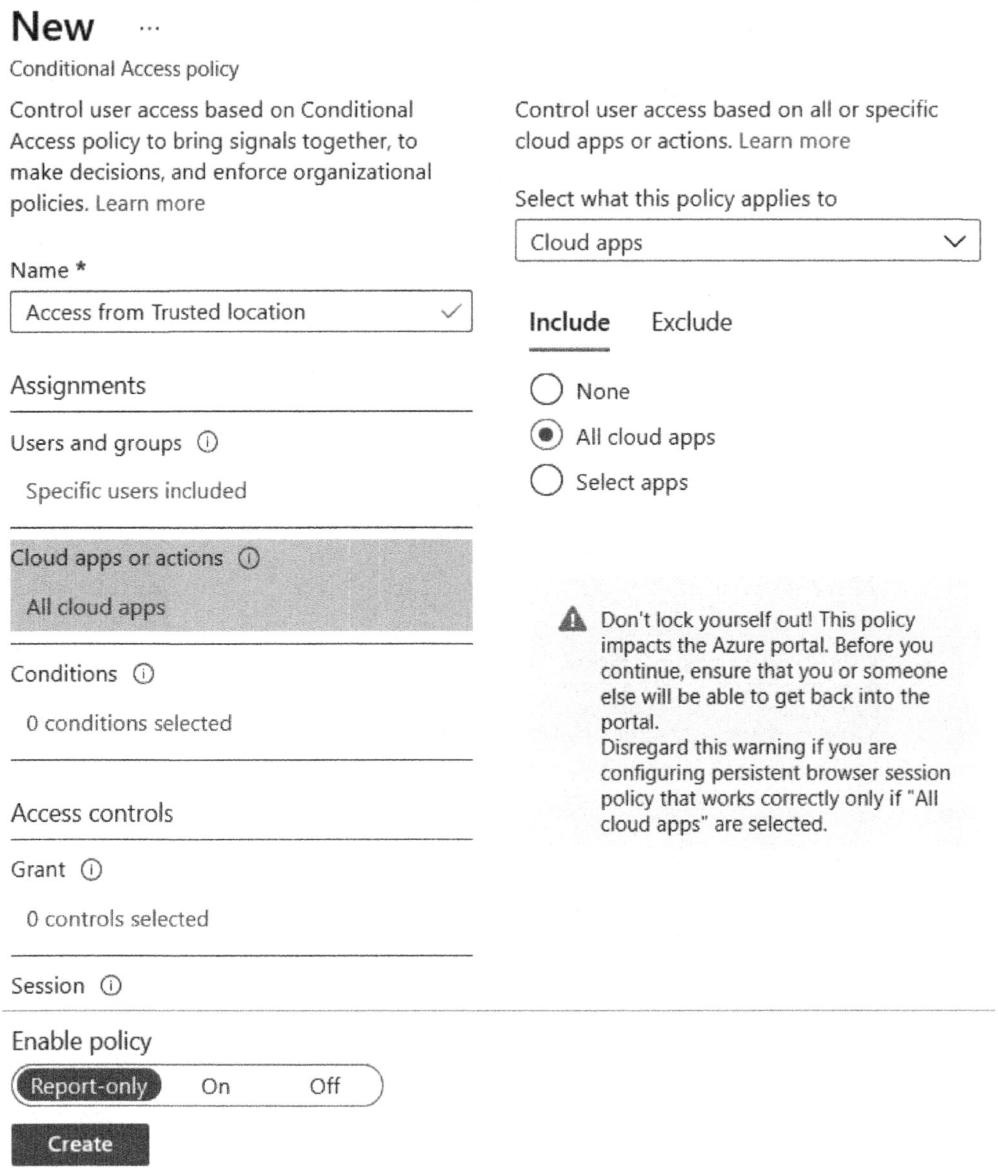

New   ...

Conditional Access policy

Control user access based on Conditional Access policy to bring signals together, to make decisions, and enforce organizational policies. Learn more

Control user access based on all or specific cloud apps or actions. Learn more

Name *

Select what this policy applies to

Cloud apps	⌄

Access from Trusted location	✓

Assignments

Include   Exclude

Users and groups ⓘ

◯ None

Specific users included

◉ All cloud apps

◯ Select apps

Cloud apps or actions ⓘ

All cloud apps

Conditions ⓘ

⚠ Don't lock yourself out! This policy impacts the Azure portal. Before you continue, ensure that you or someone else will be able to get back into the portal.

0 conditions selected

Disregard this warning if you are configuring persistent browser session policy that works correctly only if "All cloud apps" are selected.

Access controls

Grant ⓘ

0 controls selected

Session ⓘ

Enable policy

(Report-only)   On   Off

Create

Figure 9.26 – Configuring all cloud apps

7. Next, we will navigate to **Conditions** and select **Device platforms**. Select **Not configured** under **Device platforms**. Change **Configure** to **Yes**, select **Device platforms**, and choose **Android**, as illustrated in the following screenshot. Then, click **Done** to save:

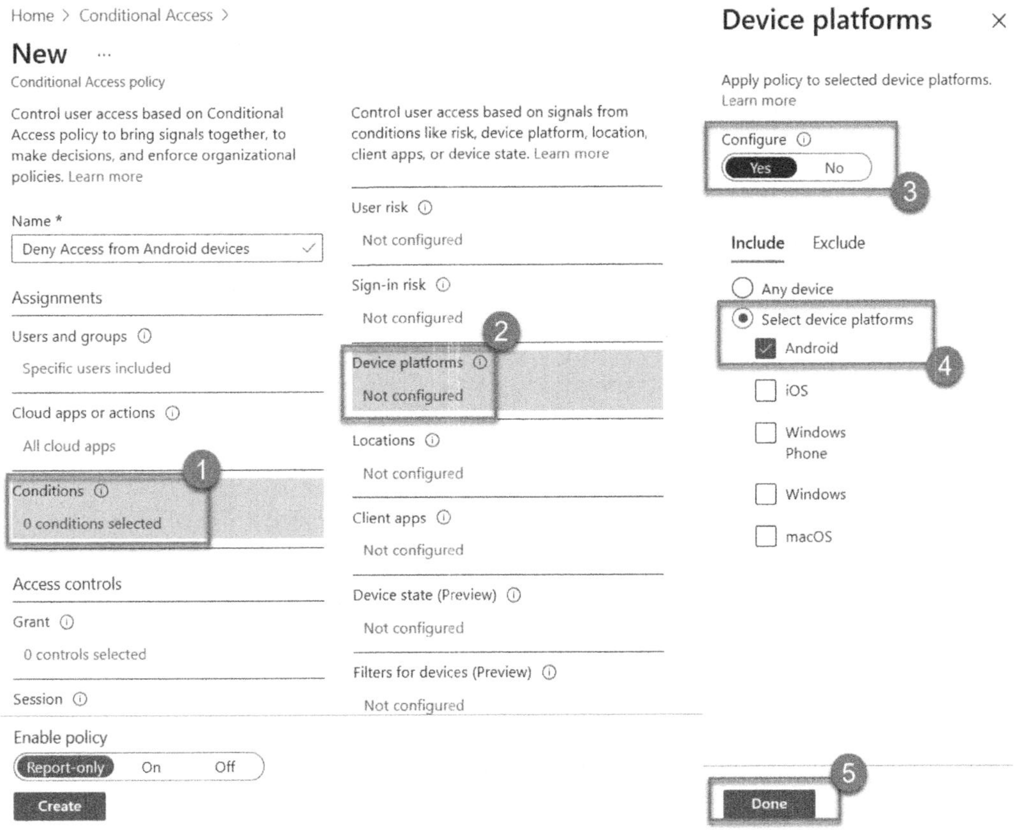

Figure 9.27 – Configuring the Android device platform

8. Under **Access controls**, select **0 controls selected** under **Grant**. Select **Block access** and click **Select** to save, as illustrated in the following screenshot:

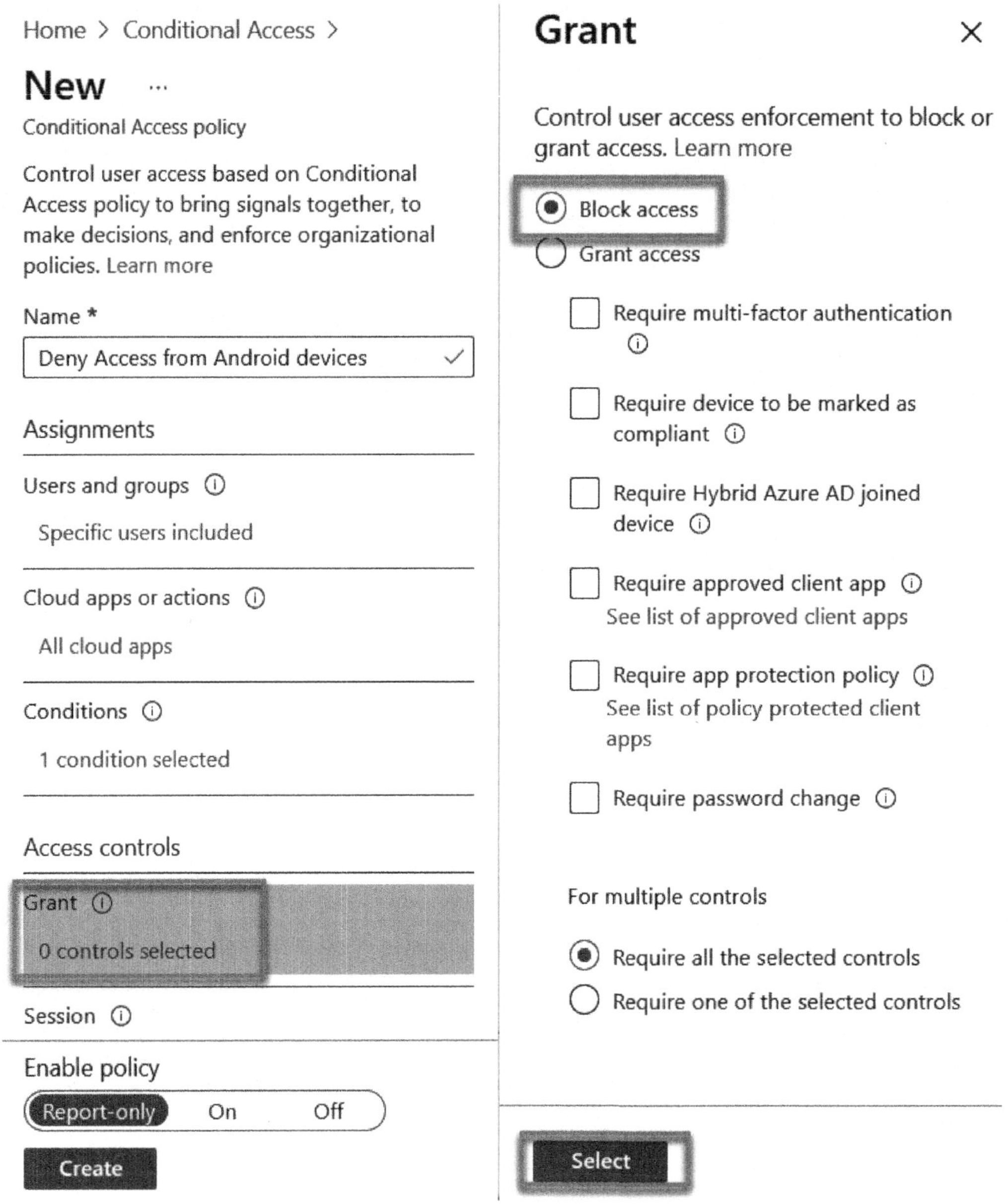

Home > Conditional Access >

New ...

Conditional Access policy

Control user access based on Conditional Access policy to bring signals together, to make decisions, and enforce organizational policies. Learn more

Name *

| Deny Access from Android devices ✓ |

Assignments

Users and groups ⓘ

  Specific users included

Cloud apps or actions ⓘ

  All cloud apps

Conditions ⓘ

  1 condition selected

Access controls

Grant ⓘ

0 controls selected

Session ⓘ

Enable policy

(Report-only) On   Off

Create

Grant ✕

Control user access enforcement to block or grant access. Learn more

◉ Block access
◯ Grant access

☐ Require multi-factor authentication ⓘ

☐ Require device to be marked as compliant ⓘ

☐ Require Hybrid Azure AD joined device ⓘ

☐ Require approved client app ⓘ
See list of approved client apps

☐ Require app protection policy ⓘ
See list of policy protected client apps

☐ Require password change ⓘ

For multiple controls

◉ Require all the selected controls
◯ Require one of the selected controls

Select

Figure 9.28 – Block access configuration

9. View the configuration, leave **Enable policy** set to **Report-only**, and click **Create** to create a Conditional Access policy. The following screenshot shows the settings that you should have:

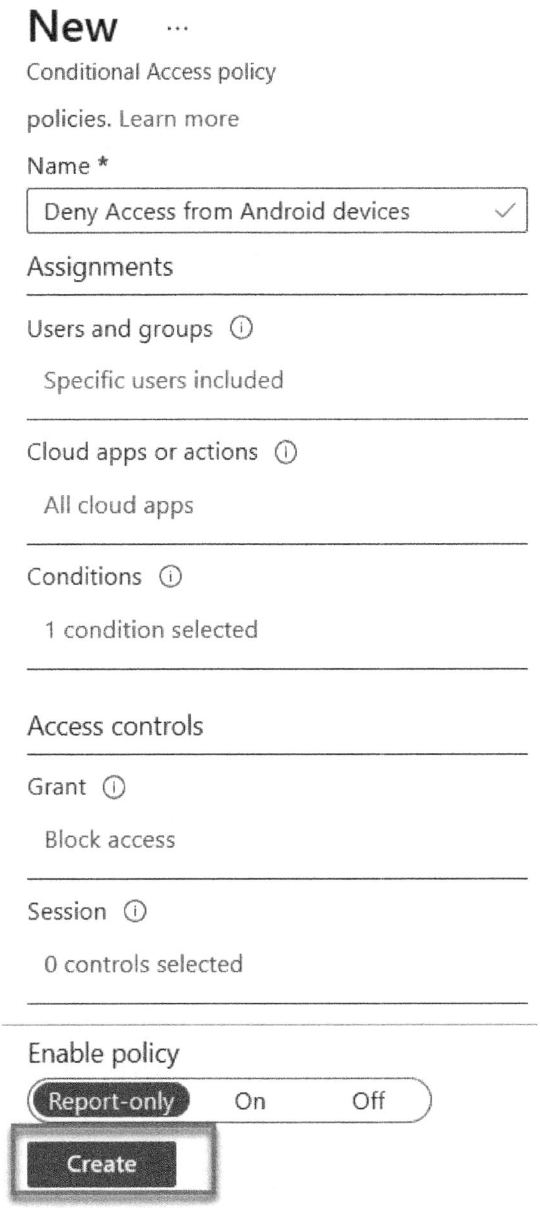

New ...

Conditional Access policy

policies. Learn more

Name *

| Deny Access from Android devices | ✓ |

Assignments

Users and groups ⓘ

  Specific users included

Cloud apps or actions ⓘ

  All cloud apps

Conditions ⓘ

  1 condition selected

Access controls

Grant ⓘ

  Block access

Session ⓘ

  0 controls selected

Enable policy

(Report-only   On   Off)

Create

Figure 9.29 – Deny access policy configuration

The next policy that we will create will be to allow cloud apps after MFA authentication.

The following screenshot shows that the **Deny Access from Android devices** policy has been created:

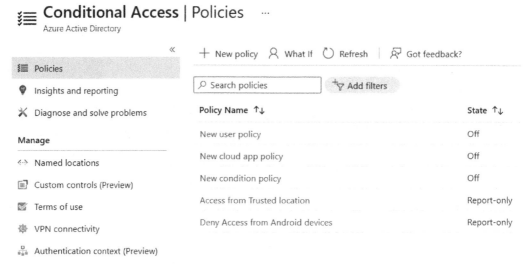

Figure 9.30 – New policy created

The final Conditional Access policy that we will cover will set up different grant access controls based on verification with MFA.

Conditional Access policy to allow access to cloud apps after verifying with MFA

The following steps will go through the configuration of a Conditional Access policy that allows access to cloud apps when accessing from a trusted location:

1. Search for **Azure AD Conditional Access** to access Conditional Access and select it, as illustrated in the following screenshot:

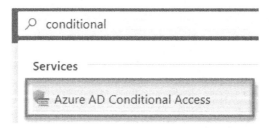

Figure 9.31 – Searching for Azure AD Conditional Access

2. Select **+ New policy** to create a **Conditional Access** policy, as illustrated in the following screenshot:

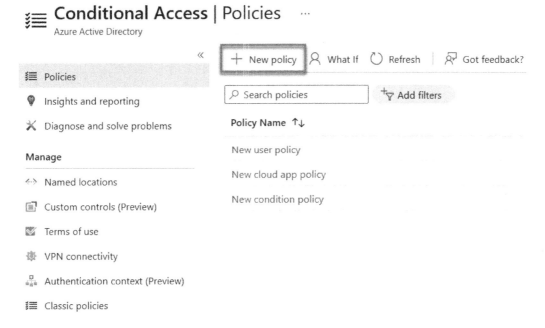

Figure 9.32 – Creating a new policy

3. Enter a name for your policy—for example, `Device compliance app policy`. This is demonstrated in the following screenshot:

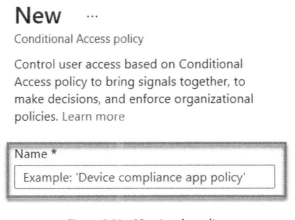

Figure 9.33 – Naming the policy

4. Select **Users and groups** under **Assignments**. Here, you can select everyone in
    Azure AD by selecting **All users**, or specific users and groups under **Select users
    and groups**. Options here include **All guest and external users**, **Directory roles**,
    and/or **Users and groups**. For this exercise, we will select **Users and groups**, **Sales
    group**, and then click **Select**, as illustrated in the following screenshot:

Figure 9.34 – Selecting a group

5. After clicking **Select**, **Sales group** will appear under the included users and groups.
    Something to note in the following screenshot is that there is also an **Exclude** tab.
    It is recommended that if the administrator is part of the included group, they be
    added as an excluded assignment to avoid being locked out of resources.

Figure 9.35 – Including the Sales group and understanding where to exclude users and groups

6. Next, we configure cloud apps or actions, which is a similar process to including users and groups. The following screenshot shows **Office 365** being selected as a cloud app. Use this as the preferred setting for this exercise:

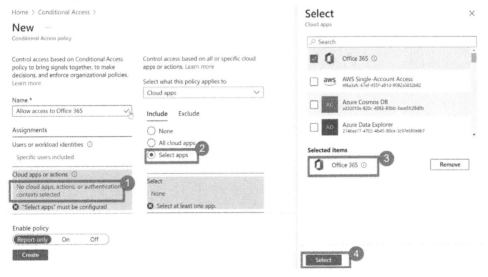

Figure 9.36 – Selecting Office 365 as a cloud app

7. Next, we will navigate to **Conditions** and select **Locations**. Change **Configure** to **Yes**, and then choose **Exclude** and **Selected locations**. Choose **Company headquarters** and click **Select** to save, as illustrated in the following screenshot. This will configure all locations except the company headquarters to be within the scope of this policy.

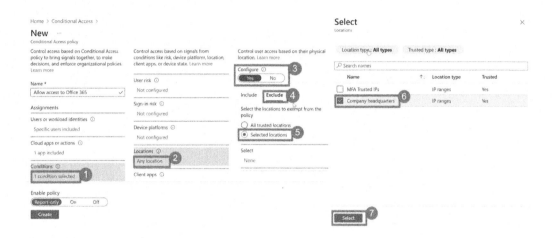

Figure 9.37 – Excluding the Company headquarters location

8. Select **Device platforms** under **Conditions**. Change **Configure** to **Yes**, and choose **iOS** and **Windows** for the selected device platforms, as illustrated in the following screenshot. Click **Done** to save.

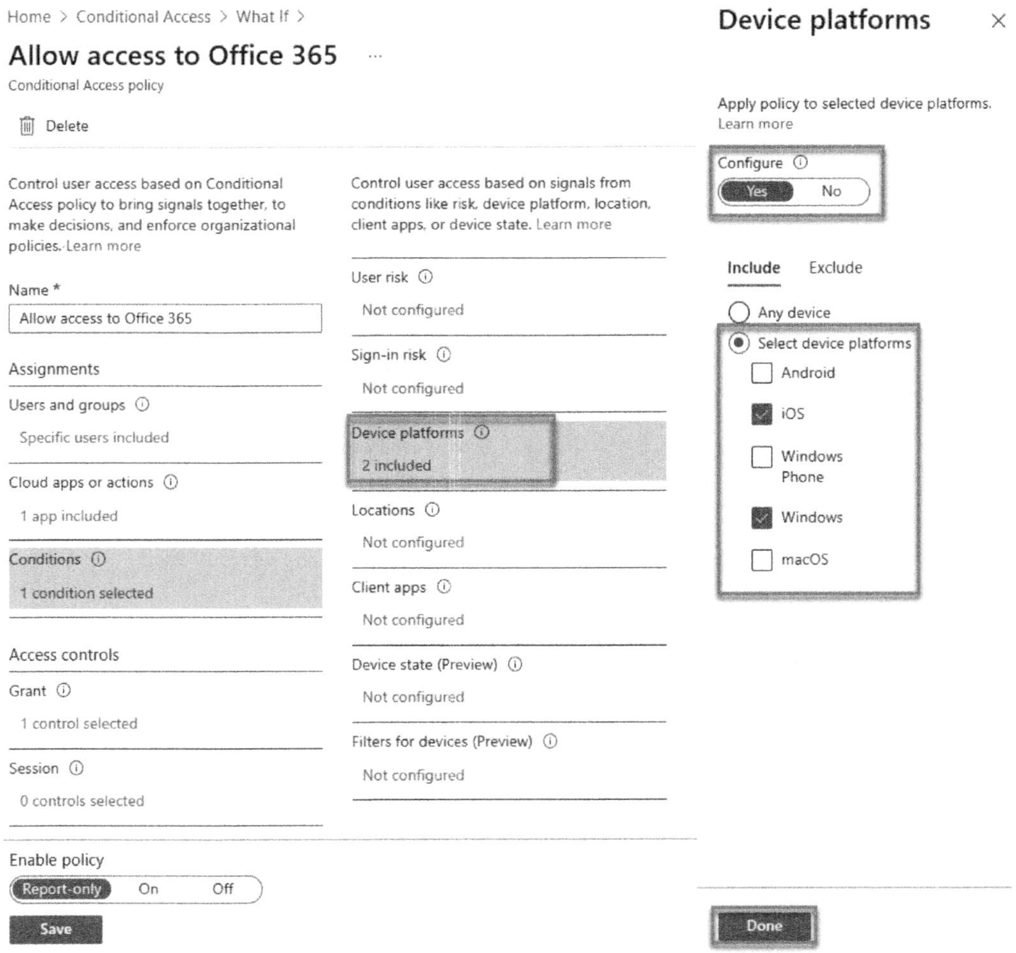

Home > Conditional Access > What If >

Allow access to Office 365   ...

Conditional Access policy

🗑 Delete

Control user access based on Conditional
Access policy to bring signals together, to
make decisions, and enforce organizational
policies. Learn more

Name *

Allow access to Office 365

Assignments

Users and groups ⓘ

Specific users included

Cloud apps or actions ⓘ

1 app included

Conditions ⓘ

1 condition selected

Access controls

Grant ⓘ

1 control selected

Session ⓘ

0 controls selected

Enable policy

Report-only   On   Off

Save

Control user access based on signals from
conditions like risk, device platform, location,
client apps, or device state. Learn more

User risk ⓘ

Not configured

Sign-in risk ⓘ

Not configured

Device platforms ⓘ

2 included

Locations ⓘ

Not configured

Client apps ⓘ

Not configured

Device state (Preview) ⓘ

Not configured

Filters for devices (Preview) ⓘ

Not configured

Device platforms   ✕

Apply policy to selected device platforms.
Learn more

Configure ⓘ

Yes   No

Include   Exclude

○ Any device

● Select device platforms

☐ Android

☑ iOS

☐ Windows
Phone

☑ Windows

☐ macOS

Done

Figure 9.38 – Configuring device platforms

9. Under **Access controls**, select **Grant**. Choose **Grant access** and select **Require multi-factor authentication**, as illustrated in the following screenshot. Click **Select** to save.

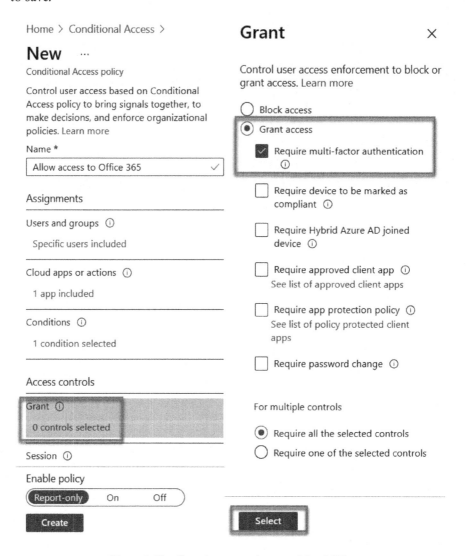

Figure 9.39 – Granting access but requiring MFA

Note

You can select multiple grant controls here to meet your needs. When you use multiple controls, you can choose whether only one or all of those control conditions must be met to grant access.

---

10. The Conditional Access policy is ready to be created. Set **Enable policy** to **Report-only** and select **Create**, as illustrated in the following screenshot:

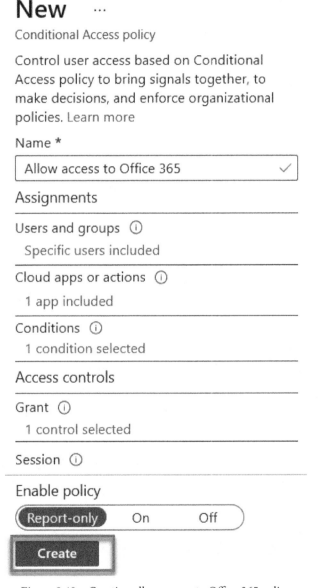

Figure 9.40 – Creating allow access to Office 365 policy

We have now created three new **Conditional Access** policies, as shown in the following screenshot:

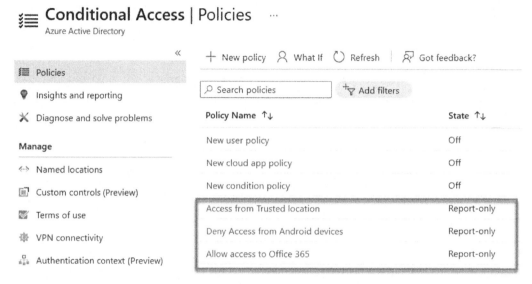

Figure 9.41 – New Conditional Access policies

In the next section, we will show how to test and view the actions of these policies using the **What If** function.

Testing a Conditional Access policy with What If

In the previous sections, we created three new Conditional Access policies. When we created these policies, we enabled them as **Report-only**. This allows us to test these policies before turning them on and unintentionally locking users out of their applications. This section will show how we can test these policies for different users, devices, and locations and evaluate the Conditional Access policies that are initiated to verify that the proper actions are taking place to enforce verification, grant access, or deny access. These are the steps we need to follow:

1. The following screenshot shows how to access **What If**. Select **What If** on the **Conditional Access | Policies** tile.

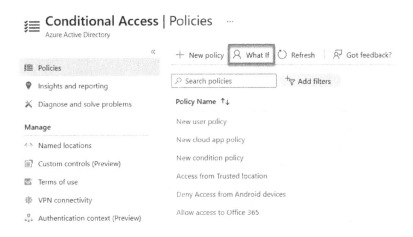

Figure 9.42 – Selecting What If

2.   On the **What If** tile, we will select a user. Our Conditional Access policy used the
     Sales group as the scope of the policy. Choose a user who is a member of your Sales
     group. Leave **Cloud apps, actions, or authentication context** on **Any cloud app**.
     For the **IP address** field, use your `whatsmyip` address and select your country.
     Under **Device platform**, select **Android**. Leave the remaining fields unselected and
     choose **What If**. The following screenshot shows the correct configuration:

Figure 9.43 – What If configuration

After choosing **What If**, the results will appear at the bottom of the tile with the policies that will apply and the policies that will not apply. As you see in the following screenshot, two of our created policies will apply to these settings:

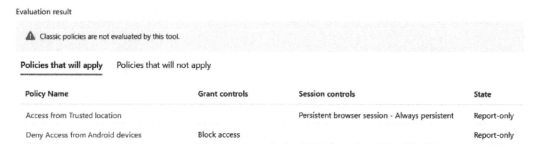

Figure 9.44 – Policies that will apply to the What If configuration

The following screenshot shows the policies that will not apply:

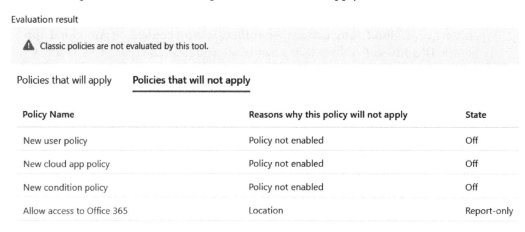

Figure 9.45 – Policies that will not apply to the What If configuration

3. Next, select **Reset** and add the same user. Leave **IP address** and **Country** blank, and select **What If** to get the evaluation results, as illustrated in the following screenshot:

Figure 9.46 – What If for all locations and apps

4. The evaluation results will show that all three of our Conditional Access policies will apply. The following screenshot shows the results:

Figure 9.47 – What If results for all locations

At this point, we have configured Conditional Access policies and tested how they would affect a user. If the results within **What If** are acceptable, we can now go back into the policies and move **Enable policy** to the **On** position. This will then enforce the policy for the users, devices, and locations that we have in scope for Conditional Access policies.

The next section will discuss the use and configuration of Smart Lockout.

Configuring Smart Lockout thresholds

In the previous sections, we went through the process of creating Conditional Access policies to protect against unauthorized users accessing applications and data while enforcing the zero-trust model for IAM. This section discusses how you can configure Smart Lockout to assist in preventing identity attacks.

Smart Lockout is a part of Azure AD Password Protection. The following screenshot shows how you can search and access this feature:

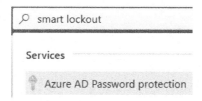

Figure 9.48 – Searching for Smart Lockout

Smart Lockout is used to protect users in a company from having their identity compromised through a brute-force dictionary attack. These attacks are executed by using the known username, which is generally an email address, and then automating login attempts with commonly used passwords. These attempts generally happen multiple times per minute in order to find a successful attempt. Smart Lockout is a way to configure the threshold of the number of attempts in a predetermined amount of time before that user's username is locked out and requires a password reset and verification code to regain access. In addition to setting a lockout threshold, you also have the ability to create a banned password list that you want users to avoid within Azure AD. The following screenshot shows the configurable settings for **Password Protection** and Smart Lockout. These settings can also be utilized in a hybrid identity infrastructure by turning **Password protection for Windows Server Active Directory** to the **Yes** position. Once the configuration is complete, you should change the mode to **Enforced** to execute the use of Smart Lockout.

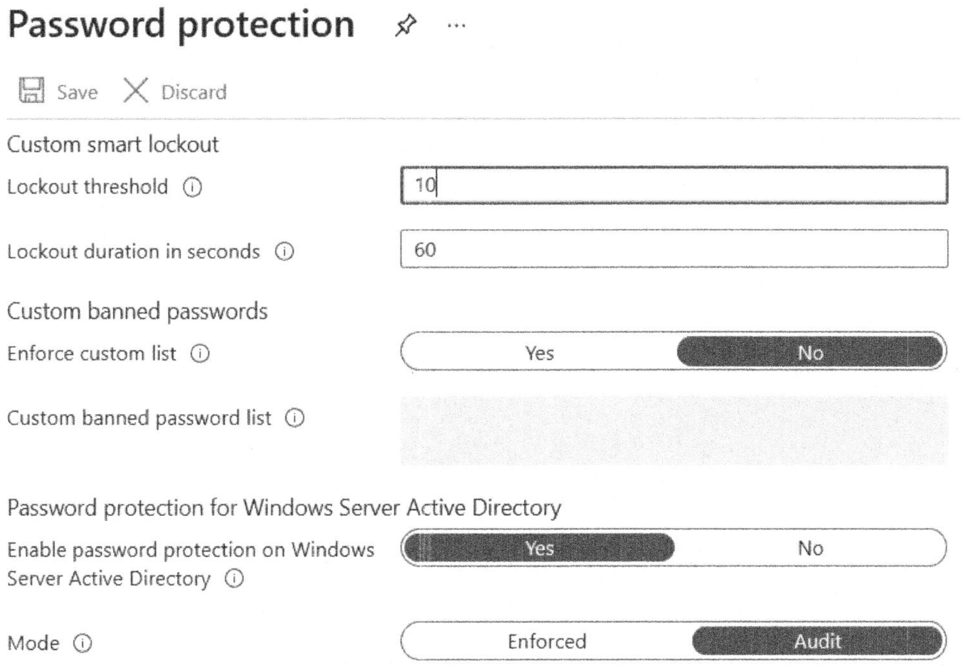

Password protection 📌 ⋯

🖫 Save   ✕ Discard

Custom smart lockout

Lockout threshold ⓘ

> 10|

Lockout duration in seconds ⓘ

> 60

Custom banned passwords

Enforce custom list ⓘ

(Yes | **No**)

Custom banned password list ⓘ

Password protection for Windows Server Active Directory

Enable password protection on Windows
Server Active Directory ⓘ

(**Yes** | No)

Mode ⓘ

(Enforced | **Audit**)

Figure 9.49 – Password protection settings

Password protection and Smart Lockout are configurable features that protect the identity of our users and help to ensure unauthorized access to our applications and resources. These features, as with Conditional Access policies, require planning and configuration for them to be effective.

In the next section, we will look at how Azure AD Identity Protection can help us to monitor suspicious activity on user accounts and how we can also use it to manage additional Conditional Access policies.

Implementing and managing a user risk policy

In order to implement and manage a user risk policy, your company requires an **Azure Active Directory Premium P2** license. This license provides the advanced identity security feature of Azure AD Identity Protection.

Azure AD Identity Protection

Azure AD Identity Protection provides additional capabilities within Azure AD to monitor user activity and recognize, through Microsoft's **machine learning** (**ML**) capabilities, anomalous and suspicious activity on user accounts. The following screenshot shows how to search for and access **Azure AD Identity Protection** within the Azure portal:

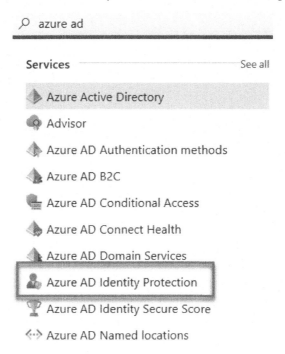

Figure 9.50 – Searching for Azure AD Identity Protection

Azure AD Identity Protection provides feedback in two areas: user risk and sign-in risk. Both are related to user behavior, but it is important to understand the differences between them, which are outlined as follows:

- User risk is concerned with activities that pertain directly to a user. This is primarily seen in the form of potentially leaked credentials, or something identified through **threat intelligence** (**TI**) attack patterns being targeted on a particular user.

- Sign-in risk identifies that a request for authentication likely isn't requested by the authorized identity owner. Some examples of a sign-in risk would include login attempts from anonymous IP addresses, atypical travel, suspicious browsers, and IP addresses linked with malware, among others.

Additional information and examples can be found at this link: `https://docs.microsoft.com/en-us/azure/active-directory/identity-protection/concept-identity-protection-risks`. It is important to identify the difference between user risk and sign-in risk for the exam.

The following screenshot shows the **Protect** and **Report** menus of Azure AD Identity Protection. We will discuss reports in the next section. To protect against attackers gaining access to resources, policies can be put in place to block access or require additional verification when a user or sign-in is flagged at a certain risk level—**Low**, **Medium**, or **High**.

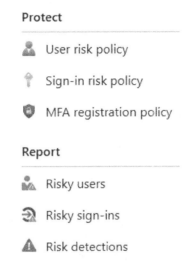

Figure 9.51 – Azure AD Identity Protection menu

These policies work the same as the Conditional Access policies that we discussed previously in this chapter. User and sign-in risk policies can be standalone policies within Azure AD Identity Protection or integrated into Conditional Access policies.

Once we have our protection in place, we also want to understand the level of risk for our users and sign-ins. The final section of our chapter will show how Azure AD Identity Protection can be used to monitor, investigate, and remediate risky users.

Monitoring, investigating, and remediating elevated risky users

If you are utilizing resources that are touching the internet, then someone is scanning them and attempting to gain access to them. There is an abundance of bad actors that have automated tools to scan usernames and attempt to authenticate with common passwords. **Azure AD Identity Protection** utilizes the Microsoft **Threat Intelligence** database and ML tools to look for these threats, identify the users affected, and identify the type of threat that exists. This information feeds into the **Identity Protection** overview dashboard shown in the following screenshot:

Figure 9.52 – Identity Protection overview

The **Report** section of the **Identity Protection** menu provides additional information on users who are at risk and what their risk level is, and allows you to drill down and investigate potential attacks that may have taken place on those user accounts. The following screenshot shows how you can view this information and select a user for more information:

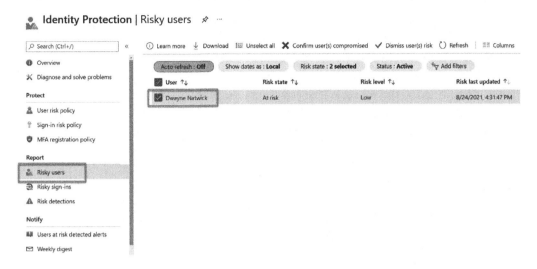

Figure 9.53 – Viewing user risk information

Once you open the details, you can view the **Basic info** tab, which provides the level of administrative roles that the user has, their status and level of risk, and when the last event took place. This information is shown in the following screenshot:

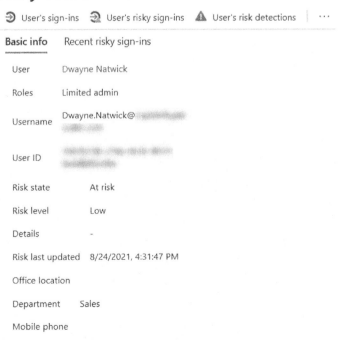

Figure 9.54 – Risky user details

Moving on to recent risky sign-ins, this provides a deeper level of information about the risk activity that took place. In the following screenshot, you can see that although risk activity took place, that attack failed. This explains why the **Risk level** setting was set to **Low** for this user, even though they were attacked. This view also shows the IP address that was identified as the source of the attack, and scrolling to the right also shows the location that the IP address is associated with. If a Conditional Access policy applied to this user that was triggered by this event, that would also be reflected here. The next two screenshots show all of the information that is provided, starting with this one:

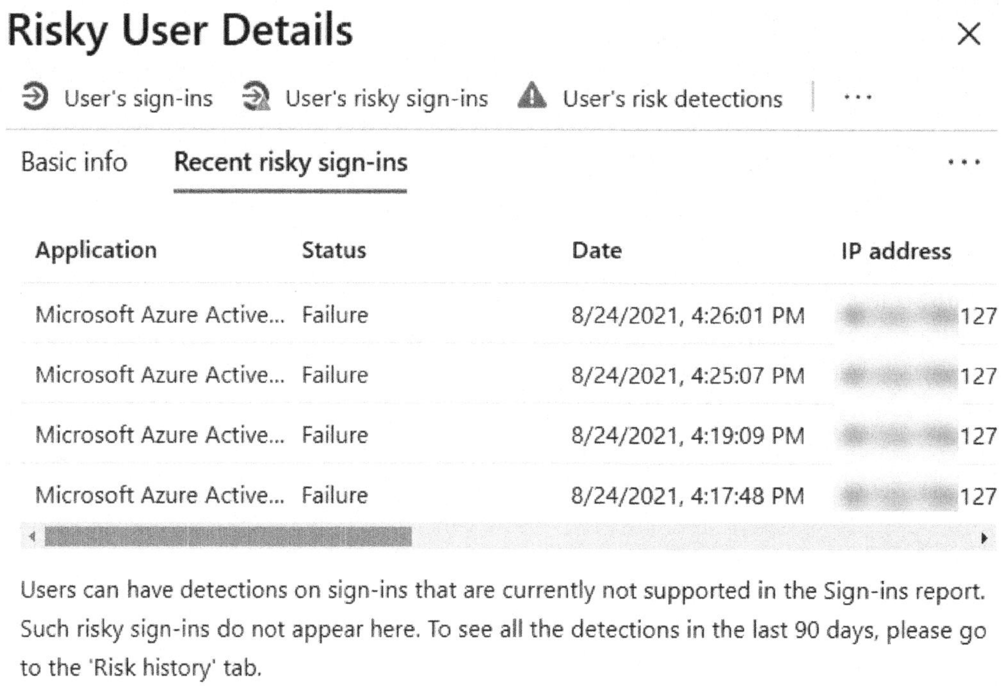

Risky User Details   ✕

⮐ User's sign-ins   🔁 User's risky sign-ins   ⚠ User's risk detections | • • •

Basic info   **Recent risky sign-ins**   • • •

Application	Status	Date	IP address
Microsoft Azure Active...	Failure	8/24/2021, 4:26:01 PM	127
Microsoft Azure Active...	Failure	8/24/2021, 4:25:07 PM	127
Microsoft Azure Active...	Failure	8/24/2021, 4:19:09 PM	127
Microsoft Azure Active...	Failure	8/24/2021, 4:17:48 PM	127

Users can have detections on sign-ins that are currently not supported in the Sign-ins report. Such risky sign-ins do not appear here. To see all the detections in the last 90 days, please go to the 'Risk history' tab.

Figure 9.55 – Risky sign-in details

This screenshot shows the additional risky sign-in details of location, risk state, and whether there was a Conditional Access policy applied:

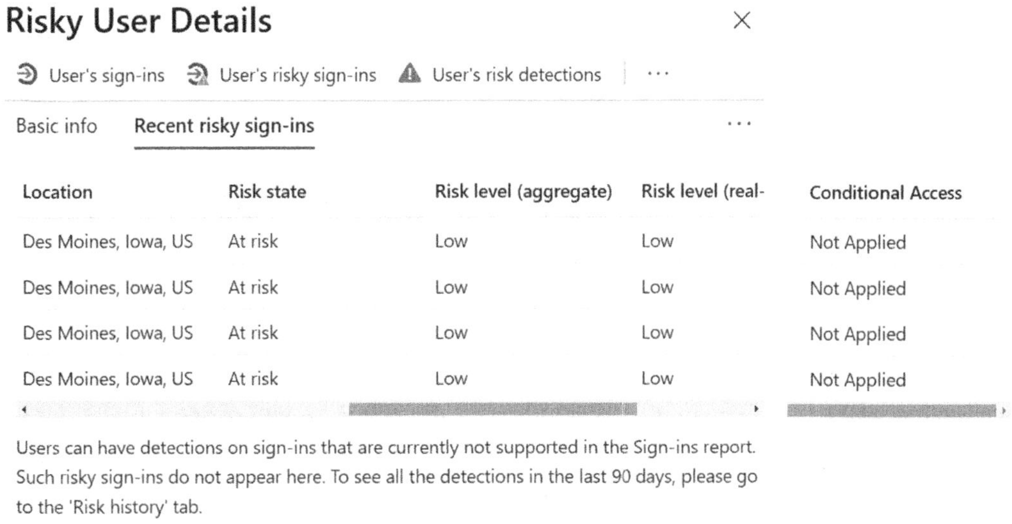

Risky User Details
User's sign-ins
User's risky sign-ins
User's risk detections
Basic info
Recent risky sign-ins
Location
Risk state
Risk level (aggregate)
Risk level (real-
Conditional Access
Des Moines, Iowa, US
At risk
Low
Low
Not Applied
Des Moines, Iowa, US
At risk
Low
Low
Not Applied
Des Moines, Iowa, US
At risk
Low
Low
Not Applied
Des Moines, Iowa, US
At risk
Low
Low
Not Applied
Users can have detections on sign-ins that are currently not supported in the Sign-ins report. Such risky sign-ins do not appear here. To see all the detections in the last 90 days, please go to the 'Risk history' tab.

Figure 9.56 – Additional risky sign-in details

A final area to discuss is what to do once we have identified users at risk and what we need to do to protect these users and our company. The following screenshot shows the selection menu for actionable items for remediating this particular user. This includes resetting their password, confirming or dismissing that the user was compromised, blocking the user entirely, or taking additional steps to investigate in **Azure Defender**.

Risky User Details
User's sign-ins
User's risky sign-ins
User's risk detections
Basic info
Recent risky sign-ins
Reset password
Confirm user compromised
Dismiss user risk
Block user
Investigate with Azure Defender
Risk level (aggregate)
Low
Low
Low
Low
Low
Not Applied
Users can have detections on sign-ins that are currently not supported in the Sign-ins report. Such risky sign-ins do not appear here. To see all the detections in the last 90 days, please go to the 'Risk history' tab.

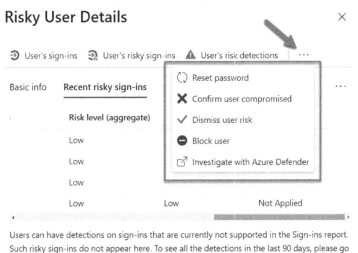

Figure 9.57 – Actionable items to remediate risk

Taking these steps will protect our Azure AD users and also our company from compromised identities.

Next, we will provide a summary of what was discussed in this chapter.

Summary

In this chapter, we discussed advanced solutions to protect identity and enforce the zero-trust model with Conditional Access policies and Azure Identity Protection. We went through the process of creating Conditional Access policies and then tested scenarios of how they would be applied with the **What If** function. We discussed how to configure Smart Lockout within Password Protection to protect against password brute-force dictionary attacks. Finally, we discussed how to license and use Identity Protection to identify and protect against user-credential leaks and risky sign-ins. In the next chapter, we will discuss the implementation of **single sign-on** (**SSO**) for enterprise applications in our hybrid infrastructure.

Section 4 – Implementing Access Management for Applications

This section will cover how to implement access management for on-premises and cloud applications across your organization.

This section of the book comprises the following chapters:

- *Chapter 10, Planning and Implementing Enterprise Apps for Single Sign-On (SSO)*
- *Chapter 11, Monitoring Enterprise Apps with Microsoft Defender for Cloud Apps*

10
Planning and Implementing Enterprise Apps for Single Sign-On (SSO)

The previous chapter covered conditional access policies, including planning for and testing these policies to verify that they are working correctly and providing the proper controls, in addition to Azure Identity Protection and using sign-in and user risk conditions with policies. In this chapter, we will discuss how we can implement enterprise applications in Azure AD with **single sign-on** (**SSO**).

In this chapter, we're going to cover the following main topics:

- Designing and implementing access management and SSO for apps
- Integrating on-premises apps using Azure AD Application Proxy
- Planning your line-of-business application registration strategy
- Implementing application registrations
- Planning and configuring multi-tier application permissions

Technical requirements

In this chapter, we will continue to explore configuring a tenant for use with **Microsoft 365** and **Azure**. You will need access to Azure Active Directory. If you have not created the trial licenses for Microsoft 365 yet, please follow the instructions provided in *Chapter 1, Preparing for Your Microsoft Exam*.

Designing and implementing access management and SSO for apps

In *Chapter 6, Implementing and Managing Hybrid Identities* you learned how to configure SSO for hybrid identity infrastructures using Azure AD Connect. This chapter will build upon SSO and how we can use SSO for enterprise applications, both on-premises and in the cloud, to provide the best user experience. The first step for any company that wants to have SSO available to their users is knowing about the applications that the company is using. In this section, we are going to discuss how Microsoft Defender for Cloud Apps (formerly Microsoft Cloud App Security) can help us discover the applications that are being accessed by users and how we can manage the applications that we want them to use.

Discovering apps with Microsoft Defender for Cloud Apps

Microsoft Defender for Cloud Apps is a cloud service for Microsoft 365 that provides Cloud Access Security Broker services. A cloud access security broker is used as an enterprise policy enforcement point between the consumers and the providers so that applications adhere to the baseline security requirements of the company. **Microsoft Defender for Cloud Apps** provides these capabilities for Microsoft, third-party cloud services, and registered on-premises applications.

Microsoft Defender for Cloud Apps is a helpful solution that aids in discovering applications that are being used within your company, both for planning for SSO integration with Azure AD and for controlling Shadow IT within your company. Shadow IT is where you use applications that are not approved by the company for use on the company network or on devices that also access company data. Microsoft Defender for Cloud Apps will identify all the applications that are being accessed through managed users and devices. These applications are then reported on the discovery dashboard. Knowing about the applications that are being used and accessed allows us to plan for SSO for authorized applications and block unauthorized applications.

For companies that have users in office locations with a firewall or a device that can log network traffic, Microsoft Defender for Cloud Apps's discovery capabilities allow you to connect these logs. Microsoft Defender for Cloud Apps will then create a discovery report that lists the applications that are being accessed. The workflow and architecture of Microsoft Defender for Cloud Apps are shown in the following diagram:

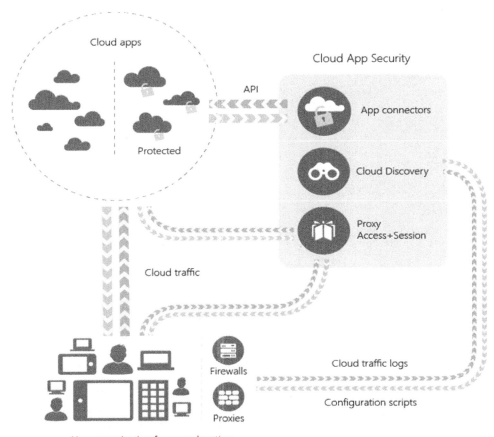

Figure 10.1 – Microsoft Defender for Cloud Apps architecture

For more information on Microsoft Defender for Cloud Apps, please go to `https://docs.microsoft.com/en-us/cloud-app-security/what-is-cloud-app-security`.

Next, we will discuss how to use Cloud Discovery to identify application use and the next steps to take.

Cloud Discovery

As we mentioned in the previous section, Microsoft Defender for Cloud Apps utilizes logs from network traffic to identify the applications that users are accessing. The traffic logs from on-premises firewalls or proxies will provide a snapshot report of the most common applications and users that are accessing these apps. Traffic from managed devices will be fed into the Microsoft Defender for Cloud Apps discovery overview dashboard, as shown in the following screenshot:

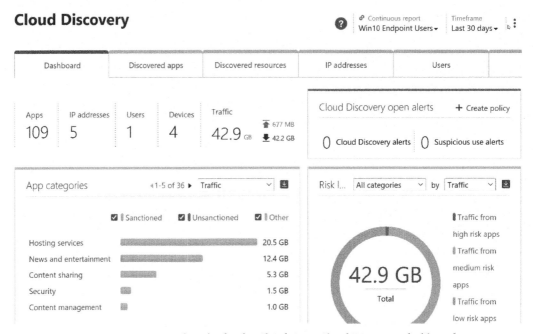

Figure 10.2 – Microsoft Defender for Cloud Apps Cloud Discovery dashboard

This information is the basis for planning and monitoring the application use within your organization. *Chapter 11, Monitoring Enterprise Apps with Microsoft Defender for Cloud Apps*, will discuss how to manage these applications and protect against shadow IT. The next section will discuss how to plan for **single sign-on** (**SSO**) for our non-Microsoft cloud and hybrid applications.

Planning for SSO for on-premises federated apps to migrate

As we discussed in the previous section, Cloud App Security logs information about the apps that are being accessed, helps us discover the applications that users are accessing, and evaluates whether they will be allowed access by users and devices logged in to Azure AD. Once we have created our list of sanctioned applications, we will want to allow users to authenticate to these applications with the same credentials that they use in Azure AD for Microsoft applications. If your company is currently utilizing SSO through Windows Active Directory and **Active Directory Federated Services (AD FS)**, you can migrate these applications to Azure AD to take advantage of the cost benefits of decreased hardware, as well as the compliance and governance services that are available within Azure AD. The following diagram shows how to utilize Windows Active Directory and AD FS for cloud and line-of-business apps. In this architecture, the users and devices on Azure AD can connect to on-premises line-of-business apps by migrating applications to Azure AD and SSO through Azure AD Application Proxy.

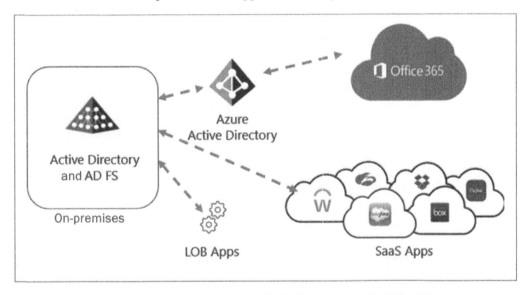

Figure 10.3 – Active Directory and Cloud Apps using AD FS for SSO

The following diagram shows the architecture after migrating these applications to Azure AD. This architecture simplifies how to manage and monitor applications and the use of SSO.

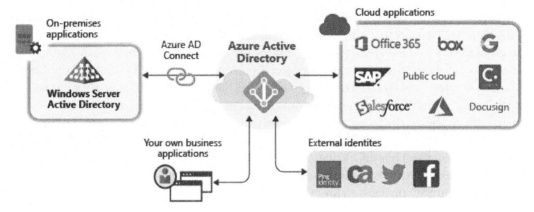

Figure 10.4 – Active Directory and Cloud Apps migrated to Azure AD for SSO

When this architecture is utilized, the company can utilize the various security, compliance, and governance tools available within Azure AD, Microsoft 365, and Azure for cloud and on-premises line-of-business applications, such as Cloud App Security, Conditional Access policies, and Azure AD Identity Protection. In the next section, we will discuss these two types of applications.

App types to migrate

When you're determining what applications will utilize SSO, it is important to understand the different types of applications that you may have in your infrastructure.

There are two types of applications you can migrate:

1. **SaaS** applications are applications that are generally procured by the company. Examples of such third-party SaaS applications include Dropbox, Salesforce, ServiceNow, and Workday. These applications have their own cloud authentication components. Many of these applications can utilize Azure AD as the authentication identity provider. The next section on implementing application registrations will discuss how to register third-party SaaS applications in Azure AD.

2. **Line-of-business** applications are applications that are developed by the organization and are not meant to be used by other companies. These can be on-premises or cloud-native applications. If they are on-premises, they may be provided with SSO capabilities through the settings within Azure AD Connect for a hybrid identity infrastructure, as discussed in *Chapter 6, Implementing and Managing Hybrid Identities*. These applications can also utilize an **Application Proxy** to register to Azure AD, which we will look at in the *Integrating on-premises apps using Azure AD Application Proxy* section.

In the next section, we will learn how to prepare line-of-business applications to utilize Azure AD for authentication.

Preparation and planning for usage and insights

If your company is currently utilizing AD FS, you can install **Usage & insights** on the local domain as part of Azure AD Connect. **Usage & insights** will identify the enterprise applications on-premises and determine the level of readiness to manage authentication with Azure AD.

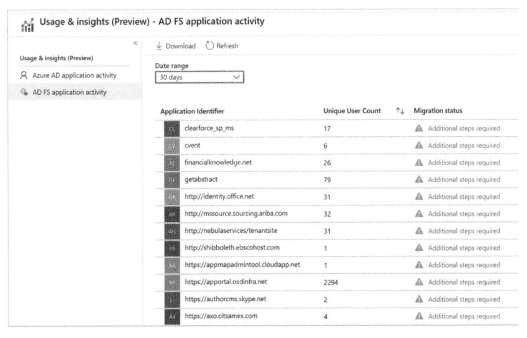

Figure 10.5 – Usage & insights report for AD FS applications

Usage & insights provides a list of on-premises applications and checks the following:

- Whether they are ready to migrate and can be fully supported by Azure AD in the current "as-is" configuration.

- Whether the reviews suggest that the application may have some settings that are capable of migrating to Azure AD, but that some settings may need to be adjusted before migration.

- Whether any additional steps are required; that is, it checks whether the application does not currently support Azure AD and whether the settings need to be adjusted to allow it to be migrated. You may find that these applications are not supported by Azure AD at all, depending on the settings of the application.

In the next section, we will discuss assigning roles for managing and creating application registrations.

App management and assigning roles

Once we have gone through the planning process and identified the apps that are ready to migrate, it is important to assign the proper roles. These roles are for creating app registrations and managing apps. Some of the main roles that are used for app management are as follows:

- The Application Administrator role, which allows users to create and manage enterprise applications, application registrations, and application proxy settings. These administrators can also grant application permissions and delegated permissions.

- The Cloud Application Administrator role can still manage enterprise applications and application registrations, but since this designation is for cloud applications, they cannot manage application proxies.

> **Note**
>
> Neither of these roles can be added as owners when you're creating new application registrations, but both can add credentials that impersonate an application's identity. Therefore, it is important to create Conditional Access policies for the users that are assigned these roles to protect against potential identity theft. Creating Conditional Access policies was discussed in *Chapter 9, Planning, Implementing, and Administering Conditional Access and Azure Identity Protection*.
>
> In addition, when assigning administrator roles to users, a best practice would be to only provide the elevated administrator roles when they are needed to perform a job function. Once that job function is complete, the administrator role is moved from active to available for the next time it is needed.

These just-in-time administrator roles are provided through **Privileged Identity Management (PIM)**, which we will discuss in more detail in *Chapter 13, Planning and Implementing Privileged Access and Access Reviews*. In the next section, we will learn how to integrate an on-premises application using Azure AD Application Proxy.

Integrating on-premises apps using Azure AD Application Proxy

In the previous sections, we went through the planning process of discovering and identifying applications that can be migrated to Azure AD for SSO. In this section, you will learn how to configure Azure AD Application Proxy to migrate on-premises applications to Azure AD for authentication and SSO. Azure AD Application Proxy provides integration between Azure AD and the on-premises application and the authentication settings in Windows Active Directory. The following diagram shows how Azure AD Application Proxy works. The difference between Azure AD Application Proxy and the hybrid identity architecture of Azure AD Connect is that this is a single registration for a single on-premises application. Rather than having a synchronization between Windows AD and Azure AD for authentication and authorization, the Azure AD Application Proxy service is used to pass the credentials to Azure AD for the user to authenticate. The Application Proxy service makes the on-premises application emulate a cloud application in Azure AD. This provides SSO authentication through Azure AD and uses Microsoft 365 and other registered cloud applications as the single identity provider.

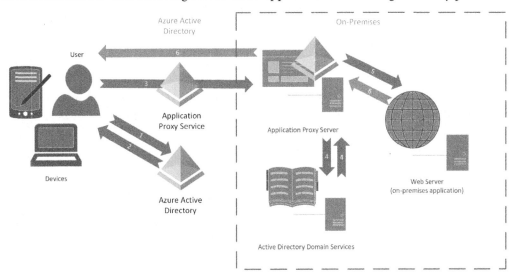

Figure 10.6 – Application Proxy diagram

As we mentioned in the previous section, the role that's required to perform this configuration is an Application Administrator or Global Administrator role. Adhering to the principle of least privilege, you should assign users who need to perform this configuration with the Application Administrator role. Once that role is activated, you can begin the configuration, as shown in the following steps:

1. Go to **Azure Active Directory** and select **Application proxy** from the **Manage** menu.

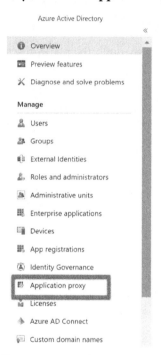

Figure 10.7 – Application proxy

2. If you receive a message stating that **Application proxy** is disabled on your tenant, it will be enabled automatically when you download and install the connector.

Figure 10.8 – Application Proxy is currently disabled for your tenant

3. Select **Download connector service**, as shown in the following screenshot:

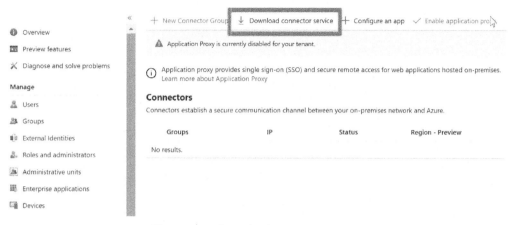

Figure 10.9 – Download connector service

4. Accept the terms and download the Application Proxy connector.

Figure 10.10 – Accept terms & Download

5. Locate the `AADApplicationProxyConnectorInstaller.msi` file in your `Downloads` folder and start the installation. Accept the license terms and click **Install**.

> **Note**
>
> Make sure that your network has been configured properly for the Application Proxy connector to communicate with Azure AD by following the steps at `https://docs.microsoft.com/en-us/azure/active-directory/app-proxy/application-proxy-deployment-plan`.

Figure 10.11 – Installing the Application Proxy Connector

6. During the installation, sign in to your Azure account (when prompted) with the account that has been assigned the Application Administrator or Global Administrator role.

Figure 10.12 – Signing in to your Microsoft Azure account

7. Once you've installed the Application Proxy connector, refresh the **Application proxy** tile in the Azure portal. Your connector will now be active, as shown in the following screenshot:

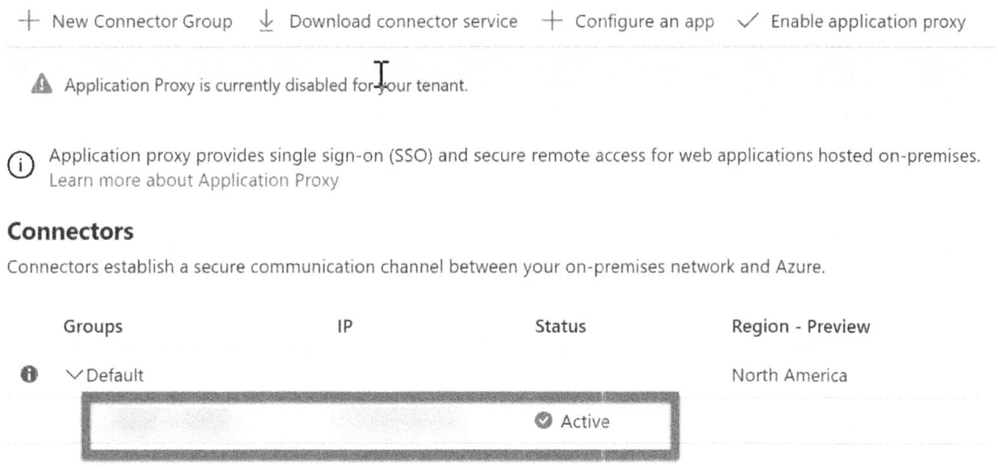

Figure 10.13 – Application Proxy is active

8. The message stating that **Application Proxy is currently disabled for your tenant** will still be visible, but **Enable application proxy** will no longer be grayed out. Select **Enable application proxy**.

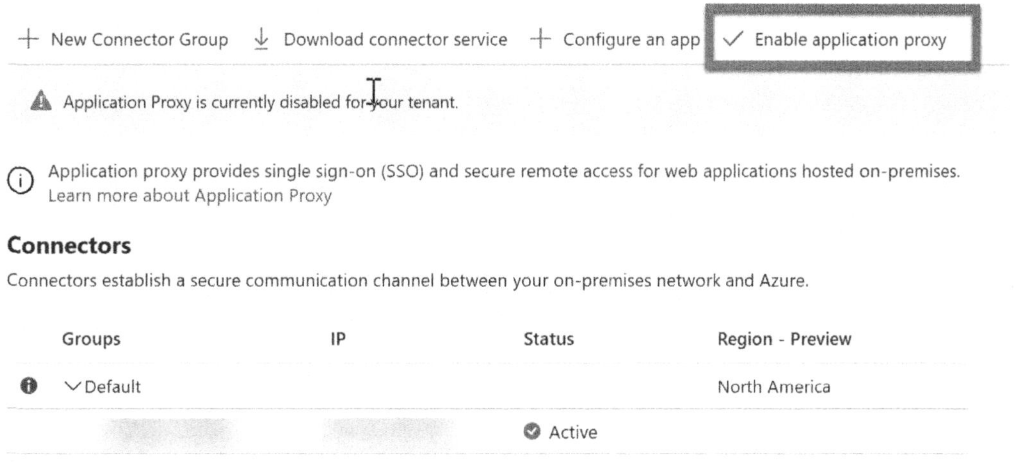

Figure 10.14 – Selecting Enable application proxy

9.   Select **Yes** when prompted to continue enabling Application Proxy.

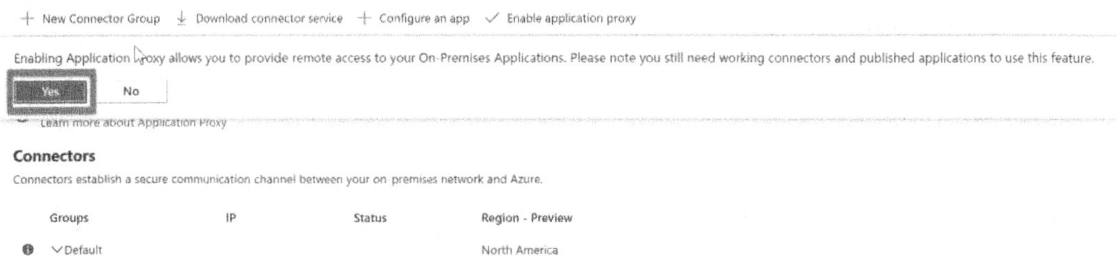

Figure 10.15 – Continuing to enable Application Proxy

10. Once Application Proxy has been enabled, the next step is to configure an app. Select **+ Configure an app**, as shown in the following screenshot:

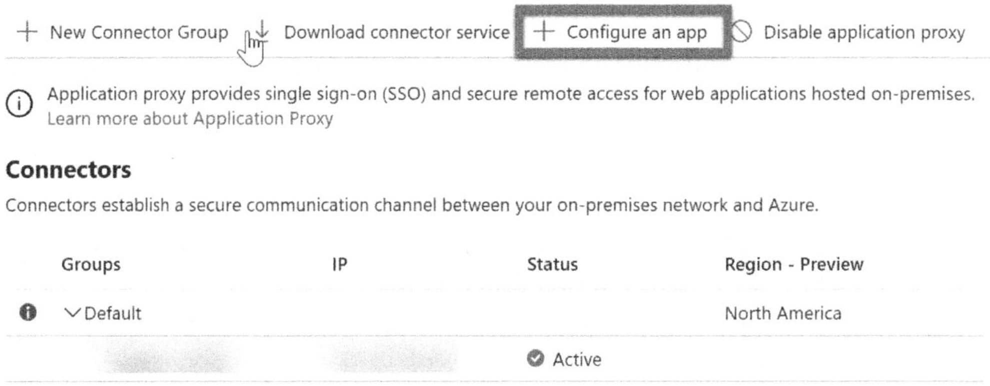

Figure 10.16 – Configure an app

11. Enter a name for your application and provide an **Internal Url** for your enterprise application. For **External Url**, you can create a name for your app and select a custom URL for your tenant from the dropdown, as shown in the following screenshot as **1**. If you do not have a custom URL to use, it will use your `tenantname.msapproxy.net` for **External Url**, shown as **2**. Once you've entered this information, select **+ Add** to add the on-premises application for SSO.

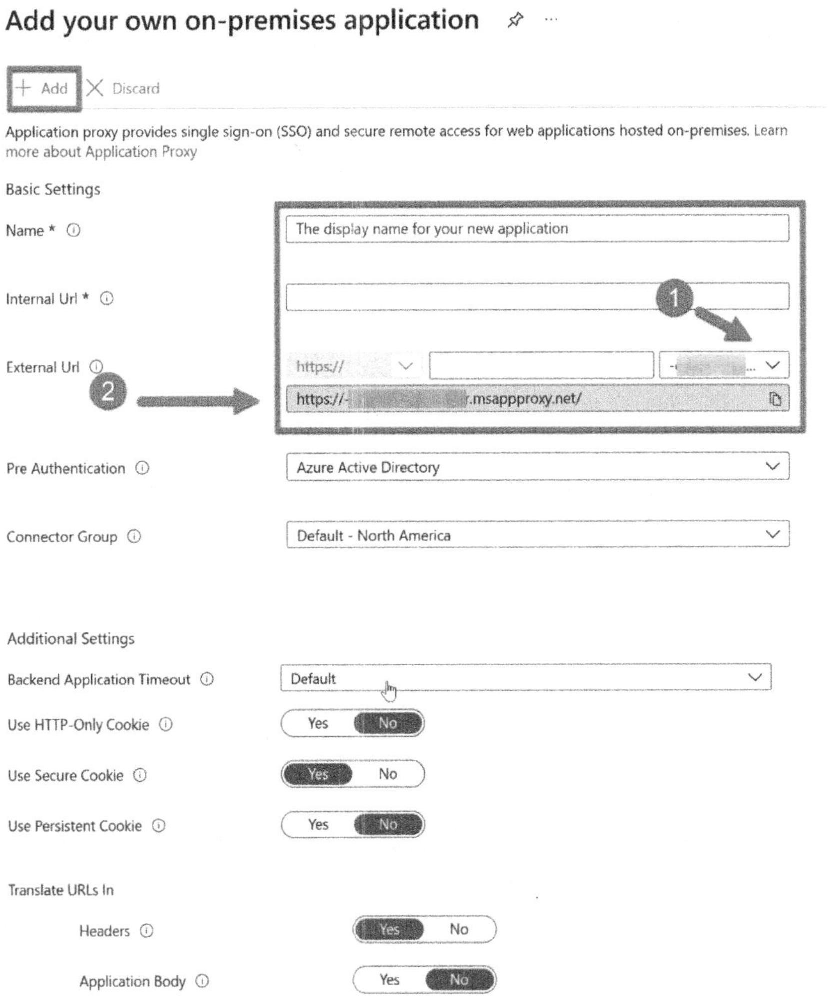

Add your own on-premises application 📌 ⋯

+ Add ✕ Discard

Application proxy provides single sign-on (SSO) and secure remote access for web applications hosted on-premises. Learn more about Application Proxy

Basic Settings

Name * ⓘ

> The display name for your new application

Internal Url * ⓘ

External Url ⓘ

https:// ⌄

https://-   r.msappproxy.net/

Pre Authentication ⓘ

> Azure Active Directory ⌄

Connector Group ⓘ

> Default - North America ⌄

Additional Settings

Backend Application Timeout ⓘ

> Default ⌄

Use HTTP-Only Cookie ⓘ   Yes **No**

Use Secure Cookie ⓘ   **Yes** No

Use Persistent Cookie ⓘ   Yes **No**

Translate URLs In

Headers ⓘ   **Yes** No

Application Body ⓘ   Yes **No**

Figure 10.17 – Configuring Application Proxy for an on-premises application

12. With that, the application has been added and can be used with Azure AD for SSO.

Note

The Application Proxy connector should be installed on more than one device in your on-premises network for additional resiliency in case of a device failure.

In the next section, we will discuss how to plan for your business application registration strategy.

Planning your line-of-business application registration strategy

As you plan for business applications to be registered to utilize Azure AD for SSO, it is important to understand the reasoning for doing so. The first is that SSO creates a better experience for users who only require a single username and password for authentication.

The second is to decrease the infrastructure that is required for authenticating to applications that are on-premises. If we can register our on-premises applications to Azure AD with Application Proxy, we no longer require a Windows Active Directory infrastructure on-premises.

The third reason is security. If we have our applications registered with Azure AD, including on-premises and third-party cloud applications, we can utilize the security solutions within Azure AD to authenticate and authorize all enterprise applications. This includes **multi-factor authentication (MFA)**, **single sign-on (SSO)**, **self-service password reset (SSPR)**, Azure AD Identity Protection, and Azure AD Conditional Access policies.

We can plan this strategy using Cloud App Security Discovery and Application Usage and Insights. Both planning and discovery options were discussed earlier in this chapter.

In the next section, we will learn how to register third-party cloud applications with Azure AD.

Implementing application registrations

In the previous sections, we discussed how to discover third-party applications through Cloud App Security. We also learned how to install application proxy connectors on-premises and add those on-premises line-of-business applications to Azure AD. In this section, we will learn how to register third-party cloud applications with Azure AD. Let's get started:

1. In the Azure portal, navigate to **Azure Active Directory** and select **Enterprise applications** from the **Manage** menu.

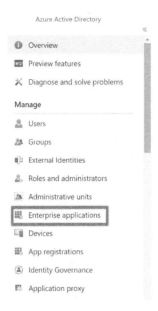

Figure 10.18 –Enterprise applications

2. In the **Enterprise applications** tile, you will see the list of current applications that are registered. Select **+ New application** to add a new application.

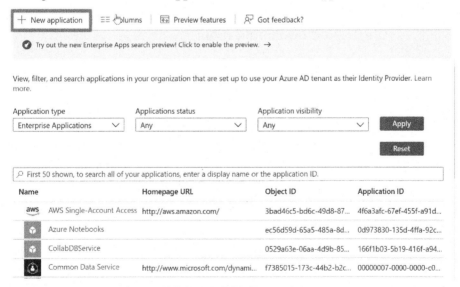

Figure 10.19 – New application

3. Scroll through the list and find the application that you need to register for. You also have the option to **+ Create your own application** at the top of the tile.

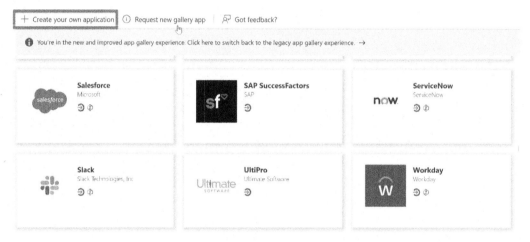

Figure 10.20 – Browsing Azure AD Gallery or the Create your own application option

4. Selecting **Create your own application** will open another tile. Within this tile, you can select a non-gallery application or register with Application Proxy. Choosing Application Proxy will take you to the same application configuration that was shown in *Figure 10.17*. The following screenshot shows the **Create your own application** tile:

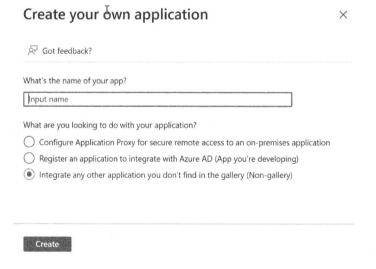

Figure 10.21 – Create your own application

5. Selecting an application from the gallery will take you to a tile for that application. Included within this tile is a link to some documentation to guide you through the registration process. This is shown in the following screenshot:

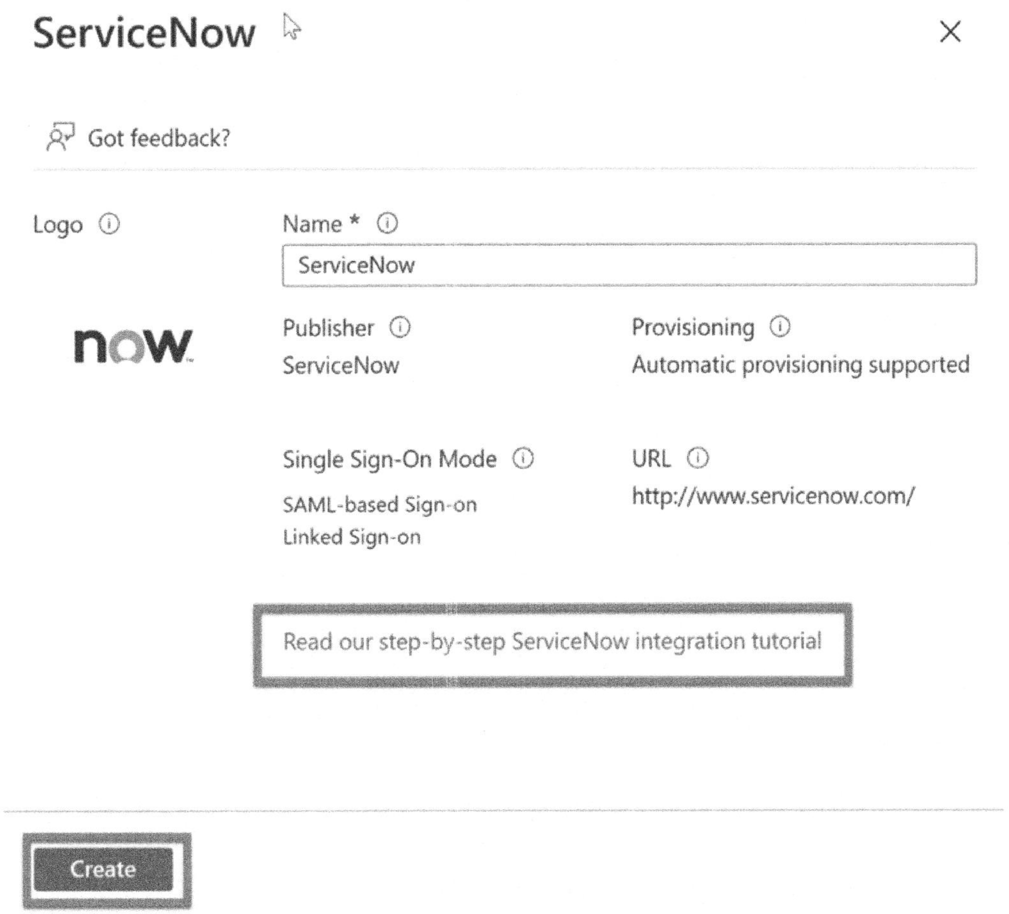

ServiceNow   ✕

🗨 Got feedback?

Logo ⓘ   Name * ⓘ

                ServiceNow

now.   Publisher ⓘ   Provisioning ⓘ
                ServiceNow   Automatic provisioning supported

                Single Sign-On Mode ⓘ   URL ⓘ
                SAML-based Sign-on   http://www.servicenow.com/
                Linked Sign-on

                Read our step-by-step ServiceNow integration tutorial

Create

Figure 10.22 – Registering for the third-party cloud application

6. Once you've registered, your application will be ready to use for SSO with Azure AD.

You must repeat these steps for each of the enterprise applications that you would like to register and utilize SSO for Azure AD within your tenant. You will need to have proper licensing for the users of the third-party cloud applications to register and allow SSO to be effective.

The next section will discuss multi-tier application permissions for applications.

Planning and configuring multi-tier application permissions

The final area that we need to consider for our application strategy is securing the applications and determining who can grant consent to them. You can do this by going to the **Enterprise applications** menu, then **Security**, and then **Consent and permissions**, as shown in the following screenshot:

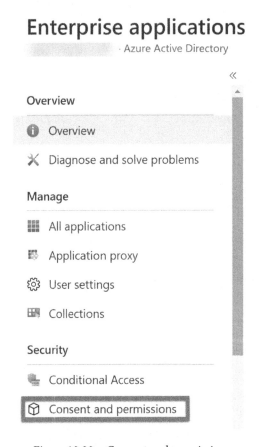

Figure 10.23 – Consent and permissions

Within **Consent and permissions**, we can configure who can grant consent. These options allow only an administrator to grant consent, allow users to grant consent to low-impact applications, or allow users to grant consent to all applications. These options are shown in the following screenshot:

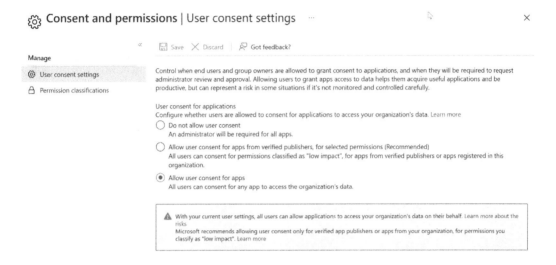

Figure 10.24 – User consent options for applications

Below these options are options for assigning group owners the appropriate permissions for granting access to users, as shown in the following screenshot:

Group owner consent for apps accessing data
Configure whether group owners are allowed to consent for applications to access your organization's data for the groups they own.
Learn more

○ Do not allow group owner consent
   Group owners cannot allow applications to access data for the groups they own.

○ Allow group owner consent for selected group owners
   Only selected group owners can allow applications to access data for the groups they own.

◉ Allow group owner consent for all group owners
   All group owners can allow applications to access data for the groups they own.

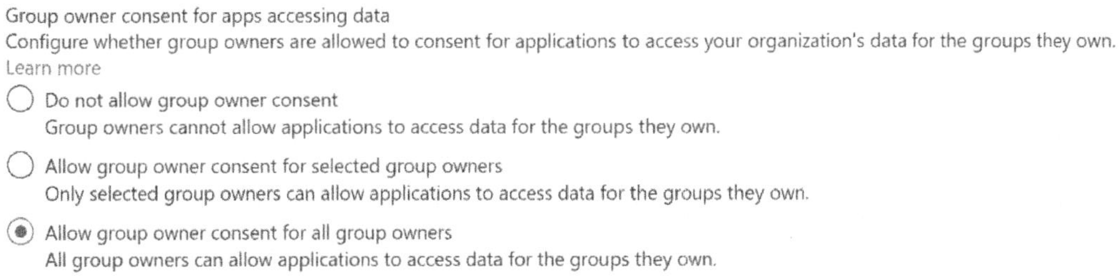

Figure 10.25 – Group owner consent options

Configuring these permissions is important if you wish to have the proper levels of security and governance over your applications. If your applications include sensitive information, then allowing users to grant application access could lead to security vulnerabilities. Planning properly and having an appropriate strategy can help you determine the level of governance that's needed for application permissions.

Next, we will summarize what was discussed in this chapter.

Summary

In this chapter, we covered the process for discovering, planning, and implementing application registrations for single sign-on to enterprise applications. These enterprise applications include on-premises applications that are accessed through Application Proxy and cloud applications. The more applications that we can register for single sign-on in Azure Active Directory, the better the user experience becomes and the more we can utilize and leverage Azure AD security solutions.

In the next chapter, we will discuss how to use third-party cloud applications within our organization and how to manage, monitor, and control them with Cloud App Security.

11
Monitoring Enterprise Apps with Microsoft Defender for Cloud Apps

The previous chapter covered how we can implement enterprise applications into **Azure Active Directory (AD)** for use with **single sign-on (SSO)**. This included utilizing **Microsoft Defender for Cloud Apps** (formerly Microsoft Cloud App Security) to discover applications that are being used on your company network. In this chapter, we will look at the advanced tools and capabilities of Microsoft Defender for Cloud Apps to monitor and manage the use of cloud applications in your company.

In this chapter, we're going to cover the following main topics:

- Planning your cloud application strategy
- Implementing cloud app security policies
- Planning and configuring cloud application permissions

- Discovering apps by using a Microsoft Defender for Cloud Apps or an **Active Directory Federated Services (ADFS)** app report

- Using Microsoft Defender for Cloud Apps to manage application access

Technical requirements

In this chapter, we will continue to explore configuring a tenant for the use of **Microsoft 365** and **Azure**. There will be exercises that will require access to Azure AD. If you have not yet created the trial licenses for Microsoft 365, please follow the directions provided within *Chapter 1, Preparing for Your Microsoft Exam*.

Planning your cloud application strategy

In *Chapter 10, Planning and Implementing Enterprise Apps for Single Sign-On (SSO)*, we discussed how Microsoft Defender for Cloud Apps can help to discover the applications being accessed by users and how we can manage the applications that we want them to use. This included on-premises and cloud applications that we registered for **SSO**. This chapter will focus more on how to develop a cloud application strategy and the reasons why we would allow or deny certain applications. Let's start by reviewing what Microsoft Defender for Cloud Apps is and how it is used to discover apps being accessed by our users and registered devices.

Discovering apps with Microsoft Defender for Cloud Apps

As mentioned in *Chapter 10, Planning and Implementing Enterprise Apps for Single Sign-On (SSO)*, Microsoft Defender for Cloud Apps is a cloud service with Microsoft 365 that provides cloud access security broker services. A cloud access security broker is used as a policy enforcement point between the consumers and the providers so that applications adhere to the baseline security requirements of the company. **Microsoft Defender for Cloud Apps** provides these capabilities for Microsoft, third-party cloud, and registered on-premises applications.

Microsoft Defender for Cloud Apps is a helpful solution to aid in the discovery of applications that are being used within your company to help you control shadow IT. Shadow IT is the use of applications that are not approved by the company for use on the company network or on devices that also access company data. Microsoft Defender for Cloud Apps will identify all applications that are being accessed through managed users and devices. These applications are then reported on the discovery dashboard. Knowing the applications that are being used and accessed allows us to plan for the use of authorized applications and block unauthorized applications.

For companies that have users in office locations with a firewall or a device that is able to log network traffic, Microsoft Defender for Cloud Apps' discovery capabilities allow you to connect these logs and it will create a discovery report that lists the applications that are being accessed. The workflow and architecture of Microsoft Defender for Cloud Apps are shown in *Figure 11.1*:

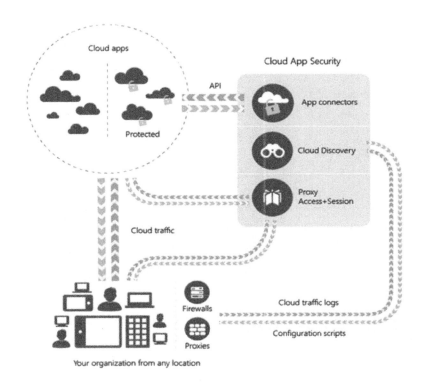

Figure 11.1 – Microsoft Defender for Cloud Apps architecture

The next sections will discuss the use of cloud app discovery for identifying application use and the next steps to take with those applications.

Cloud app discovery

As stated in the previous section, Microsoft Defender for Cloud Apps utilizes logs from network traffic to identify the applications that users are accessing. Traffic logs from on-premises firewalls will provide a snapshot report on the most common applications and the users that are accessing these apps. Traffic from devices managed with Microsoft Intune will be fed into the Microsoft Defender for Cloud Apps discovery overview dashboard, as shown in *Figure 11.2*:

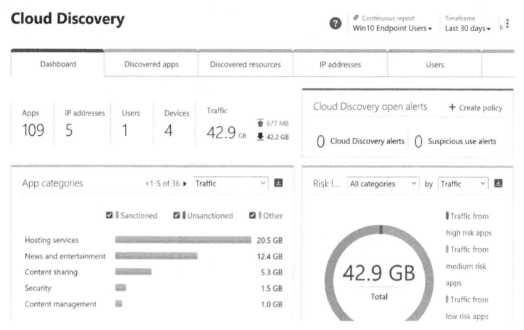

Figure 11.2 – Microsoft Defender for Cloud Apps Cloud Discovery dashboard

This information is the basis for planning and monitoring application use within your organization. You can build documentation on user usage and habits, and then evaluate the legitimate need for various applications to be used on company resources. In the *Using Microsoft Defender for Cloud Apps to manage application access* section, we will discuss more about evaluating the app score to determine whether to sanction or un-sanction apps. For additional information on the discovery of cloud apps, please visit this link: `https://docs.microsoft.com/en-us/cloud-app-security/set-up-cloud-discovery`.

Once we have determined the applications that we are going to allow as a company, we can create a plan and enforce policies utilizing Microsoft Defender for Cloud Apps. *Figure 11.3* shows the architecture of monitoring applications within Azure AD. This architecture simplifies the management and monitoring of applications through Microsoft Defender for Cloud Apps:

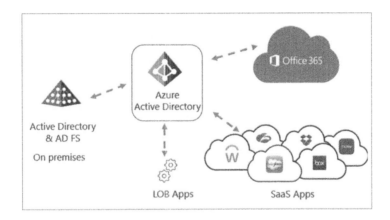

Figure 11.3 – AD and cloud apps managed by Microsoft Defender for Cloud Apps

When this architecture is utilized, the company can take advantage of the various security, compliance, and governance tools available within Azure AD, Microsoft 365, and Azure for the cloud and on-premises line of business applications, such as Microsoft Defender for Cloud Apps, Conditional Access policies, and Azure AD Identity Protection.

The next section will go through the process of creating security policies for cloud apps within Microsoft Defender for Cloud Apps.

Implementing cloud app security policies

In the previous sections, we went through the planning process of discovering and identifying applications that can be migrated to Azure AD for SSO. This section goes through the process of configuring an Azure AD application proxy to migrate on-premises applications to Azure AD for authentication and SSO.

Conditional Access policies in Microsoft Defender for Cloud Apps

Microsoft Defender for Cloud Apps allows us to create additional control for cloud apps through policies specific to the cloud apps that we are monitoring. Creating these policies can be done from within the **Control** menu within the **Microsoft Defender for Cloud Apps** portal, as shown in *Figure 11.4*. There are also a number of built-in templates, which can be found under **Templates** in the **Control** menu:

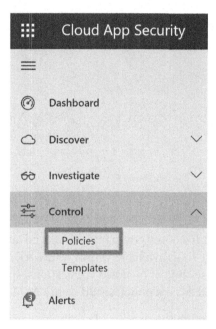

Figure 11.4 – Conditional Access policies in Cloud App Security

For more on the use case for creating a Conditional Access policy, please review *Chapter 9, Planning, Implementing, and Administering Conditional Access and Azure Identity Protection,* of this book. Let's go through the process of creating a new policy within the Microsoft Defender for Cloud Apps portal. We will then look at how to utilize one of the templates to create a new policy:

1. The first step is to navigate to **Control** on the Microsoft Defender for Cloud Apps menu and select **Policies**, as shown in *Figure 11.4*.

2. Note that within the policy dashboard there are several threat-detection policies that are already enabled within Microsoft Defender for Cloud Apps. These policies are used to alert and protect our environment from known malicious activity. We will discuss these alerts later in the *Policy alerts and response in Microsoft Defender for Cloud Apps* section. *Figure 11.5* shows this dashboard. To create a new policy, select the **+ Create policy** dropdown:

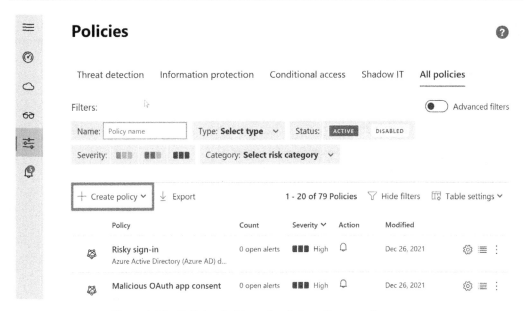

Figure 11.5 – Policies dashboard and the + Create policy option

3. Within the + **Create policy** dropdown are several selections to determine the type of policy that you would like to create. We will discuss the use of each of these in the *Types of Microsoft Defender for Cloud Apps app policies* section. For this exercise, select **File policy** from the list:

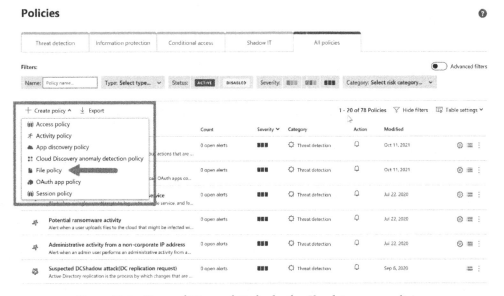

Figure 11.6 – Types of Microsoft Defender for Cloud Apps app policies

4. Unlike a Conditional Access policy within Azure AD, Microsoft Defender for
    Cloud Apps policies provide templates that you can utilize to create your policy and
    provide several preconfigured filters, as shown in *Figure 11.7*. For this exercise, we
    will select the **File shared with personal email addresses** template:

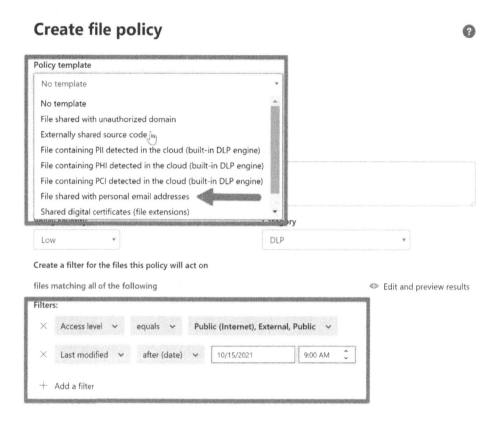

Figure 11.7 – Creating a file policy from a template

5. When asked to confirm that this will overwrite all existing values, select **Apply
    template**, as shown in *Figure 11.8*:

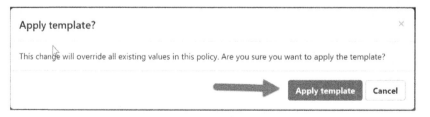

Figure 11.8 – Confirming that you want to apply template

6. The template completes the required fields, but you have the option to change these as needed for your company policy. For example, you may want this policy to be of medium or high severity instead of the default low, as shown in *Figure 11.9*. Change **Policy severity** to **Medium** for this exercise:

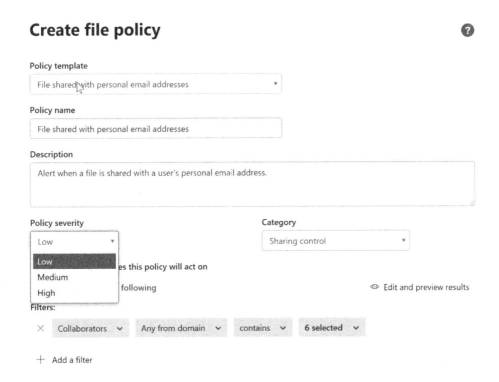

Figure 11.9 – Changing Policy severity

7. Scrolling down on the **Create file policy** tile, you will find additional configurable drop-down selections and checkboxes to customize your policy, as shown in *Figure 11.10*:

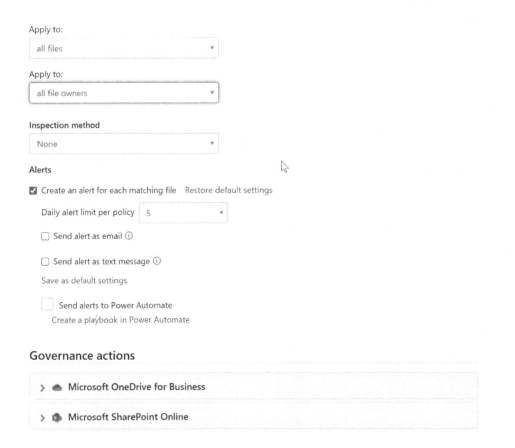

Figure 11.10 – Customizing the file policy

8. The next step is to configure the files to apply the policy within OneDrive for Business and SharePoint. This can be all files, selected folders, or all files excluding selected folders. *Figure 11.11* shows these selections; we will select all files for this exercise:

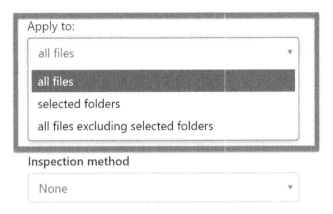

Figure 11.11 – Applying to all files

9. After selecting the scope of the files, we now set **Apply to:** to owners to determine the files that are in scope, based on the owners of the files. This includes all file owners within the scope, a user group, or an excluded group. If you have a sales group created in your Azure AD, select that group for this exercise. If not, select all file owners, as shown in *Figure 11.12*:

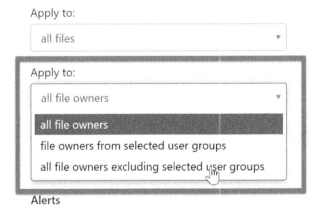

Figure 11.12 – Applying to all file owners

10. The next option is **Inspection method**. Since the file policy is a threat protection policy, we can configure **Inspection method** to utilize an existing data loss prevention policy and also data classification services that are configured within Microsoft 365. **Data Loss Prevention (DLP)** is out of scope for this exam, so we will choose **None** for this exercise, as shown in *Figure 11.13*:

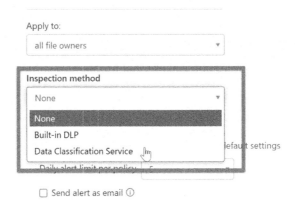

Figure 11.13 – Inspection method

11. The next section to configure is **Alerts**. These alerts are typical for policy templates. You have the ability here to set an alert limit, specify the alert to be sent as an email or text message, and utilize a pre-created Power Automate workflow. Select **Send alert as email** and enter your email address for this exercise:

Figure 11.14 – Configuring Alerts

12. The next two sections are **Governance actions**. The first is for **Microsoft OneDrive for Business**. These include several options, as shown in *Figure 11.15*. We will leave these unselected for this exercise:

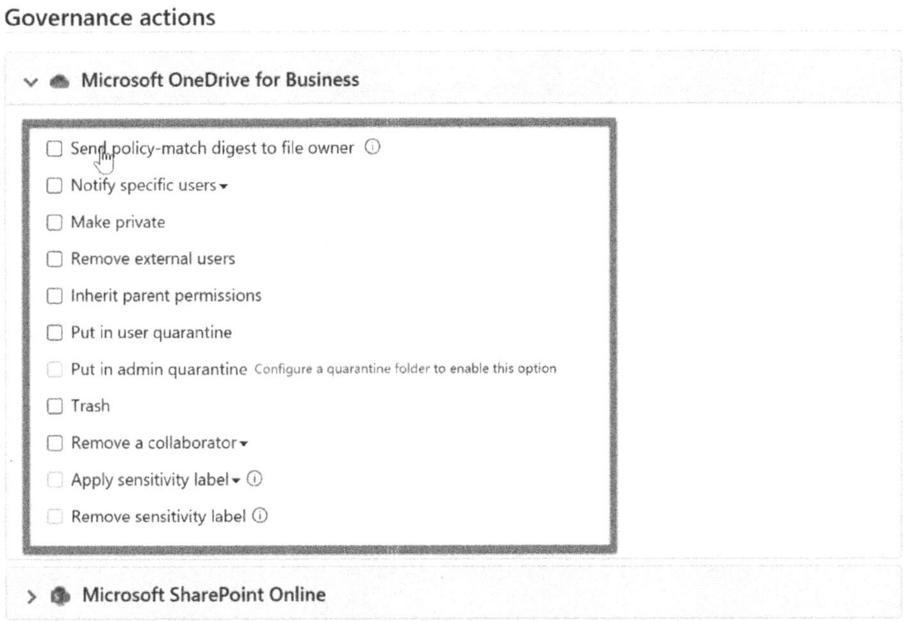

Governance actions

Figure 11.15 – OneDrive for Business governance actions

13. The **Governance actions** options for **Microsoft SharePoint Online** are the same as **Microsoft OneDrive for Business**. Again, leave these as the defaults:

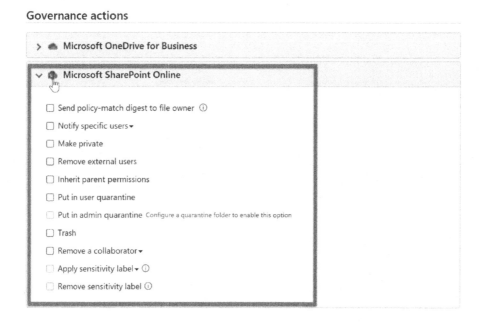

Figure 11.16 – SharePoint Online governance actions

14. The final action is to create the policy. There is a note in the portal that clarifies that this policy will only scan online files and folders and nothing external, per Microsoft privacy standards:

Figure 11.17 – Creating the policy

Those were the steps to create a file policy within Microsoft Defender for Cloud Apps. The next section will provide an additional definition of the other optional policy types within Microsoft Defender for Cloud Apps.

Types of Microsoft Defender for Cloud Apps app policies

When you navigate to the policy tile within Microsoft Defender for Cloud Apps, there are several different policies and templates that you can utilize. Each of these policies is categorized by the area of protection that the policy governs and the type of policy that will be implemented. The following are the types of policies that are available. More information can be found here: `https://docs.microsoft.com/en-us/cloud-app-security/control-cloud-apps-with-policies`.

The **access policy** is in the Conditional Access category. These policies work in the same way as Azure AD Conditional Access policies. They monitor the users and devices that have access to applications in Microsoft Defender for Cloud Apps in real-time.

The **activity policy** is in the threat detection category. These policies monitor particular activities from various users that take place across different apps and resources. These policies require the configuration of monitoring APIs to be connected to Microsoft Defender for Cloud Apps.

The **app discovery policy** is a shadow IT policy. Shadow IT is those applications that may not be on the list of allowed applications within the company policy. App discovery policies can monitor applications being accessed outside of these policies and report through alerts and notifications when unsanctioned apps are accessed by users and devices.

The **Cloud Discovery anomaly detection policy** is another shadow IT policy. These policies look for unusual activity on discovered apps. These may be on sanctioned and unsanctioned apps. An example would be a large amount of data being downloaded suddenly or impossible travel with a login event from two different countries within a short period of time.

The **file policy** is an information protection policy. These policies allow you to scan files within the policy scope and to verify that proper data protection is in place for potentially sensitive information within those files. Refer to *Figure 11.7* on how to filter these templates for customized alerts.

The **OAuth app policy** is a threat protection policy. These policies investigate permissions and whether they are enabled on the app. The policy can then approve or revoke that permission. These policies are built-in.

The **session policy** is a Conditional Access policy. These policies monitor the activity on apps in real time and control the activity on those apps as allowed through the policy.

Now that we know the different policy types and categories, we will look at the policy alert and response dashboard in Microsoft Defender for Cloud Apps.

Policy alerts and response in Microsoft Defender for Cloud Apps

Once you have created policies to govern your cloud and enterprise apps, you need to make sure that you are monitoring and responding to these alerts. The Microsoft Defender for Cloud Apps Policies dashboard provides access to this information for policy alert and response. *Figure 11.18* shows this dashboard and the built-in policies that are in place, along with alerts on those policies:

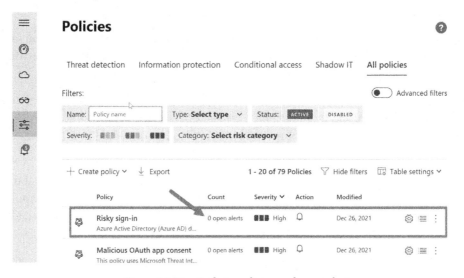

Figure 11.18 – Built-in policies and open alerts

If you look on the left-hand side menu, there is a bell icon that will show whether there are any active alert notifications that you need to review. *Figure 11.19* shows the active alerts and where to find these notifications:

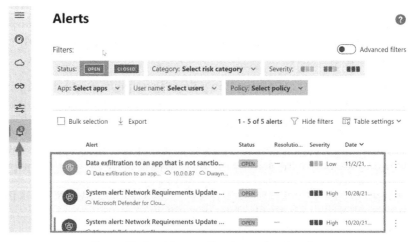

Figure 11.19 – Alert notification and active alerts

From this dashboard, you can review and respond to these alerts, and add governance actions based on policy alerts.

In the next section, we will discuss the planning and configuring of cloud application permissions.

Planning and configuring cloud application permissions

The permissions for enterprise applications were discussed in *Chapter 10, Planning and Implementing Enterprise Apps for Single Sign-On (SSO)*, but we will review them again here. There are two primary roles to consider for cloud applications, application administrator and cloud application administrator:

- The **application administrator** role, which allows users to create and manage enterprise applications, application registrations, and application proxy settings. These administrators can also grant application permissions and delegated permissions.

- The **cloud application administrator** role can still manage enterprise applications and application registrations, but since this designation is for cloud applications, they do not have the ability to manage application proxies.

When determining the role to assign to an administrator, you should determine whether that administrator is going to be required to manage on-premises enterprise applications that are registered with an application proxy. If so, they should be assigned the application administrator role. If they are only managing cloud-native applications, then the cloud application administrator will be the proper permission needed to adhere to the principle of least privilege.

The next section will go through the steps to discover apps in Microsoft Defender for Cloud Apps and ADFS app reports.

Discovering apps by using Microsoft Defender for Cloud Apps or an ADFS app report

In this section, we show how to discover third-party applications through Cloud App Security with Microsoft Defender for Cloud Apps reporting and ADFS app reports.

Discovering apps with Microsoft Defender for Cloud Apps app report

Microsoft Defender for Cloud Apps utilizes logs from network traffic to identify the applications that users are accessing. Traffic logs from on-premises firewalls will provide a snapshot report on the most common applications and the users that are accessing these apps. Additional information on app discovery can be found at this link: `https://docs.microsoft.com/en-us/cloud-app-security/set-up-cloud-discovery`. Traffic from managed devices will be fed into the Microsoft Defender for Cloud Apps Cloud Discovery overview dashboard, as shown in *Figure 11.20*:

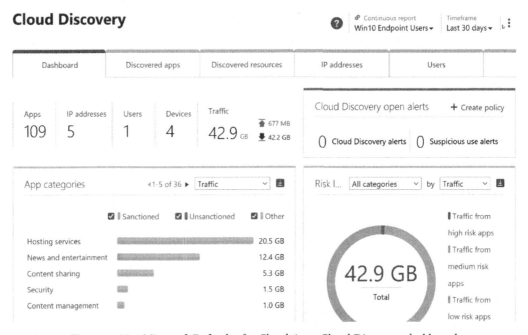

Figure 11.20 – Microsoft Defender for Cloud Apps Cloud Discovery dashboard

This information is the basis for planning and monitoring application use within your organization. In addition, you can review the **Discovered apps** tab within the **Cloud Discovery** menu to identify apps based on configured user groups, as shown in *Figure 11.21*:

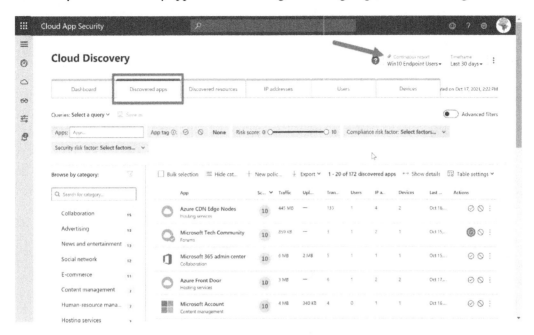

Figure 11.21 – Discovered apps dashboard

The next sections will discuss the use of Cloud App Discovery for identifying application use through on-premises resources.

Discovering apps with an ADFS app report

As stated in the previous section, Microsoft Defender for Cloud Apps utilizes logs from network traffic to identify the applications that users are accessing. Traffic logs from on-premises firewalls will provide a snapshot report on the most common applications and the users that are accessing these apps. The report can be initiated through the home dashboard of Microsoft Defender for Cloud Apps. You will need access to your firewall to generate this report. *Figure 11.22* shows where you initiate the creation of this report:

Figure 11.22 – Creating a Cloud Discovery report

This information is the basis for planning and monitoring your application use within your organization. The next section will discuss how to manage these applications and protect against shadow IT.

Using Microsoft Defender for Cloud Apps to manage application access

The final area that we need to consider for our application strategy is securing the applications and determining which applications will be allowed or denied access by our users and registered devices.

Discovered app scoring

As a company, you have a responsibility to protect against the sharing of personally identifiable information and company data by users. This includes the potential exposure of this data through unsanctioned cloud applications that are being accessed from devices. Cloud App Security provides an easy-to-follow scoring system for cloud applications, where the level of protection that each app provides has a score based on **GENERAL**, **SECURITY**, **COMPLIANCE**, and **LEGAL** criteria. *Figure 11.23* shows the scoring for **Microsoft Office Online**:

Figure 11.23 – Microsoft Office Online score

Sanctioning and unsanctioning apps

Once you have evaluated the applications that are discovered as being accessed by your company users and devices, you can review their scores and determine whether these will be sanctioned or unsanctioned for use. Sanctioned apps will continue to be allowed for use by users and devices. Unsanctioned apps will be blocked on registered devices or devices that registered users are logged into. This includes apps that are installed locally, accessed on a web browser, and accessed on a private browser session. *Figure 11.24* shows the sanctioned and unsanctioned selection area for an app:

Figure 11.24 – Sanctioned and unsanctioned apps

When unsanctioning an app in Microsoft Defender for Cloud Apps, the access to the application is blocked on devices that are registered to Azure AD and/or users that are logged into Azure AD on those devices. This includes blocking access to installing these applications on these devices or access through web browsers, both public and private sessions.

Next, we will provide a summary of what was discussed in this chapter.

Summary

In this chapter, we covered the use of third-party cloud applications within our organization, and how to manage, monitor, and control them with Cloud App Security. This included how to create app policies and discover apps to sanction or unsanction on a Microsoft tenant. In the next chapter, we will discuss entitlement management and managing the terms of use for users.

Section 5 – Planning and Implementing an Identity Governance Strategy

The objective of Section 5 is to help you set up your development environment and create a working platform for the later phases. It is often referred to as the board *bring-up* phase.

This section of the book comprises the following chapters:

- *Chapter 12, Planning and Implementing Entitlement Management*
- *Chapter 13, Planning and Implementing Privileged Access and Access Reviews*

12
Planning and Implementing Entitlement Management

The previous chapter covered the advanced tools and capabilities of **Microsoft Defender for Cloud Apps**, formerly **Microsoft Cloud App Security**, to monitor and manage the use of cloud applications in your company. In this chapter, we will discuss the planning and implementation process for entitlement management as an important part of Identity Governance. This includes life cycle management for external users and managing the terms of use.

In this chapter, we're going to cover the following main topics:

- Defining catalogs and access packages
- Planning, implementing, and managing entitlements
- Implementing and managing terms of use
- Managing the life cycle of external users in Azure AD Identity Governance settings

Technical requirements

In this chapter, we will continue to explore configuring a tenant to use **Microsoft 365** and **Azure**. There will be exercises that will require access to Azure **Active Directory (AD)**. If you have not yet created the trial licenses for Microsoft 365, please follow the directions provided within *Chapter 1, Preparing for Your Microsoft Exam*.

Defining catalogs and access packages

Up to this point, you have worked on planning and implementing various aspects of security identity and access throughout the company tenant. This has included providing access to the tenant for members and external users. When adding a member or external user, you need to govern that they have the authorization to access immediately upon authenticating them to the company tenant. The catalogs that are created define the resources that a user or group is authorized to use. This allows clear governance of the resources that a user or group has access to use once they authenticate to the tenant. Entitlement management provides this governance through the creation of catalogs and access packages that you can build for these groups of users. Entitlement management is a premium feature and requires Azure AD Premium P2 licenses to assign to users and groups. Entitlement management is found under Identity Governance within Azure AD. *Figure 12.1* shows the **Getting started** tile of this service and where **Entitlement management** is found in the menu:

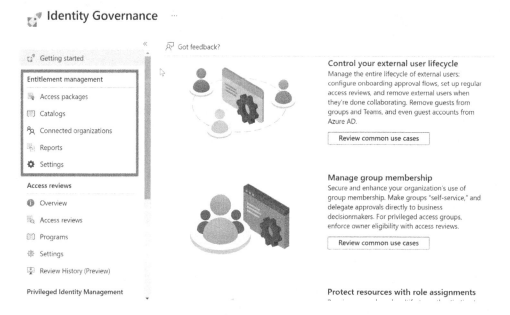

Figure 12.1 – Identity Governance services

For additional information, please refer to this link: `https://docs.microsoft.com/en-us/azure/active-directory/governance/entitlement-management-overview`. Let's discuss how catalogs and access packages work to provide this governance.

Catalogs

The first step in entitlement management is to create catalogs. If you do not create a catalog for your access packages, users will have access to the general catalog. If you want to clearly define the catalog, then one should be created because you cannot move an access package to another catalog once it is created. Additional information can be found at this link: `https://docs.microsoft.com/en-us/azure/active-directory/governance/entitlement-management-access-package-create#basics`. These catalogs can be created within the Identity Governance services within Azure AD under the **Entitlement management** menu, as shown in *Figure 12.2*:

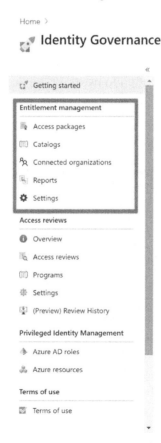

Figure 12.2 – Entitlement management menu

Catalogs are a collection of users and groups, SaaS applications (Salesforce, Workday, ServiceNow, and others), enterprise applications, and SharePoint sites. To create these catalogs, you must be assigned the Identity Governance Administrator role or Global Administrator role. Previously, the User Administrator role was authorized to create these catalogs, but that is currently being phased out. In the *Planning, implementing, and managing entitlements* section, we will go through the steps to create catalogs. Let's define each of the areas that make up this catalog. For additional information and examples, refer to this link: `https://docs.microsoft.com/en-us/azure/active-directory/governance/entitlement-management-access-package-create#overview`.

Users and groups are assigned to catalogs in order to access the applications and sites that are within the catalog. These users and groups can include internal and external users. The ability to create catalogs with internal and external users allows us to use entitlements for project-based access or other applications, such as branch offices and departmental assignments.

Applications are the enterprise and cloud applications that are registered through the steps that were completed in *Chapter 10*, *Planning and Implementing Enterprise Apps for Single Sign-On (SSO)*. The applications that are added to the catalog provide the users and groups assigned with the authorization to use these applications.

SharePoint sites can be added to a catalog. These sites can be a project-based internally created SharePoint site, a file share site on SharePoint, or any SharePoint URL that you determine should be assigned to the catalog. Multiple sites can be added to a single catalog.

Once these three areas are configured, we have our catalog prepared and ready to be assigned. You will go through the configuration process in the *Implementing entitlements* section of this chapter.

The next section will discuss the next step of entitlement management, which is the access package.

Access packages

As discussed in the previous section, catalogs define the groups and teams, applications, and SharePoint sites within Identity Governance. Creating a catalog does not establish access to these catalogs. You must go through the creation of access packages to approve and allow access to these catalogs. As stated in the previous section, once an access package is created and assigned to a catalog, this cannot be changed.

When creating an access package, at a minimum, you define the catalog that the access package governs, how requests are handled, and the life cycle of the access package, as shown in *Figure 12.3*:

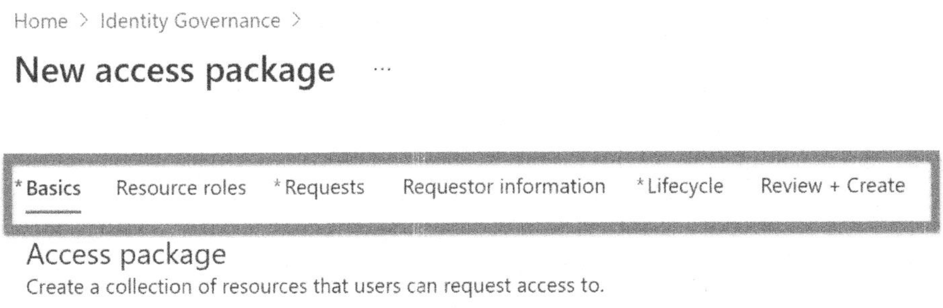

Home > Identity Governance >

New access package   ⋯

| *Basics | Resource roles | *Requests | Requestor information | *Lifecycle | Review + Create |

Access package
Create a collection of resources that users can request access to.

Figure 12.3 – Access Package creation tabs

The configuration and assignment of an access package will be shown in the *Implementing entitlements* section.

The next section will go through the process of planning, implementing, and managing entitlements.

Planning, implementing, and managing entitlements

In the previous sections, we discussed and defined how catalogs and access packages are used for Identity Governance within entitlement management. This section will discuss how to plan for these entitlements, how they are implemented, and how to manage access and review these entitlements.

Planning entitlements

Before creating catalogs and access packages, you should plan and determine how they are going to be used within your company. Entitlement management can be a helpful tool for companies that have projects that utilize internal and external users, departments that utilize different and specialized resources that other departments don't require access to, and branch and global offices that have their own users, groups, and partners.

As someone in charge of Identity Governance, you should work with stakeholders to plan these catalogs and access packages, as well as determine how often they will be reviewed for continued use and access. Proper planning with stakeholders based on the business model will allow the stakeholders to quickly provide users with access to the resources that are required for a given project or department once they are onboarded.

Something that is going to be important in the meeting with stakeholders will be to determine the internal and external users that will make up the group that will be assigned to the catalog. Stakeholders should be asked what the job roles for the users that need access are and what the list of applications that they need to be authorized to use is. This may need to be created prior to the implementation of the entitlement. Stakeholders should also provide the list of applications and SharePoint sites that the entitlement will be required to access.

The next section will go through the process of creating a catalog and access package.

Implementing entitlements

After planning with the necessary groups about what is needed for catalogs and access packages within your company, they are ready to be implemented. To better understand how catalogs and access packages are created, let's go through the steps to create a catalog that identifies the users and groups with access and the applications and SharePoint sites that they have access to. Then, you will step through how to assign that catalog through the creation of an access package:

1.   Select **Catalogs** from the **Entitlement management** menu.

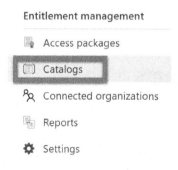

Figure 12.4 – Selecting Catalogs

2. From the **Catalogs** tile, select **+ New catalog**, as shown in *Figure 12.5*:

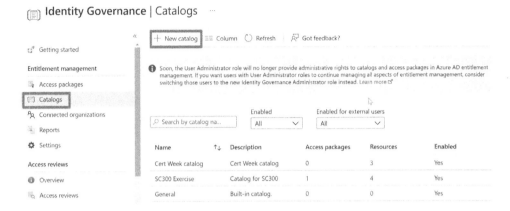

Figure 12.5 – Adding a new catalog

3. Enter a name and description for your catalog. These two fields are required information. Then, you will select whether to enable the catalog and whether to enable this catalog for external users who are assigned to the groups within the catalog. After filling out this information, select **Create**.

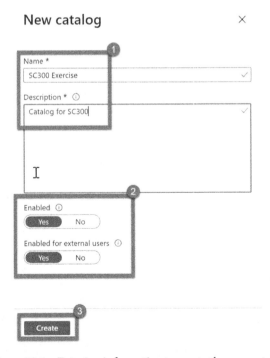

Figure 12.6 – Entering information to create the new catalog

4. The catalog will now be shown within the catalog list along with the **General** catalog, a built-in catalog that is there by default. Select the catalog to begin the configuration.

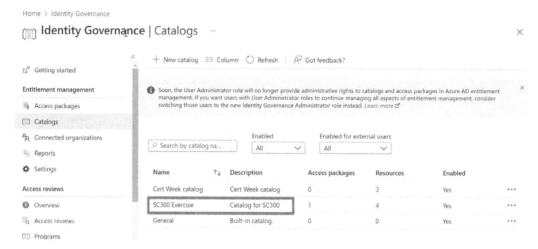

Figure 12.7 – Selecting the catalog from the list of catalogs

5. Selecting the catalog will take you to a new tile, as shown in *Figure 12.8*. This tile provides an overview of the catalog configuration, which includes the resources assigned, the access packages, and the roles and administrators that are able to manage this catalog.

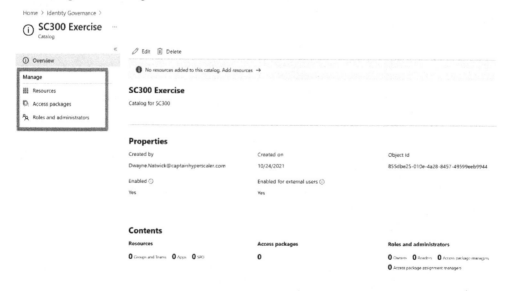

Figure 12.8 – Catalog overview

6. Under the **Manage** menu, select **Resources**.

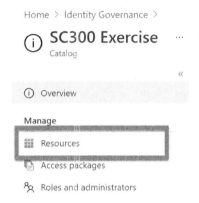

Figure 12.9 – Selecting Resources under the Manage catalog menu

7. Within **Resources**, select + **Add resources**.

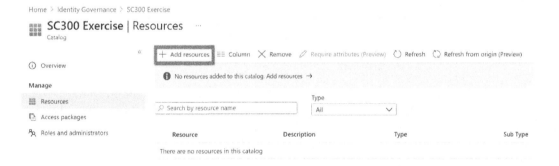

Figure 12.10 – Adding resources to the catalog

8. In the **Add resources** tile, you can now add groups and teams, applications, and SharePoint sites to your catalog. Here is where you will fully define the catalog that will govern the access and authorization for the assigned groups. The following screenshot shows where you will add these resources to the catalog:

Figure 12.11 – Adding catalog resources

9. Select **+ Groups and Teams**. Select the security groups and teams that will be assigned and authorized to this catalog.

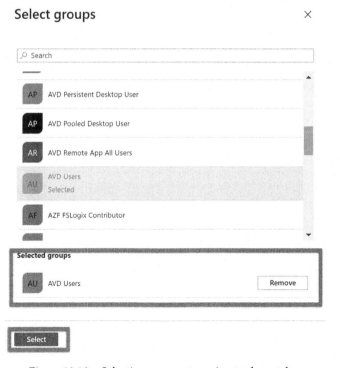

Figure 12.12 – Selecting a group to assign to the catalog

10. Select + **Applications**. Select the enterprise and cloud applications that will be authorized for use within this catalog. The allowed applications will be those enterprise and cloud applications that you registered when completing the steps that were discussed in *Chapter 10, Planning and Implementing Enterprise Apps for Single Sign-On (SSO)*.

Figure 12.13 – Selected applications for the catalog

11. Select **+ SharePoint sites**. Some companies have different SharePoint sites specific to departments or projects. If your company has these sites created in SharePoint Online, they can be assigned here.

Figure 12.14 – Selecting SharePoint sites

12. After each of these areas has been configured, select **Add** to complete the configuration of the catalog, as shown in *Figure 12.15*:

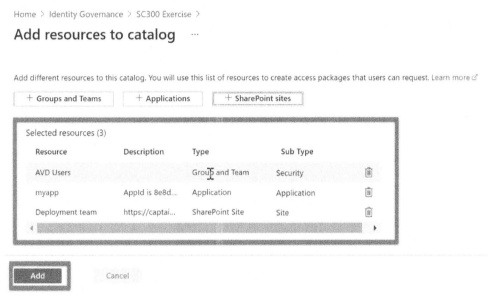

Figure 12.15 – Adding selected resources

This completes the process of creating a catalog. Next, you will implement the access package that will have this catalog as the assignment:

1. To create an access package, select **Access packages** from the **Entitlement management** menu within Identity Governance, as shown in *Figure 12.2*. Since you are still within the catalog tile, you can select **Access packages** here as well, as shown in *Figure 12.16*:

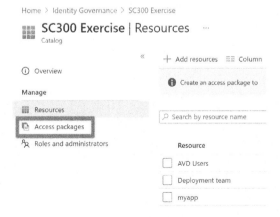

Figure 12.16 – Selecting Access packages

2. Select **+ New access package**:

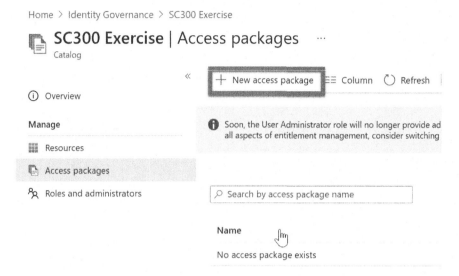

Figure 12.17 – Creating a new access package

3. You will step through the wizard to create your access package, starting with the name and description. Enter a name and description and select **Next: Resource roles**:

Figure 12.18 – Name and description for an access package

4. The **Resource roles** tile allows you to assign different **Member** and **Owner** roles for the access package. This can be the groups and teams that were assigned to the catalog or other groups and teams that are not assigned to the catalog. When using dynamic groups, you will not see any other roles available other than the owner role. *Figure 12.19* shows the previous catalog group as well as a group from outside the catalog being added and the assignment of the **Owner** or **Member** role from the dropdown. This section is not required. Select **Next: Requests**:

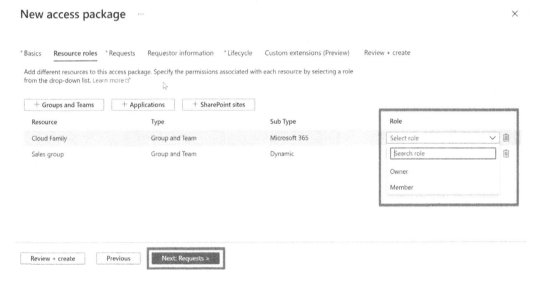

Figure 12.19 – Resource role assignments

5.   The **Requests** tile is where you will define how members of the catalog will gain access to the catalog. In this exercise, you will select **For users in your directory** and **All members (excluding guests)**. You can require approval and configure levels of approval to this access package. For this exercise, you will leave this as **No** and set **Enable** to **Yes**, as shown in *Figure 12.20*. Select **Next: Requestor Information**:

Home > Identity Governance > SC300 Exercise >

New access package   ···

* Basics   Resource roles   *Requests   Requestor information   *Lifecycle   Review + Create

Create a policy to specify who can request an access package, who can approve requests, and when access expires. Additional request policies can be created. Learn more ☐

Users who can request access

◉ **For users in your directory**	○ **For users not in your directory**	○ **None (administrator direct assignments only)**
Allow users and groups in your directory to request this access package	Allow users in connected organizations (other directories and domains) to request this access package	Allow administrators to directly assign specific users to this access package. Users cannot request this access package

○ Specific users and groups
◉ All members (excluding guests)
○ All users (including guests)

Approval

Require approval * ⓘ   Yes   No

Enable

Enable new requests * ⓘ   Yes   No

Review + Create   Previous   Next: Requestor Information >

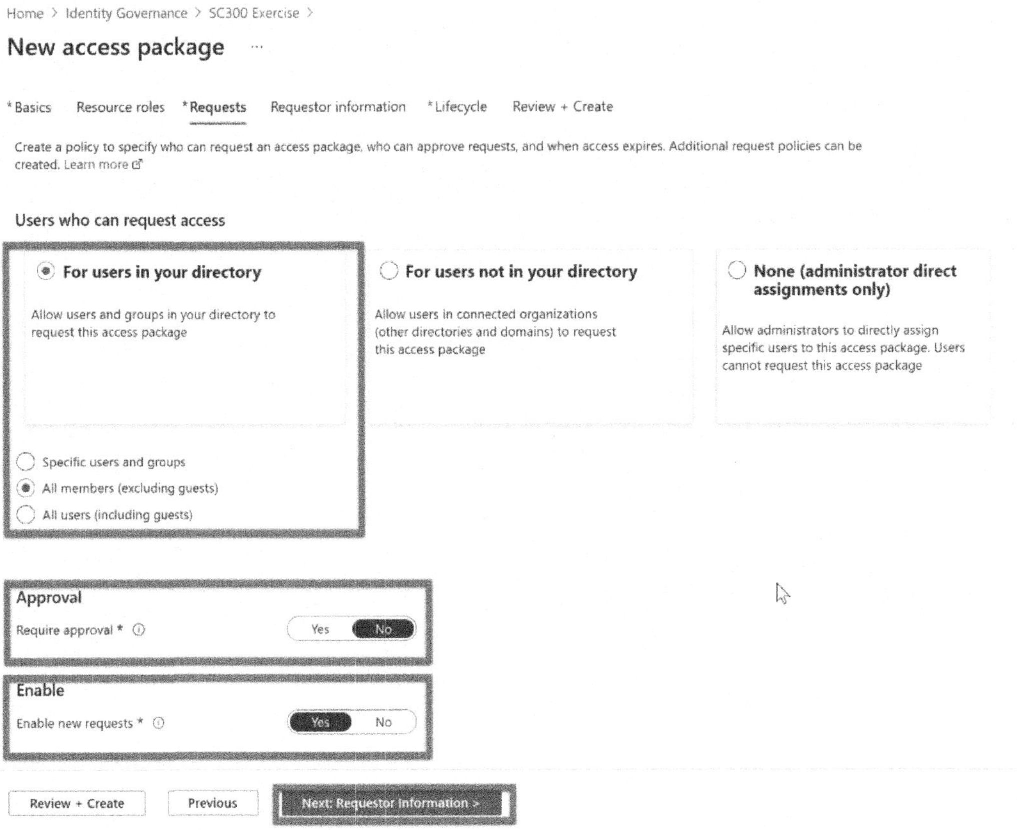

Figure 12.20 – Configuring requests

6. The **Requestor information** tile is another optional tile to configure. Here, you can create attributes for a question-and-answer response that is required from users to be authorized to the access package. More information can be found at this link: `https://docs.microsoft.com/en-us/azure/active-directory/ governance/entitlement-management-access-package- create#enable-requests`. Select **Next: Lifecycle**:

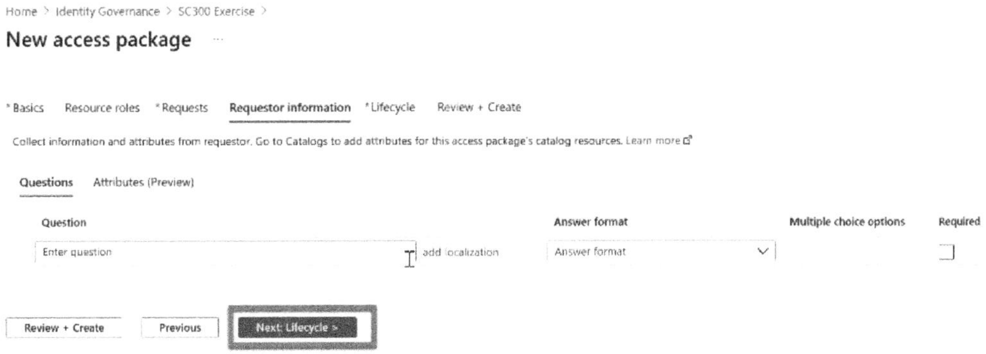

Home > Identity Governance > SC300 Exercise >

New access package   ...

*Basics   Resource roles   *Requests   **Requestor information**   *Lifecycle   Review + Create

Collect information and attributes from requestor. Go to Catalogs to add attributes for this access package's catalog resources. Learn more ☐

Questions   Attributes (Preview)

Question		Answer format		Multiple choice options	Required
Enter question	T add localization	Answer format	∨		☐

[Review + Create]   [Previous]   [**Next: Lifecycle >**]

Figure 12.21 – Optional requestor information

7. The **Lifecycle** section is where we can set an expiration date for the access package.
    When creating an access package for a specific project, you can define an expiration
    that aligns with the completion of the project. You can also add access reviews to the
    access package to review the membership to the access package, as shown in *Figure
    12.22*. Select **Next: Review + Create**:

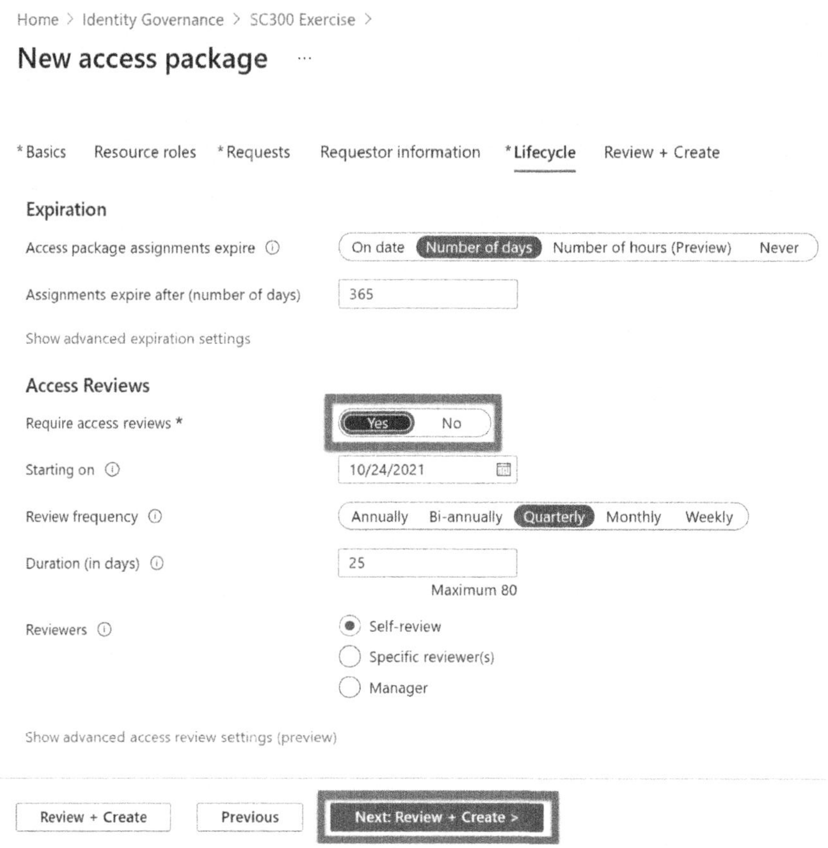

Home > Identity Governance > SC300 Exercise >

New access package   ...

*Basics   Resource roles   *Requests   Requestor information   *Lifecycle   Review + Create

Expiration

Access package assignments expire ⓘ   (On date   **Number of days**   Number of hours (Preview)   Never)

Assignments expire after (number of days)   365

Show advanced expiration settings

Access Reviews

Require access reviews *   (**Yes**   No)

Starting on ⓘ   10/24/2021

Review frequency ⓘ   (Annually   Bi-annually   **Quarterly**   Monthly   Weekly)

Duration (in days) ⓘ   25
                                            Maximum 80

Reviewers ⓘ   ⦿ Self-review
                                      ◯ Specific reviewer(s)
                                      ◯ Manager

Show advanced access review settings (preview)

[Review + Create]   [Previous]   [**Next: Review + Create >**]

Figure 12.22 – Configuring the access package life cycle

8. **Review + Create** provides a summary of the configuration that you just completed. Select **Create** to create the access package:

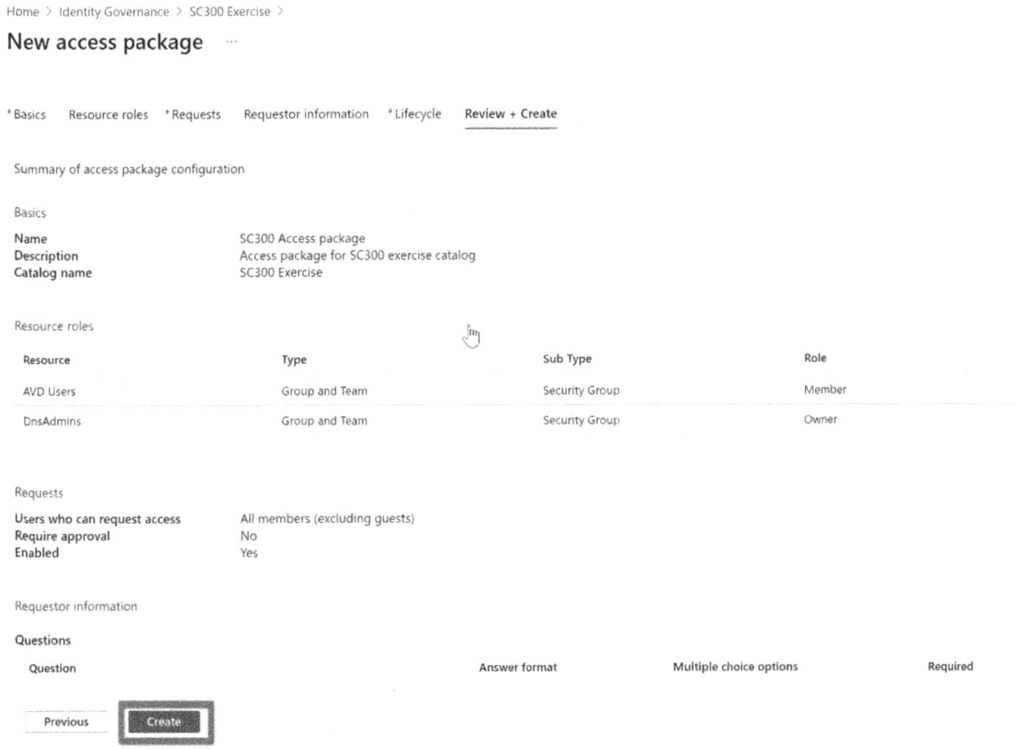

Home > Identity Governance > SC300 Exercise >

New access package   ...

*Basics   Resource roles   *Requests   Requestor information   *Lifecycle   **Review + Create**

Summary of access package configuration

Basics

Name	SC300 Access package
Description	Access package for SC300 exercise catalog
Catalog name	SC300 Exercise

Resource roles

Resource	Type	Sub Type	Role
AVD Users	Group and Team	Security Group	Member
DnsAdmins	Group and Team	Security Group	Owner

Requests

Users who can request access	All members (excluding guests)
Require approval	No
Enabled	Yes

Requestor information

Questions

Question	Answer format	Multiple choice options	Required

Previous   Create

Figure 12.23 – Review + Create summary

9.   After creating the access package, the access package overview tile opens. From within this tile, you can manage and modify the configuration that you just created. Also within this overview is **My Access portal link**. This URL is provided to the group members assigned to this access package for easy access to applications and SharePoint sites in the catalog.

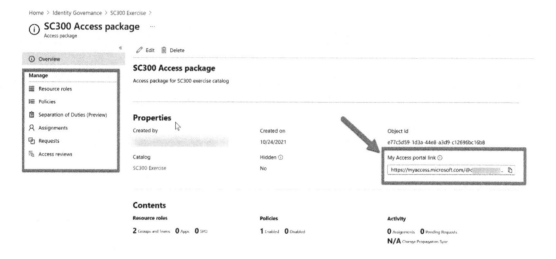

Figure 12.24 – New access package management tile

Now that you have configured your catalog and access package, you will want to understand how to manage these entitlements; this includes how to request access and validate access. The next section will go through how you can manage access packages, catalogs, and entitlements.

Managing entitlements

In the previous section, you configured your catalog and access package. Once the access package has been created and enabled, you should understand how to manage these entitlements.

After creating an access package, you are taken to the management tile for that specific access package, as shown in *Figure 12.24*. For users who are in the group assigned to the access package, there is a URL created for direct access to the applications and SharePoint sites in the catalog. This URL is pointed out in *Figure 12.24*. For administrators that need to manage the access package, you will use the **Manage** menu shown in *Figure 12.25*:

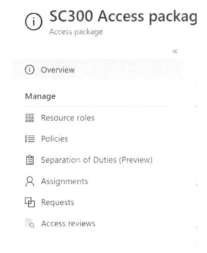

Figure 12.25 – Access package manage menu

In this menu, you can adjust the configuration of the resource roles, requests, and access reviews. There are also additional management areas to configure policies, separation of duties, and assignments for the access package. If you select **Policies**, you will see that an initial policy is assigned to the access package. This policy is created based on the access package configuration and can be selected to view, as shown in *Figure 12.26*:

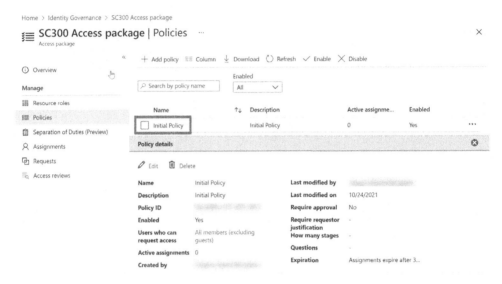

Figure 12.26 – Viewing the initial access package policy

If you require additional policies, assignments, and separation of duties, select those sections and add them as needed for additional access policy governance. For more information on managing Identity Governance and entitlement management, see the Microsoft Docs link here: https://docs.microsoft.com/en-us/azure/active-directory/governance/identity-governance-overview.

In the next section, we will discuss implementing and managing terms of use within Identity Governance.

Implementing and managing terms of use

If your company requires particular terms of use for the applications or sites that are being accessed by member and guest users, Azure AD Identity Governance allows companies to assign these terms of use and tie them to a Conditional Access policy to allow access to the application. *Figure 12.27* shows where to find the terms of use within the **Identity Governance** menu. You can select **+ New terms** to add new terms:

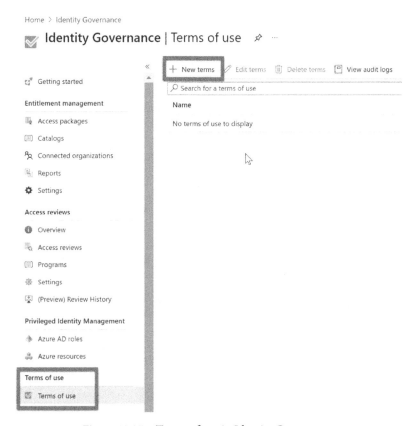

Figure 12.27 – Terms of use in Identity Governance

When you select **+ New terms**, the configuration wizard tile will open for adding the terms of use. This document is a PDF that can be in multiple languages. This is shown in *Figure 12.28*. At the bottom of this tile is where you can create a Conditional Access policy to enforce acceptance of the terms of use before accessing an application:

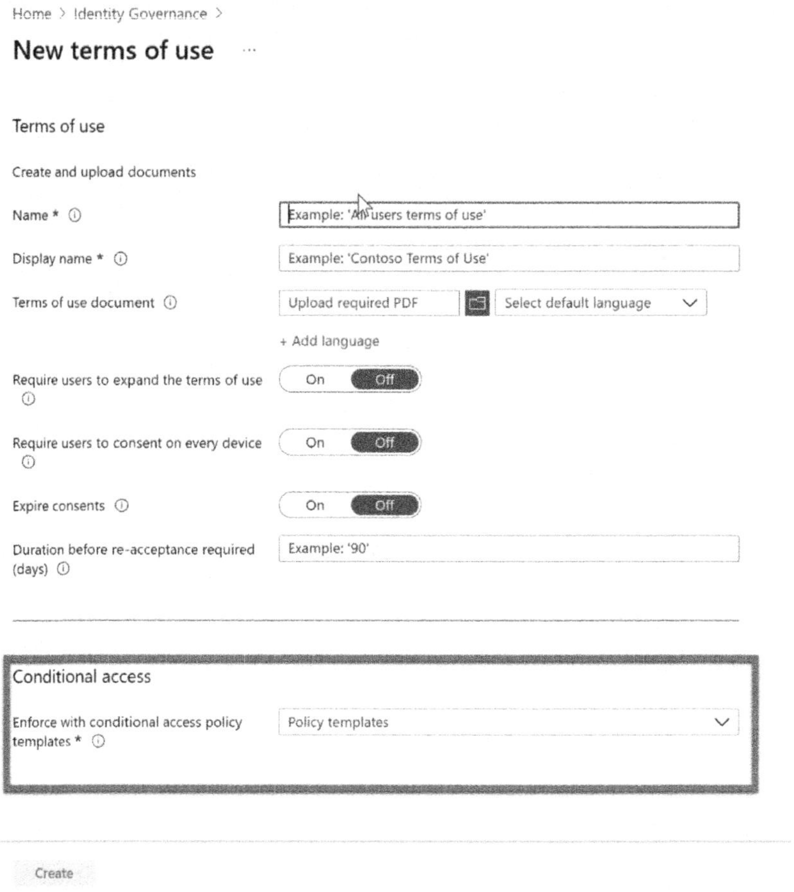

Figure 12.28 – Configuring the terms of use with Conditional Access

More information on how to implement and manage the terms of use can be found at this link: `https://docs.microsoft.com/en-us/azure/active-directory/conditional-access/terms-of-use`.

The next section will discuss managing the life cycle of external users in the Identity Governance settings.

Managing the life cycle of external users in Azure AD Identity Governance settings

When discussing Azure AD Identity Governance, the key concepts in managing governance are how we are managing privileged roles, access packages, and the life cycle of access. You configured access packages earlier in this chapter. This chapter will discuss managing privileged roles and access. In terms of the access life cycle, you should consider the access life cycle of your member users and your guest users. These should be handled differently as the life cycle of our member users is based on the employment within the company and the access that is required for the department or team that they belong to.

Guest users are provided access based on a partnership and external collaboration trust relationship. This access can be due to a managed services contract, a particular project, or perhaps a merger/acquisition. In any case, these relationships have a life cycle that will eventually come to an end. Therefore, you should have governance in place to manage this life cycle. Within Identity Governance, this is managed through the creation of access reviews.

Access reviews

Access reviews can manage the access life cycle. Azure AD Identity Governance provides an **Overview** dashboard showing the status of access reviews, as shown in *Figure 12.29*:

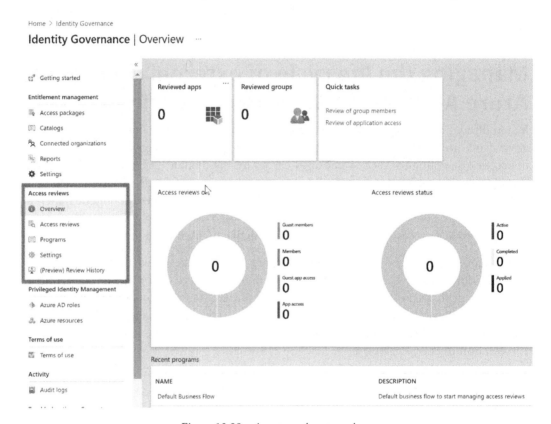

Figure 12.29 – Access review overview

Under the **Access reviews** menu, you can select **Access reviews** to configure an access review for guest users. You can select **+ New access review** to create your guest user access review. The tile will open to configure the access review for guest users. *Figure 12.30* shows this tile and how to configure an access review for guest users:

Home > Identity Governance >

New access review   ···

Review type   Reviews   Settings   Review + Create

Schedule an access review to ensure the right people have the right access to access packages, groups, apps, and privileged roles.
Learn more

Select what to review *   Teams + Groups   ∨

Select review scope *   ◉ All Microsoft 365 groups with guest users
                                   ◯ Select Teams + groups

Group   + Select group(s) to exclude

Select user scope *   ◉ Guest users only
                                  ◯ All users ①

Next: Reviews

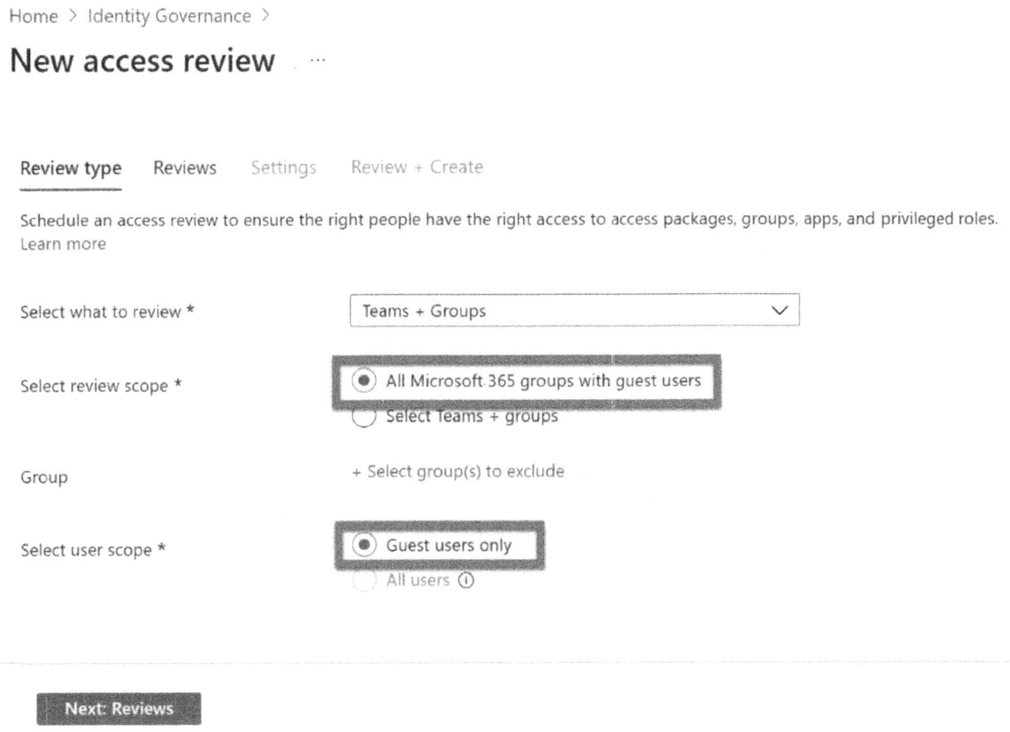

Figure 12.30 – Guest user access review

The next tile is where you configure who reviews and approves access, how often access will be reviewed, and when access will expire. Guest users should not review their access. An internal member user should be assigned to review guest access. This is shown in *Figure 12.31*:

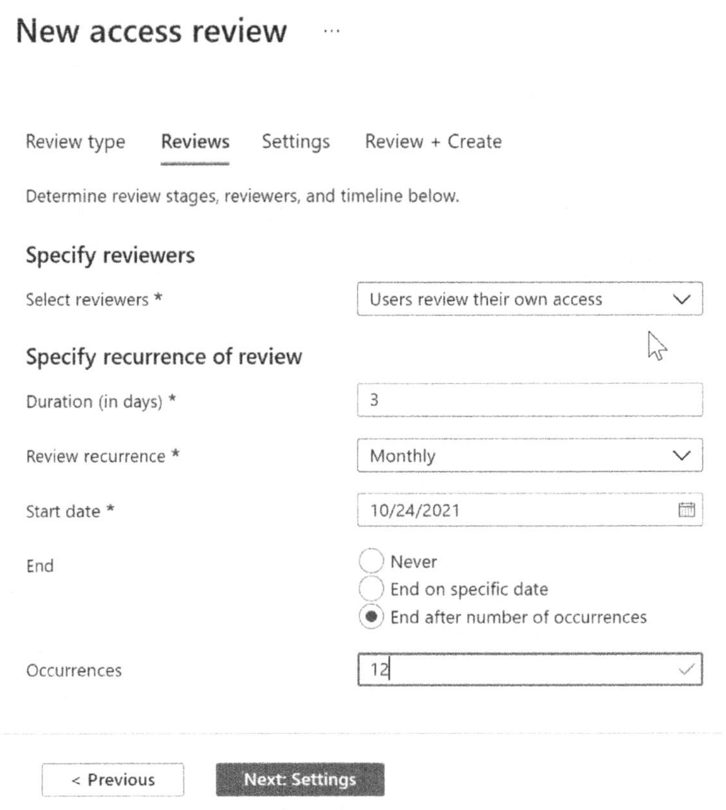

Figure 12.31 – Review settings

Finally, you will configure the settings for how the review will take place and what happens when the guest user responds or does not respond. This is shown in *Figure 12.32*:

New access review ⋯

Review type   Reviews   **Settings**   Review + Create

Set additional information regarding your access review such as decision helpers, completion and advanced settings.

Upon completion settings

Auto apply results to resource ⓘ   ☑

If reviewers don't respond ⓘ   [No change   ⌄]

(Preview) At end of review, send notification to   + Select User(s) or Group(s)

Enable reviewer decision helpers

No sign-in within 30 days ⓘ   ☑

Advanced settings

Justification required ⓘ   ☑

Email notifications ⓘ   ☑

Reminders ⓘ   ☑

Additional content for reviewer email ⓘ   [   ]

[< Previous]   [Next: Review + Create]

Figure 12.32 – Settings for the access review

Once you review and create the access review, this will show as an access review in the list. It will also show within the access review overview dashboard as a guest member review.

Next, we will provide a summary of what was discussed in this chapter.

Summary

In this chapter, we covered the areas of entitlement management and guest access life cycle management within Azure AD Identity Governance. This included creating new catalogs and access packages for providing entitlement management of users, applications, and SharePoint site access. You went through an exercise on implementing a new catalog and an access package. We then discussed how to manage entitlements and the access life cycle for access packages and guest user access. In the next chapter, we will discuss **privileged identity management (PIM)** within Azure AD Identity Governance.

13
Planning and Implementing Privileged Access and Access Reviews

The previous chapter covered the planning and implementation process for entitlement management. This includes life cycle management for external users and managing the terms of use. In this chapter, we will discuss planning and implementing our privileged access for administrator accounts and managing them with access reviews. This will include the benefits of using Privileged Identity Management and how to audit these privileged assignments.

In this chapter, we're going to cover the following main topics:

- Defining a privileged access strategy for administrative users
- Configuring Privileged Identity Management for Azure AD roles and Azure resources
- Creating and managing break-glass accounts
- Planning for and automating access reviews
- Analyzing PIM audit history and reports

Technical requirements

In this chapter, we will continue to explore configuring a tenant for use in **Microsoft 365** and **Azure**. There will be exercises that will require access to Azure AD. If you have not yet created the trial licenses for Microsoft 365, please follow the directions provided within *Chapter 1, Preparing for Your Microsoft Exam*.

Defining a privileged access strategy for administrative users

In the previous chapter, we discussed Identity Governance as it pertains to user access packages for applications and SharePoint sites. A major area of identity governance that we need to manage is privileged access based on administrative user accounts. Within this book, we have identified administrator roles necessary for managing services within Azure AD. As we continue to add and activate these administrative roles within our tenant, we begin to increase the attack surface in that someone who gains unauthorized access to a compromised account may have elevated privileges.

As identity and access administrators, it is our duty to protect and defend this layer through utilizing the concepts of zero trust and the principle of least privilege to assign and manage these administrator accounts. You should have a clear strategy with defined job tasks for every administrator account to plan for the proper assignment of these roles. This strategy should include meetings with stakeholders and discussing the roles that each department member requires to complete their job tasks. This will determine the level of just enough access that a user requires. It is easy to make everyone a global administrator, but that is not the best practice in securing access to information and resources. In addition, you should be monitoring the activity of these accounts and verifying the continued requirement for users to have these privileged access roles.

To enforce the concepts of zero trust, you have the capability to assign Conditional Access policies to these accounts. This was discussed in *Chapter 9, Planning, Implementing, and Administering Conditional Access and Azure Identity Protection*. To address and protect privileged assignments, Azure AD provides **Privileged Identity Management (PIM)** within the set of Identity Governance solutions.

PIM provides just-in-time privileged access to users, which means users are administrators for a short period of time, rather than the practice in the past of permanently setting a user as an administrator. Since users are only set active administrator roles for a short window of time, this reduces the attack surface and potential for these user accounts to expose privileged access to an attack. PIM provides an approval and justification process for activating privileged role assignments, which includes notifications when a role is activated and an audit trail of these activations.

PIM requires an Azure AD Premium P2 license. To assign PIM to member accounts, each user must have this license. However, for guest users who require privileged access with PIM, five guests can be assigned PIM roles for every Azure AD Premium P2 license that you have in your tenant. For additional information on licensing for PIM, you can visit this link: `https://docs.microsoft.com/en-us/azure/active-directory/ privileged-identity-management/subscription-requirements`.

PIM can be accessed directly by searching for `Privileged Identity Management` in the search bar in the Azure portal or it can be found in the **Azure AD Identity Governance** tile, as shown in *Figure 13.1*:

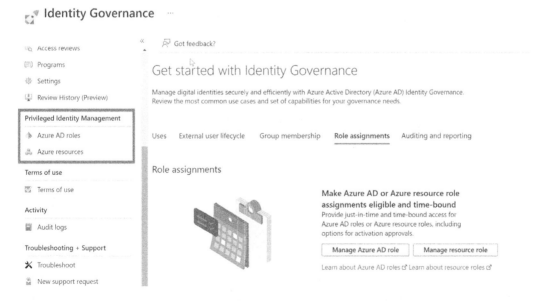

Figure 13.1 – PIM within Identity Governance services

Let's now discuss how to configure PIM and assign roles to users.

Configuring PIM for Azure AD roles and Azure resources

In the previous section, we discussed planning role assignments and defined PIM. This section will discuss how to configure PIM for Azure AD roles and resources:

1. Navigate in the search bar for `Privileged Identity Management`. Under the **Quick start** menu, select **Manage**, as shown in *Figure 13.2*:

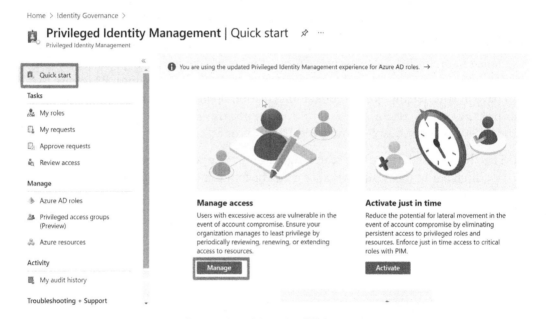

Figure 13.2 – Managing PIM access

2. Select **Roles** under **Manage** in the menu bar and then select **+ Add assignments** to
    create a new PIM role assignment:

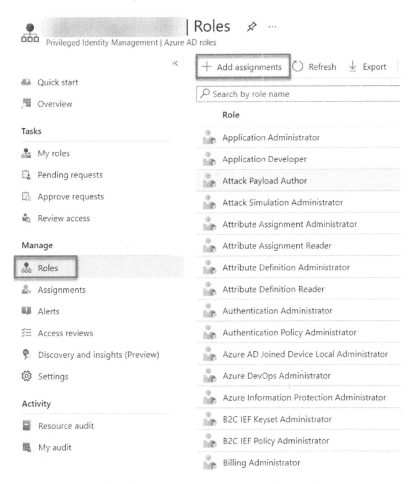

Figure 13.3 – Adding a new PIM assignment

3. In the **Add assignments** tile, choose the **Select role** dropdown and find **Privileged Role Administrator**:

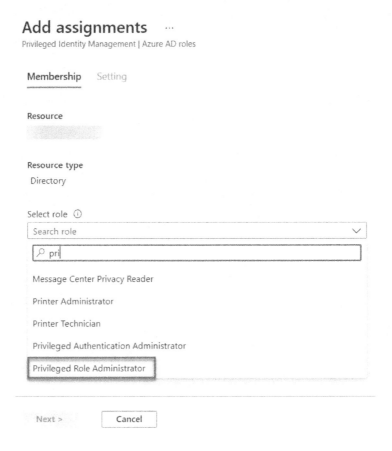

Figure 13.4 – Selecting the Privileged Role Administrator role

4. Select **No member selected** under **Select member(s)** and choose a user or group to assign this role:

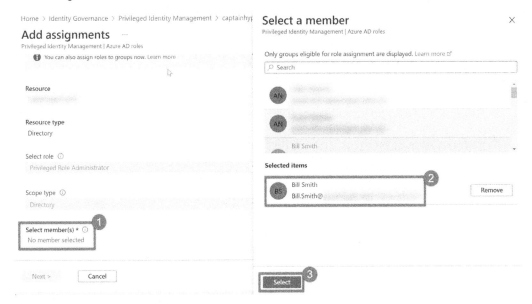

Figure 13.5 – Selecting members for role assignment

5. Select **Next** to navigate to the next step in the configuration process:

Figure 13.6 – Selecting Next to continue the assignment configuration

6. On the next tile, verify that **Eligible** is the **Assignment type** option and deselect the **Permanently eligible** checkbox. Leave the assignment start and end dates as their default values, as shown in *Figure 13.7*. Select **Assign**:

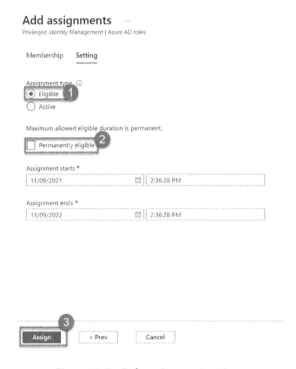

Figure 13.7 – Role assignment settings

7. The new role assignment will appear in the assignments tile under the **Eligible assignments** tab. To change this eligible assignment to active, choose **Update**, as the arrow shows in *Figure 13.8*:

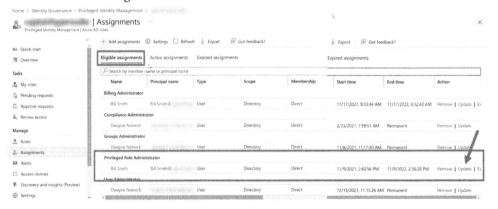

Figure 13.8 – Updating the role assignment

8. In **Membership settings**, change the **Assignment type** dropdown to **Active**, deselect **Permanently assigned**, set an **Assignment ends** date, and provide a justification. Select **Save** to save the changes:

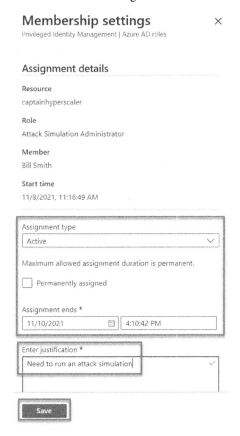

Figure 13.9 – Changing membership settings to Active

9. On the **Assignments** tile, navigate to the **Active assignments** tab, and you will see the now active role assignment for your user with the end date that you set:

Figure 13.10 – Active assignments

You have now created a **Privileged Role** assignment and activated it within Privileged Identity Management. Once the end time is reached, the privileged role is automatically removed and given eligible status. No administrator intervention is required.

In the next section, we will discuss creating and managing break-glass accounts.

Creating and managing break-glass accounts

As we continue to secure our identities with security and governance features, such as Multi-Factor Authentication, Conditional Access policies, Identity Governance, and PIM solutions, it is important to make sure that we do not mistakenly get locked out of Azure AD. To protect against potential lockout and to make sure that access is still available in a potential emergency situation, you should configure at least two emergency-access or *break-glass* accounts. These accounts are accounts of high privileges with access at the level of a global administrator. These accounts are not protected with Multi-Factor Authentication, meaning that they can gain access quickly to resources when other administrator accounts cannot gain access. They should also be excluded from all Conditional Access policies. The use of these accounts should be limited to this scenario and the credentials should be locked away and kept in a secure location, such as a password vault, until the time that they are absolutely needed.

Break-glass accounts are member accounts that are tied directly to the Azure AD tenant. Therefore, they can be utilized in situations where federated identity providers are being utilized for authentication and there is an outage to that identity provider. Other use cases would be that the global administrator has lost access to their MFA device to verify their identity, a global administrator has left the company and it is needed to delete that account, and a storm has taken down cellular services and you cannot verify with MFA.

Additional information on emergency-access or break-glass accounts can be found at this link: https://docs.microsoft.com/en-us/azure/active-directory/roles/security-emergency-access.

Break-glass accounts should not be associated with any particular users within the Azure AD tenant. The steps to create and secure these accounts are as follows:

1. The first step in creating a break-glass account is to create the user account in Azure AD. Go to **Azure AD | Users** and select **+ New user**:

Figure 13.11 – Creating a new user

2. Create the emergency admin user. Do *NOT* use the custom domain for this account; use the `tenant.onmicrosoft.com` domain, where the tenant is the name of your tenant. When creating a password, use a strong password generator to create the password. Save that password and lock it away in a safe place.

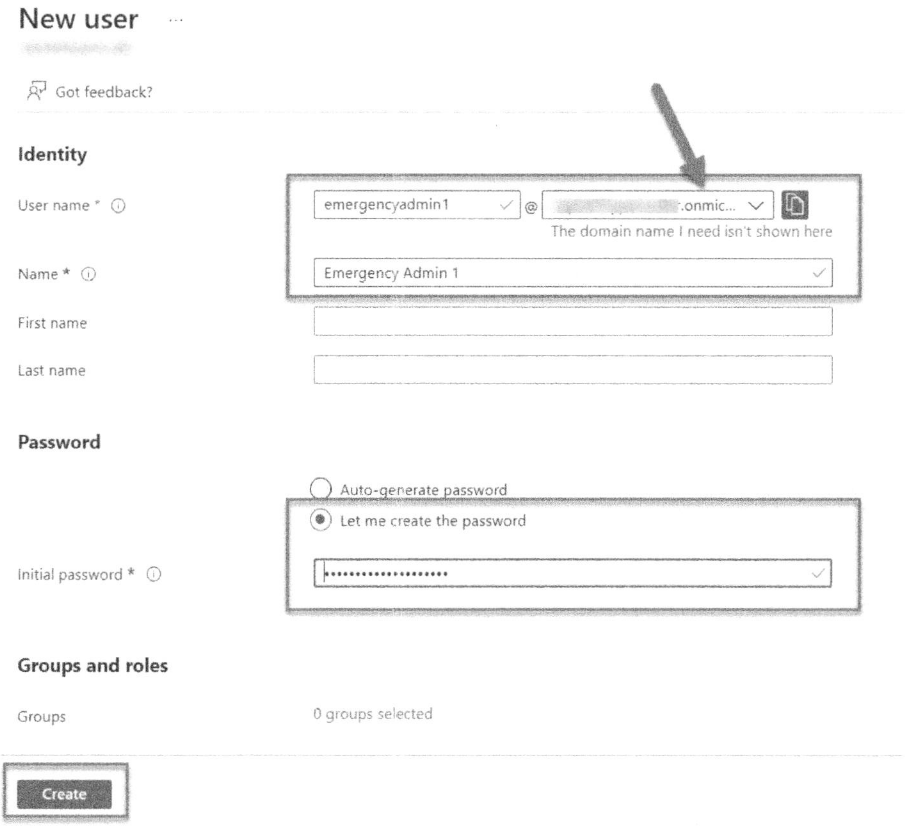

New user ...

Got feedback?

Identity

User name *   ⓘ

| emergencyadmin1 ✓ | @ | .onmic... ⌄ | 🗋 |

The domain name I need isn't shown here

Name * ⓘ

Emergency Admin 1 ✓

First name

Last name

Password

○ Auto-generate password

◉ Let me create the password

Initial password * ⓘ

••••••••••••••••••• ⌄

Groups and roles

Groups   0 groups selected

Create

Figure 13.12 – Creating the username and password

3. After creating the user, return to PIM and add the **Global Administrator** role to the users:

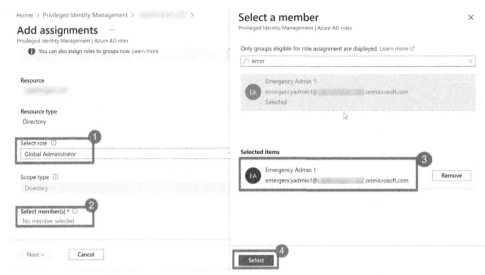

Figure 13.13 – Creating the Global Administrator role assignment

4. Select **Next** to configure the assignment settings:

Figure 13.14 – Selecting Next to continue

5. When configuring the role assignment, it should be made active and permanent to avoid being locked out:

Figure 13.15 – Creating a permanent assignment for the account

You have now configured a break-glass or emergency-access account. You should secure the credentials in a safe place and have directions on how to access the account within your company business continuity plan. Additional information on monitoring these accounts can be found here: `https://docs.microsoft.com/en-us/azure/active-directory/roles/security-emergency-access#monitor-sign-in-and-audit-logs`.

The next section will discuss planning and automating access reviews for privileged access users.

Planning for and automating access reviews

In terms of an access life cycle, you should consider the access life cycle of your member users and your guest users, and especially your privileged administrators. These should be handled differently, as the life cycle of our member users is based on employment within the company being terminated or changes in a role, and the access that is required for the department or team that they belong to. Guest users are provided access based on a partnership and external collaboration trust relationship. *Chapter 12, Planning and Implementing Entitlement Management*, discussed using access reviews for member and guest user entitlements.

Privileged administrative user access should be regularly reviewed in a similar manner. Since these are elevated access assignments, the review of these should be done on a consistent basis as identified by the policies of the company. Unused and unnecessary privileged assignments should be removed as soon as possible. Automated removal should also be configured for users who are no longer with the company or have changed departments within the company. The steps for access review configuration and automation are provided as follows:

1. **Access reviews** can manage the access life cycle. Within **Privileged Identity Management**, this is found under the **Manage** menu, as shown in *Figure 13.16*:

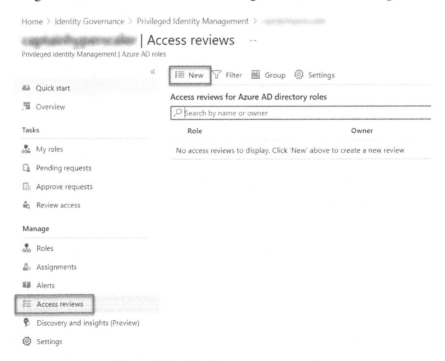

Figure 13.16 – Creating a new access review

2. Name the access review and set the start date and frequency. Duration is how long the access review will run before it expires. You can set the end to be a specific date or after a number of occurrences. The example is creating a monthly review for all users and groups. Then, select the user scope of the access review, as shown in *Figure 13.17*:

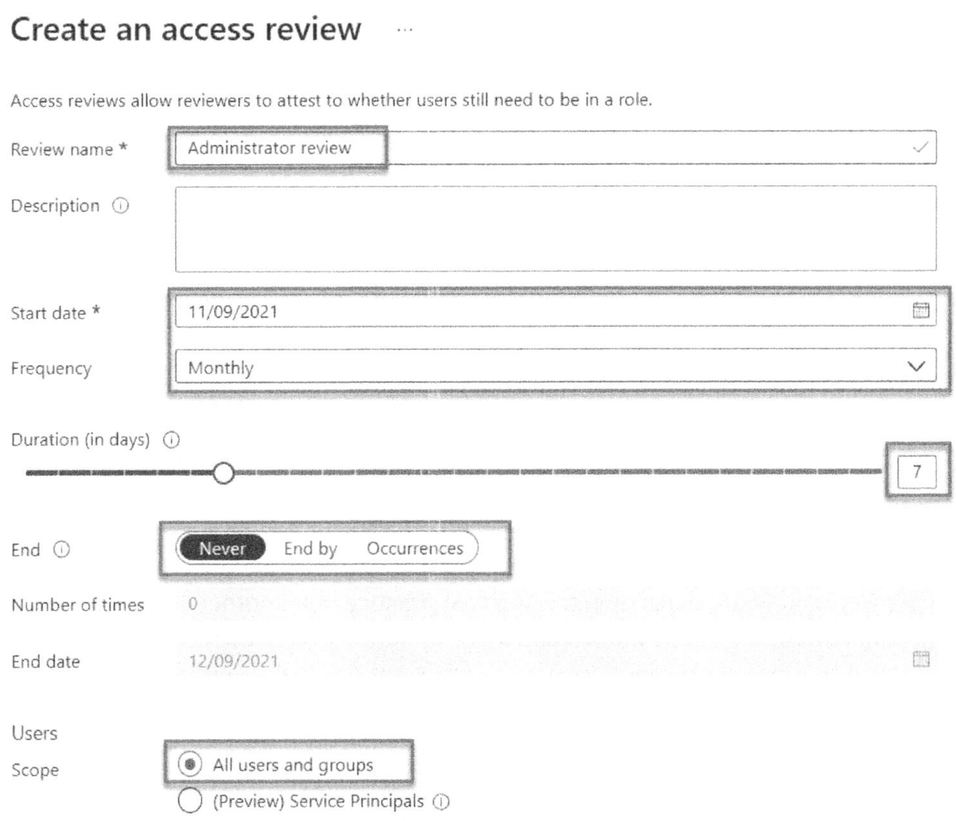

Create an access review   ...

Access reviews allow reviewers to attest to whether users still need to be in a role.

Review name *	Administrator review
Description ⓘ	
Start date *	11/09/2021
Frequency	Monthly
Duration (in days) ⓘ	7
End ⓘ	**Never** End by Occurrences
Number of times	0
End date	12/09/2021
Users	
Scope	● All users and groups
	○ (Preview) Service Principals ⓘ

Figure 13.17 – Configuring the access review

3. Select the scope for the roles that will be part of this scope. You can add all roles or only select specific roles for certain reviews, with administrator roles being the primary focus:

Figure 13.18 – Selecting the roles to review

4. The next step is to determine the reviewers. These reviewers can be the member themselves, who will do a self-review, or can be assigned to supervisors if reviewing access for an entire department. It is a best practice that another administrator completes these reviews rather than a self-review. You can also set the action when a reviewer does not respond to automatically remove that privileged access from the member. A best practice would be to remove a review when no response is received.

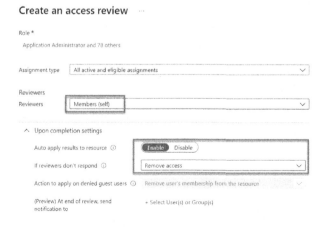

Figure 13.19 – Settings for the access review

5. The advanced settings allow you to put a message as part of the review, as shown in *Figure 13.20*. Select **Start** to initiate the access review:

Figure 13.20 – Advanced access review settings

6. When the access review is created, the access review list will populate with the roles and owners of the reviews, as shown in *Figure 13.21*:

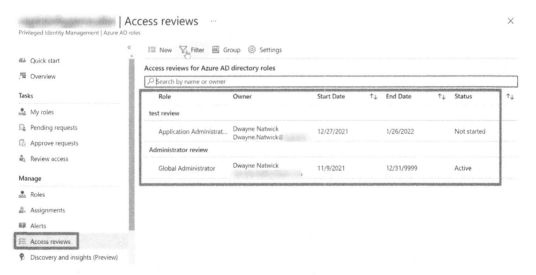

Figure 13.21 – Access reviews active

7. Members who are being reviewed will receive an email, similar to *Figure 13.22*:

Figure 13.22 – Access review action email

8. Selecting an access review of one of the roles will provide the status of these access reviews. *Figure 13.23* shows the current review of **Global Administrator** roles:

Figure 13.23 – Status of the access review

Additional information on creating access reviews can be found at this link: `https://docs.microsoft.com/en-us/azure/active-directory/privileged-identity-management/pim-create-azure-ad-roles-and-resource-roles-review`.

The next section will discuss how to use reports and audit history to analyze PIM.

Analyzing PIM audit history and reports

A key benefit to utilizing PIM is the ability to audit the use of privileged access to administrator roles. Since the activation of a PIM role requires justification, this creates an audit history that you can review and create reports to review.

You can access this history and create your reports from the **Activity** menu of **Privileged Identity Management** by choosing **Resource audit**, as shown in *Figure 13.24*:

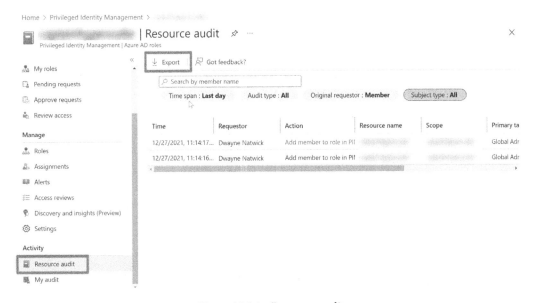

Figure 13.24 – Resource audit

From this tile, you can sort by users and filter the information for different time spans and requestor information. You can export the results to provide reports to management. Additional information can be found at this link: `https://docs.microsoft.com/en-us/azure/active-directory/privileged-identity-management/pim-email-notifications#weekly-privileged-identity-management-digest-email-for-azure-ad-roles`.

Next, we will provide a summary of what was discussed in this chapter.

Summary

In this chapter, we covered the areas of PIM. This included creating just-in-time administrator access with PIM and how to create break-glass or emergency-access accounts. Since these accounts provide elevated privileges within our company, it is very important to manage and govern these administrator accounts to protect against internal and external threats. Internal users with elevated access privileges have the potential to expose information that they are not authorized to access. We discussed how to do this through access reviews and by analyzing the audit history and reports for PIM. In the next chapter, we will further discuss how to analyze and investigate sign-in logs and elevated-risk users within Azure AD.

Section 6 – Monitoring and Maintaining Azure Active Directory

This section will focus on the monitoring, management, and maintenance of Azure Active Directory.

This section of the book comprises the following chapters:

- *Chapter 14, Analyzing and Investigating Sign-in Logs and Elevated Risk Users*
- *Chapter 15, Enabling and Integrating Azure AD Logs with SIEM Solutions*
- *Chapter 16, Mock Test*

14
Analyzing and Investigating Sign-in Logs and Elevated Risk Users

The previous chapter covered planning and implementing our privileged access for administrator accounts and managing them with access reviews. This included the benefits of using privileged identity management and how to audit these privileged assignments. In this chapter, we will discuss how to analyze, review, and investigate our logs and events for protecting against risky sign-ins and elevated risk users.

We're going to cover the following main topics:

- Analyzing and investigating sign-in logs to troubleshoot access issues
- Reviewing and monitoring Azure AD audit logs
- Analyzing Azure Active Directory workbooks and reporting

Technical requirements

In this chapter, we will continue to explore configuring a tenant for **Microsoft 365** and **Azure**. There will be exercises that will require access to Azure Active Directory. If you have not yet created the trial licenses for Microsoft 365, please follow the directions provided within *Chapter 1, Preparing for Your Microsoft Exam*.

Analyzing and investigating sign-in logs to troubleshoot access issues

In *Chapter 9, Planning, Implementing, and Administering Conditional Access and Azure Identity Protection*, we discussed how user and sign-in risk can be used as a condition for access and authorization to applications. Azure Identity Protection utilizes the activity logs to determine potential threats, vulnerabilities, and anomalous behavior among users. Sign-in logs are based on two types of reporting: activity and security.

Activity reporting within Microsoft shows what is taking place within the infrastructure. The various activities include the following:

- Sign-ins, which is the usage information of managed applications and user sign-in activities within Azure AD or a hybrid identity architecture.

- Audit logs that provide system activity for users and groups, managed applications, and directory activities.

- Provisioning logs enable customers to monitor activity that pertains to the provisioning service for enterprise and cloud applications. For example, if someone created a group in **Salesforce** or imported a user into **ServiceNow**.

Security reporting pertains to the identity protection activity within Azure AD. These include the risky sign-ins and user risks that are logged:

- Risky sign-ins indicate that a sign-in attempt might not have been made by the legitimate owner of the account. This is generally found through an anonymous IP address being used or an impossible travel event, where the legitimate user has signed in from a known IP address and another sign-in attempt takes place moments later from a location that is hours away.

- Users flagged as risky users are an indicator that the user's account has potentially been compromised. This activity can determine potential brute force attacks on a user account.

Activity and security report data can be accessed by the following Azure AD roles: **Security Administrator**, **Security Reader**, **Global Reader**, and **Report Reader**. Users that only require the ability to view these reports should be assigned the reader roles. Security Administrator allows a user to create and respond to alerts and configure reports for others to view. **The Global Administrator** role also has full access to these reports, but it is not recommended to assign someone that only requires access to these reports with this role when adhering to the principles of least privilege.

The ability to access sign-in activity is available with all Azure AD licenses. However, if you require the capabilities of Azure Identity Protection, such as sign-in risk and user risk detection, you will require the Azure AD Premium P2 license.

In the following steps, you will see how to access these reports to monitor sign-in activity and determine any sign-in patterns that may signify a potential threat:

1. Go to `portal.azure.com` and select **Azure Active Directory**:

Figure 14.1 – Navigate to Azure Active Directory

2. On the **Azure Active Directory** menu, scroll down to **Monitoring** and select **Sign-ins logs** to open and view the sign-ins report. Reports may not be available if you have created your Azure AD tenant within the past 2 hours. The sign-in reports display sign-ins where a user manually enters a username and password, also known as interactive sign-ins. These reports do not display service-to-service authentication or non-interactive sign-ins:

Figure 14.2 – Sign-in logs under Monitoring

3. On the **Sign-in logs** report tile, there is a default list of headings in the view that includes the sign-in date, user, application, sign-in status, the status of any risk or failure, and the status of multi-factor authentication:

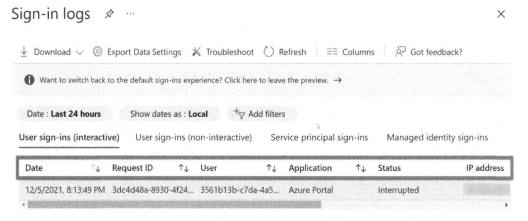

Figure 14.3 – Log headings

4. Selecting **Columns** in the toolbar allows you to customize this view:

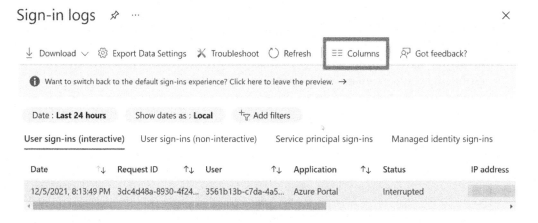

Figure 14.4 – Customize the columns

5. *Figure 14.5* shows some of the additional columns that you can add or remove for the report view:

Figure 14.5 – Additional columns to add

6. In the sign-in report view, select an item row to view the detailed information about the event:

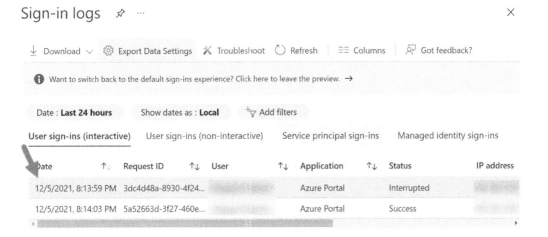

Figure 14.6 – Select a row to review details

7. The detailed view provides additional filtering tabs that can be used to review additional information, including location, device, authentication details, conditional access, and additional details that might be helpful in troubleshooting. For this exercise, select and review tabs, such as the **Basic info** or **Conditional Access** tab and review the information that is provided. The **Basic info** tab is shown in *Figure 14.7*:

Activity Details: Sign-ins   ✕

| Basic info | Location | Device info | Authentication Details | Conditional Access | Report-only | ... |

Date	12/5/2021, 8:13:59 PM	User	
Request ID		Username	
Correlation ID		User ID	
Authentication requirement	Multi-factor authentication	Sign-in identifier	
Status	Interrupted		
Continuous access evaluation	No	User type	Member
		Cross tenant access type	None
Additional Details	This is an expected part of the login flow, where a user is asked if they want to remain signed into this browser to make further logins easier. For more details, see https://techcommunity.microsoft.com/t5/Azure-Active-Directory/The-new-Azure-AD-sign-in-and-Keep-me-signed-in-experiences/td-p/128267	Application	Azure Portal
		Application ID	
		Resource	Windows Azure Service Management API
		Resource ID	
		Resource tenant ID	
	Follow these steps:		

Figure 14.7 – Activity details for sign-in

8. In the **Basic info** tab, note that **Client app** presents the method that was used to connect to the tenant. This information can be used to identify whether an application that supports modern authentication was used to sign in:

Figure 14.8 – Sign-in activity client app

9. These activities can be downloaded into a `.csv` or `.json` file from within the tile by selecting **Download**. When downloading the sign-in activity, a message will provide information on the maximum number of records that can be downloaded. This number is a constraint set by the Azure AD report retention policies:

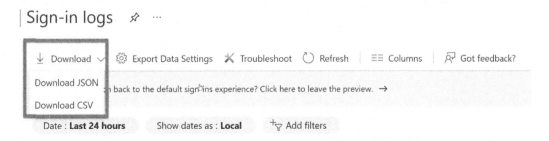

Figure 14.9 – Download sign-in logs

10. In addition to filtering and downloading sign-in activity data, Azure AD and the Azure portal provide data shortcuts to review and investigate additional points of sign-in data. These shortcuts provide graphical representations of sign-in activity and can be found in the following locations within the portal interface:

- The identity security protection overview within the Azure AD portal.

- The Azure AD **Users** overview provides user sign-in data.

- The Azure AD **Groups** overview provides group sign-in data.

- The Azure AD Identity Protection overview provides potential risky sign-in data.

- The **Enterprise Applications** overview provides sign-in activity for registered enterprise applications.

Sign-in activity log data has a default retention period of 30 days, and the graph shows activity for those 30 days. Within the sign-in activity graphs, you have the capability to select a specific day and review the data for that day. Additional information about data retention can be found at this link: `https://docs.microsoft.com/azure/active-directory/reports-monitoring/reference-reports-data-retention`. PowerShell commands to view these logs are also available at this link: `https://docs.microsoft.com/en-us/powershell/module/azuread/get-azureadauditdirectorylogs?view=azureadps-2.0-preview`.

The sign-in activity data shows the following information:

- The user that has signed in

- The application that the user was targeting to sign in to

- The status of the sign-in to that application

- Whether MFA was enforced as part of the sign-in

Figure 14.10 shows these options:

Figure 14.10 – Authentication details

When you select one of the options, you can view the details of the user ID, user, username, application ID, application, client, location, IP address, date, MFA required, and sign-in status. On the user's page, the complete overview of all user sign-ins can be accessed by selecting the sign-ins within the **Activity** section.

The IP address does not provide a definitive connection between the IP address and the physical location of the device used to sign in. IP address mapping can be complicated by mobile provider information and VPN connections that are not necessarily the physical IP address of the device. Azure AD reports provide a best-effort conversion of an IP address to a physical location based on traces, registry data, reverse lookups, and other information.

If you want to gain insights into the usage of managed applications, there is an application-centric view of the sign-in data that provides the following:

- The users that are accessing the applications.

- A list of the top three applications used within the company.

- Information on how new applications are doing based on sign-in activity. This data can be viewed within the top three application data.

The **Enterprise applications** overview provides an entry point to access the data for application usage graphs for the past 30 days. *Figure 14.11* shows **Enterprise applications** in the **Azure Active Directory** menu:

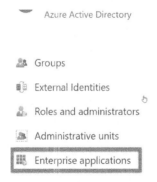

Figure 14.11 – Enterprise applications

Select a day on the graph to get detailed information on sign-in activities, as shown in
Figure 14.12:

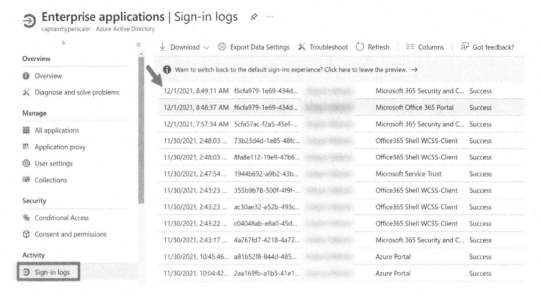

Figure 14.12 – Enterprise applications Sign-in logs

The sign-in activity for that day gives you an overview of the sign-in events for your
enterprise applications.

Now that you have an understanding of sign-in logs and the information that they provide,
in the next section, we will discuss how to review and monitor Azure AD audit logs.

Reviewing and monitoring Azure AD audit logs

In the previous section, we discussed sign-in logs and the information that they provide
in terms of user and application sign-in activity. This section will discuss Azure AD audit
logs and the information that they provide for reviewing and monitoring compliance.

Azure AD reports provide information that you will need to monitor and determine what
is taking place within your environment and how it is doing. Azure AD audit logs provide
information and records that pertain to activities for compliance.

The following steps cover how to access the audit reports and review the information:

1. Within `portal.azure.com`, navigate to **Azure Active Directory** and select **Audit logs** under the **Monitoring** section of the menu:

Figure 14.13 – Audit logs

2. View the default view that lists the following information: the data and time of the occurrence, the service that logged the occurrence, the category and name of the activity, the status of the activity (**Success** or **Failure**), the target, and the initiator/actor of the activity. This view is shown in *Figure 14.14*:

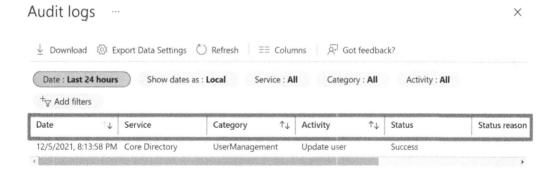

Figure 14.14 – Audit log columns

3. The audit logs can be filtered by the fields **Service**, **Category**, **Activity**, **Status**, **Target**, **Initiated by**, and date range, as shown in *Figure 14.15*:

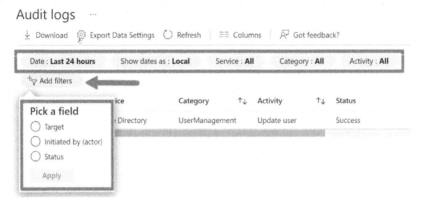

Figure 14.15 – Filter settings and additional filters

4. When selecting the **Service** filter, you have an additional list of selections that includes all services: **AAD Management UX**, **Access Reviews**, **Account Provisioning**, **Application Proxy**, **Authentication Methods**, **Azure AD Recommendations**, **B2C**, **Conditional Access**, **Core Directory**, **Entitlement Management**, **Hybrid Authentication**, **Identity Protection Invited Users**, **MIM Service**, **MyApps**, **PIM**, **Self-service Group Management**, **Self-service group Management**, **Self-service Password Management**, and **Terms of use**. This list allows you to review, monitor, and remediate potential compliance issues within your environment. Part of this list is shown in *Figure 14.16*:

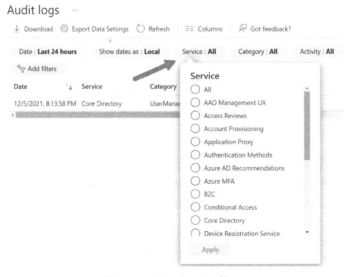

Figure 14.16 – Service filters

5. The category filter allows you to filter additional information that pertains to authentication and authorization categories, such as **AdministrativeUnit, ApplicationManagement, Authentication, Authorization, Contact, Device, DeviceConfiguration, DirectoryManagement, EntitlementManagement, GroupManagements, KerberosDomain, KeyManagement, Label, PermissionGrantPolicy, Policy, ResourceManagement, RoleManagement, UserManagement, Other,** or **All selected**. This is shown in *Figure 14.17*:

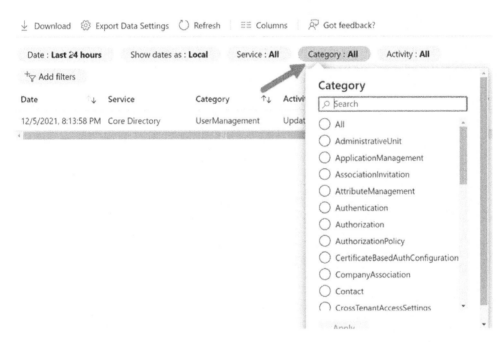

Figure 14.17 – Category filters

6.   The activity filter provides information based on the category and activity filters that you selected in the previous steps. From this view, you can select a specific activity, or you can choose all activities. The following link provides the list of all audit activities. These audit activities can be viewed through the Graph API: `https://graph.windows.net//activities/auditActivityTypesV2?api-version=beta`.

Additional filters include the status filter, target filter, initiated by filter, and date range. These filters allow you to drill down into information based on different operations. The status filter can be set to all, success, or failure. The target filter searches a particular target name or **User Principal Name** (**UPN**). Initiated by defines the actor's name or UPN starts with identifier. The target name and initiated by filters are case-sensitive. The date range will filter data based on date windows of 7 days, 24 hours, or a custom range. A custom date timeframe allows you to configure a start time and end time.

The fully filtered audit report can be seen in *Figure 14.18*:

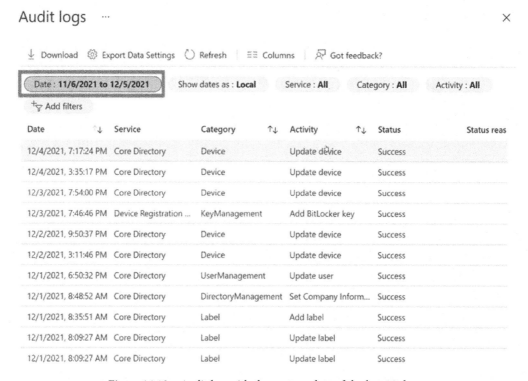

Figure 14.18 – Audit log with the custom date of the last 30 days

By selecting the **Download** button, filtered data can then be downloaded to a `.csv` or `.json` file for up to 250,000 records. The number of records is a constraint defined by Azure AD report retention policies.

The preceding steps explain how to access audit logs through Azure AD in the Azure portal. Audit data can also be accessed within the users and groups, and enterprise applications tiles.

To access audit logs within users and groups, navigate to one of these sections within Azure AD, as shown in *Figure 14.19*:

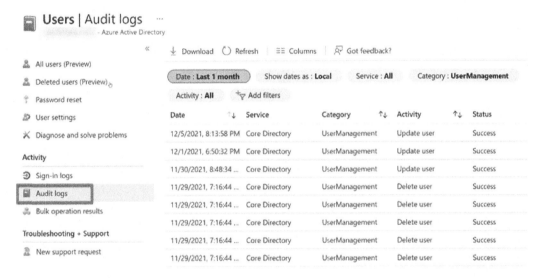

Figure 14.19 – Users Audit logs

These audit logs can be found under the **Activity** section of the **Users** tab, as shown in *Figure 14.19*. These audit logs provide information regarding the types of updates applied to users, users that were changed and how many, password changes and how many, administrator activity within the directory, groups that have been added, group membership changes, owner changes within groups, and licenses assigned to groups or users. User information can be found within **UserManagement** and group information is in the **GroupManagement** category.

The final audit logs to discuss are the **Enterprise applications** audit logs. These application-based audit reports provide you with updates and additions to applications, removed applications, changes in application service principals, application name changes, and consent given to an application and by who. Access to review this data can be found in the filtered view under **Audit logs**, which is found in the **Activity** section of the **Enterprise applications** tile, as shown in *Figure 14.20*:

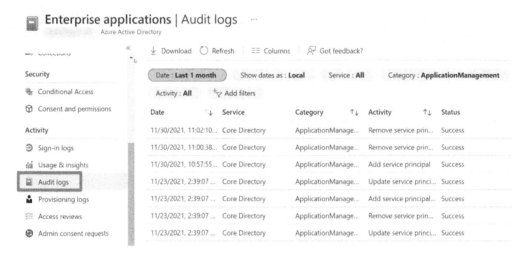

Figure 14.20 – Enterprise applications Audit logs

Selecting an application type provides the entry point to a preselected enterprise application and the targets of the application, as shown in *Figure 14.21*:

Figure 14.21 – Application audit log details

You now know how to access the audit logs to review and monitor identity and access compliance within Azure AD. In the next section, we will learn how to analyze Azure AD workbooks and provide additional reports from these workbooks.

Analyzing Azure Active Directory workbooks and reporting

The previous section explained how to access the different audit reports within Azure AD to review and monitor compliance. Activity logs and audit logs provide reports for our usage and compliance within Azure AD for users, groups, and applications. In addition to these reports, usage and insights reports can provide additional application-centric views into sign-in data.

The information within usage and insights can provide information such as the following:

- The most used applications within the company
- Applications that have the most failed sign-ins
- The top sign-in errors for each of your applications

The licensing within your tenant to access usage and data reports required is either an Azure AD Premium P1 or P2 license. Users are required to have the role of Security Administrator, Security Reader, Report Reader, or Global Administrator. As stated throughout this book, you should adhere to the principles of least privilege by only assigning the minimum level of access needed by the user. The Global Administrator role should be the last role that is considered if the user only requires access to Azure AD usage and insights. Individual users with an Azure AD Premium P1 or P2 license assigned and not one of the prior mentioned roles do have access to their own sign-in usage and insights.

The following steps are used to access usage and insights reports:

1. From within the Azure portal, navigate to **Azure Active Directory** and select **Enterprise applications** from the menu:

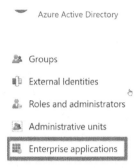

Figure 14.22 – Enterprise applications in Azure AD

2. In the **Enterprise applications** tile menu, under **Activity**, select **Usage & insights**:

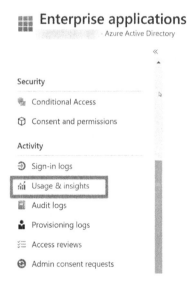

Figure 14.23 – Enterprise applications Usage & insights

3. The **Usage & insights** report shows the list of applications that have one or more sign-in attempts:

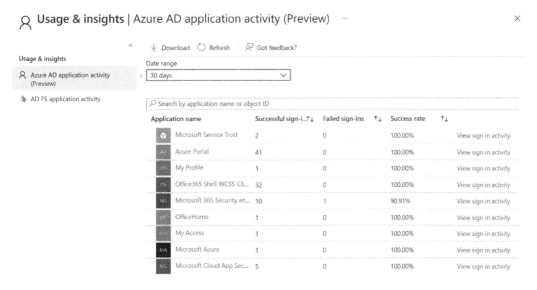

Figure 14.24 – Azure AD application activity

4. The columns within the report can be used to sort the report based on successful sign-ins, failed sign-ins, and the success rate:

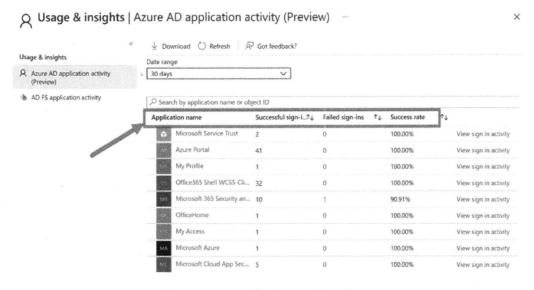

Figure 14.25 – Application activity columns

5. The report can be focused on dates, up to 30 days, or specific applications. Select **Azure Portal** from the list:

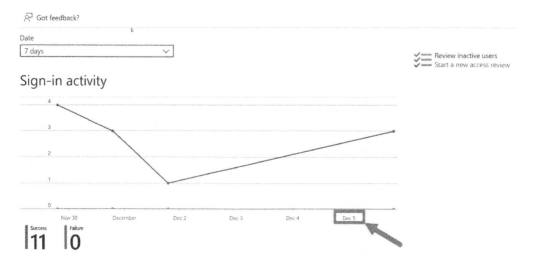

Usage & insights - Azure Portal ...

Got feedback?

Date

7 days

Review inactive users
Start a new access review

Sign-in activity

Nov 30   December   Dec 2   Dec 3   Dec 4   Dec 5

Success **11**   Failure **0**

Figure 14.26 – Azure portal sign-in activity

6. On the graph, you can select a specific day for the detailed list of sign-in activities for an application:

Usage & insights - Azure Portal ...

Got feedback?

Date

7 days

Review inactive users
Start a new access review

Sign-in activity

Nov 30   December   Dec 2   Dec 3   Dec 4   Dec 5

Success **11**   Failure **0**

Figure 14.27 – Select today's date in the graph

7. *Figure 14.28* shows the details for a selected date:

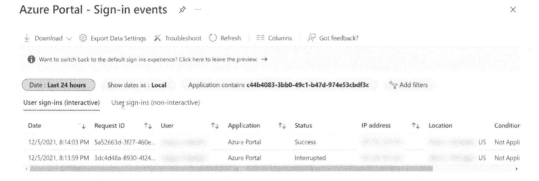

Figure 14.28 – Azure portal event list

After you have set up and are able to view the usage and insights, you may want to configure notifications and alerts regarding issues on the **Azure Active Directory Domain Services (Azure AD DS)** domain. Within the monitoring of Azure is the ability to monitor the health status of Azure AD DS. From this health status, email notifications can be configured to report on health alerts as soon as an issue is detected on the domain. The notifications specify in the email the managed domain that has the alert, the time that the issue was detected, and a link to the health page in the Azure portal. You can then troubleshoot within the portal based on the advice provided to resolve the issue.

Before selecting any links within an email, be sure that the email has been sent by Microsoft by verifying the sender's address. These notifications will come from the `azure-noreply@microsoft.com` address.

Azure AD DS notifications are sent for important updates within the domain that are urgent issues that impact the service within the domain and that should be addressed immediately. These alerts are also located within the Azure portal on the Azure AD DS health page. Open alerts that are left unresolved will be resent every 4 days. Additional information on service health alerts for Azure AD DS can be found at this link: `https://docs.microsoft.com/azure/active-directory-domain-services/check-health`. Information on how to use the alerts to troubleshoot can be found at this link: `https://docs.microsoft.com/azure/active-directory-domain-services/troubleshoot-alerts`.

Email notifications should be sent to a list of administrators that should be responding to alerts and issues. There is a limit of five email recipients for these notifications. A distribution group can be created to send to additional recipients.

The following steps show how to configure email notification recipients. There is a cost to creating Azure AD Domain Services. You can go through these steps to create them, or you can simply read these steps for understanding and reference at a later date. This is not a major component of the exam:

1. Within the Azure portal, search and navigate to **Azure AD Domain Services**:

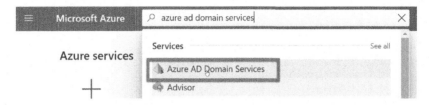

Figure 14.29 – Search for Azure AD Domain Services

2. Select your managed domain or create a managed domain, if you have not already. Create a managed domain named `aaddsdomain.com`:

Figure 14.30 – Create an Azure AD Domain Service

3. On the left menu of the **Azure AD Domain Services** tile, select **Notification** settings.

4. Select **Add email recipient** and enter the email address.

5. Select **Save** to save the changes. Any changes that are made in the notification settings affect the entire managed domain, not just you as the user.

You now understand how to configure an Azure AD DS domain and configure notifications. Next, we will provide a summary of what was discussed in this chapter.

Summary

In this chapter, we covered how to analyze and investigate sign-in logs and elevated risk users within Azure AD. This included sign-in logs and audit logs, and how to configure and filter reports for these logs. We looked at how to review usage and insights workbooks for activity. We also reviewed how to monitor, troubleshoot, and configure alert notifications for Azure AD Domain Services managed domains.

In the next chapter we will learn how to enable and integrate Azure AD Logs with SIEM Solutions.

15
Enabling and Integrating Azure AD Logs with SIEM Solutions

The previous chapter covered how to analyze, review, and investigate our logs and events to protect against risky sign-ins and elevated-risk users. This included creating reports and reviewing insights for user activity to recognize potential vulnerabilities and alert against possible threats. In this chapter, we will discuss how to integrate and enable the use of these logs with Microsoft Sentinel or a third-party **security incident and event management (SIEM)** solution. This will include how to use Log Analytics with Kusto queries to review activity in Microsoft Sentinel.

In this chapter, we're going to cover the following main topics:

- Enabling and integrating Azure AD diagnostic logs with Log Analytics and Microsoft Sentinel
- Exporting sign-in and audit logs to a third-party SIEM
- Reviewing Azure AD activity by using Log Analytics and Microsoft Sentinel

Technical requirements

In this chapter, we will continue to explore configuring a tenant for use of **Microsoft 365** and **Azure**. There will be exercises that will require access to Azure **Active Directory** (**AD**). If you have not yet created the trial licenses for Microsoft 365, please follow the directions provided in *Chapter 1, Preparing for Your Microsoft Exam*.

Enabling and integrating Azure AD diagnostic logs with Log Analytics and Microsoft Sentinel

In the previous chapter, we discussed how to access and use activity logs and audit logs to review user activity and filter that activity for monitoring, reporting, and managing potential vulnerabilities and threats. In this chapter, we will discuss how we can use this information within Microsoft Sentinel and third-party SIEM solutions to provide an integration of these logs to handle security operations more efficiently in one location.

This section will provide guidance on how to export logs to Microsoft Sentinel. The next section will discuss how to export logs to third-party security tools, if you are not utilizing Microsoft Sentinel. Let's start by explaining Microsoft Sentinel and what SIEM and **security orchestration automated response** (**SOAR**) solutions are.

A SIEM is a solution within a security operations center that gathers logs and events from various appliances and software within an information technology infrastructure. The SIEM solution reviews the logs and events for potential threats by searching for behavior that is not typical to best practices or may be seen as anomalous. The benefit of having and utilizing a SIEM is that without one, security operations personnel would need to review each of these log and event files manually. Since there are thousands of log and event files within a company, this option has the potential for mistakes as fatigue becomes an issue when scrolling through these files. A SIEM picks out the logs and events that could be a threat and security personnel can then investigate these potential threats, decreasing the time to recognize a threat or vulnerability and allowing the security operations team to be more efficient and effective in their investigations.

A SOAR solution is a complementary solution to a SIEM. SOAR solutions can add automation to the response of potential events identified as threats in the log files by initiating a workflow. An example of this would be an activity log from a device that has been accessed from a location that has been flagged as a threat. The SOAR can initiate a workflow to take that device offline and send an alert to the security operations response team to investigate.

Microsoft Sentinel is a scalable, cloud-native SIEM and SOAR solution. Microsoft Sentinel provides a full view across the company to recognize increasingly sophisticated attacks, increasing volumes of alerts, and long-resolution time frames, making your company more efficient in responding to and eliminating threats.

Microsoft Sentinel is made up of the following workflow:

1. **Collect** data at cloud scale across all users, devices, applications, and infrastructure in Azure, Microsoft 365, on-premises, and multiple clouds.

2. **Detect** previously undetected threats and minimize false positives using Microsoft's analytics and global threat intelligence.

3. **Investigate** threats with machine learning and artificial intelligence and hunt for suspicious activities at a global scale, utilizing the intelligence gathered through the cybersecurity work at Microsoft.

4. **Respond** to incidents rapidly with built-in orchestration and automation of common tasks:

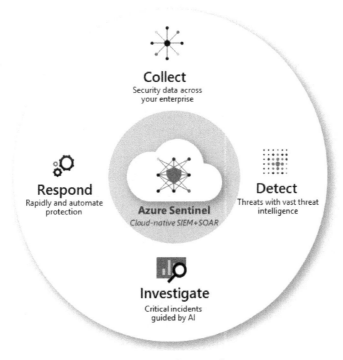

Figure 15.1 – Microsoft Sentinel processes

There are some requirements for licensing and administrative roles before you can start using Microsoft Sentinel. These are as follows:

- All Azure AD licenses (Free/O365/P1/P2) support the ability to ingest sign-in logs into Microsoft Sentinel. Microsoft Sentinel's pricing is based on per-gigabyte charges for the logs and data connector points that are ingested into Log Analytics and Microsoft Sentinel. For companies that collect a large number of logs on a daily basis, there are tiered discounts that can be applied. This link provides a list of logs that are free to ingest into Microsoft Sentinel: `https://docs.microsoft.com/en-us/azure/sentinel/billing#free-data-sources`.

- The Azure Sentinel Contributor role on the workspace must be assigned to your user account.

- The Global Administrator or Security Administrator role must be assigned to your user account on the tenant where you will be streaming the logs. Adhering to the principles of least privilege, assigning the Security Administrator role would be preferred.

- Read and write permissions to the **Azure AD diagnostic** settings must be assigned to the user account to be able to see the connection status.

- A Log Analytics workspace is an essential part of Microsoft Sentinel and is required to be configured and associated with Microsoft Sentinel. This configuration will be discussed in the step-by-step exercise.

Additional information on Microsoft Sentinel can be found at this link: `https://docs.microsoft.com/en-us/azure/sentinel/overview`.

Now that we understand Microsoft Sentinel and what the requirements are from a licensing and role perspective, we will go through the step-by-step configuration of Microsoft Sentinel for Azure AD sign-in activity logs and audit logs:

1. Navigate to `portal.azure.com` and search for `Microsoft Sentinel`:

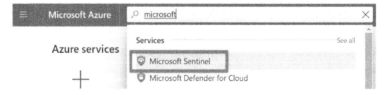

Figure 15.2 – Navigate to Microsoft Sentinel

2. Select + **Create** and **Create Microsoft Sentinel**:

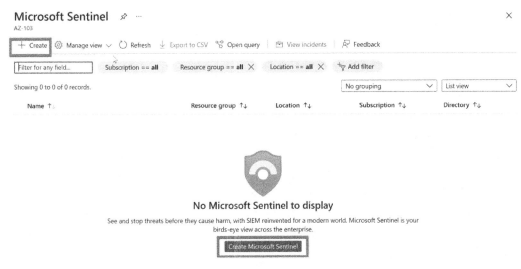

Figure 15.3 – Create a new Microsoft Sentinel service

3. The first step in the setup process of Microsoft Sentinel is to connect a Log Analytics workspace. In this exercise, select + **Create a new workspace** and **Create a new workspace**:

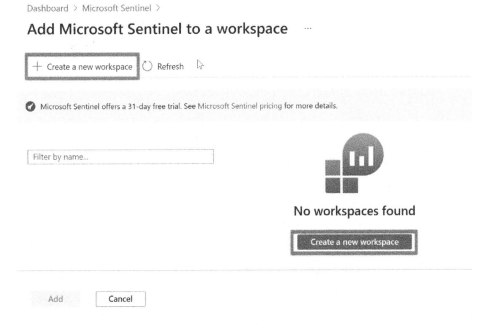

Figure 15.4 – Create a new Log Analytics workspace

4. Enter the information for the resource group and name for Microsoft Sentinel. Select **Review + Create**:

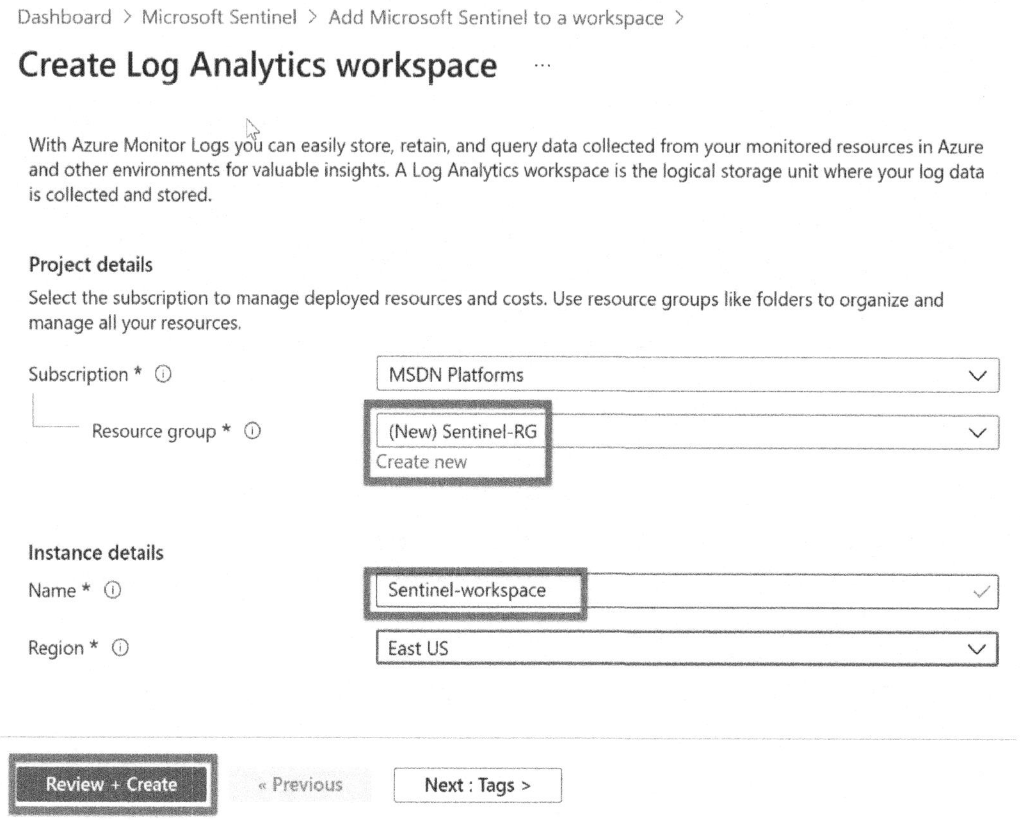

Dashboard > Microsoft Sentinel > Add Microsoft Sentinel to a workspace >

Create Log Analytics workspace ⋯

With Azure Monitor Logs you can easily store, retain, and query data collected from your monitored resources in Azure and other environments for valuable insights. A Log Analytics workspace is the logical storage unit where your log data is collected and stored.

Project details

Select the subscription to manage deployed resources and costs. Use resource groups like folders to organize and manage all your resources.

Subscription * ⓘ   MSDN Platforms

Resource group * ⓘ   (New) Sentinel-RG
                          Create new

Instance details

Name * ⓘ   Sentinel-workspace

Region * ⓘ   East US

Review + Create   « Previous   Next : Tags >

Figure 15.5 – Create Log Analytics workspace

5.   After the validation completes, select **Create** to create the workspace:

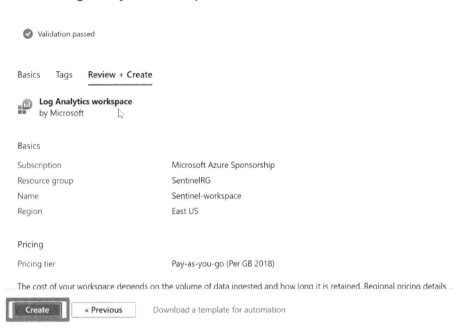

Figure 15.6 – Validate and create the workspace

6. After the Log Analytics workspace is created, you will return to the **Add Microsoft Sentinel to a workspace** creation page. If you receive a notification that the Log Analytics workspace has been created and it does not appear, select **Refresh**. Select the Log Analytics workspace that was created and select **Add**:

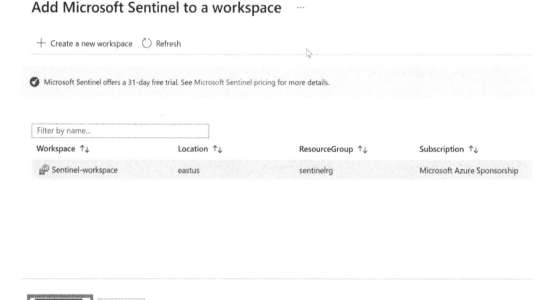

Figure 15.7 – Add Microsoft Sentinel to a workspace

7. After selecting **Add**, you will be taken to Microsoft Sentinel and a 30-day trial of Microsoft Sentinel will be activated. Select **OK** to begin using Microsoft Sentinel:

Figure 15.8 – Microsoft Sentinel trial activated

8.   The Microsoft Sentinel getting started page will open. This page provides the steps to configure Microsoft Sentinel. The first step is to collect data. Select **Connect** to go to the data connectors, as shown in *Figure 15.9*:

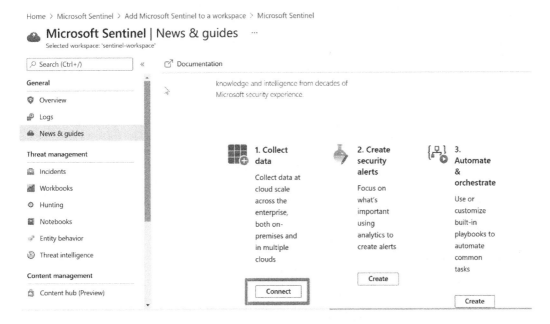

Figure 15.9 – Connect data to collect data

9.   Connecting data can also be done by accessing the **Data connectors** page under the **Configuration** menu:

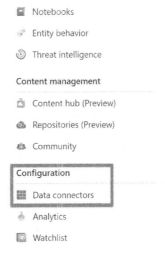

Figure 15.10 – Data connectors configuration

10. In this exercise, we are connecting Azure AD as the data connector. On the **Data connectors** page, use the search bar and type `Azure Active Directory`:

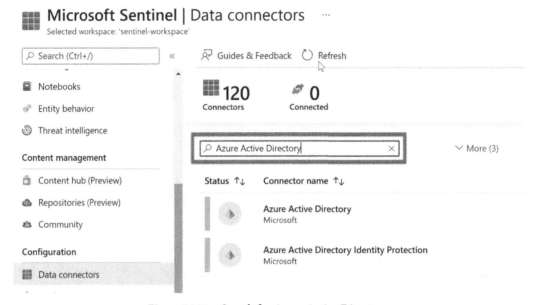

Figure 15.11 – Search for Azure Active Directory

11. Select **Azure Active Directory**. A new tile will open on the right, showing information about the Azure AD connector:

Figure 15.12 – Azure AD connector information

12. Scroll down on this tile and select **Open connector page**:

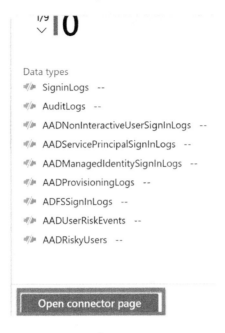

Figure 15.13 – Open connector page

13. The connector page provides the prerequisites and configuration to connect this data source. *Figure 15.14* shows that the prerequisites for connecting this data source have been met:

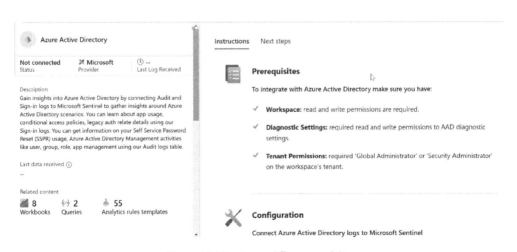

Figure 15.14 – Azure AD prerequisites

14. Next, select all of the sign-in logs and activity logs checkboxes, and select **Apply Changes** to save:

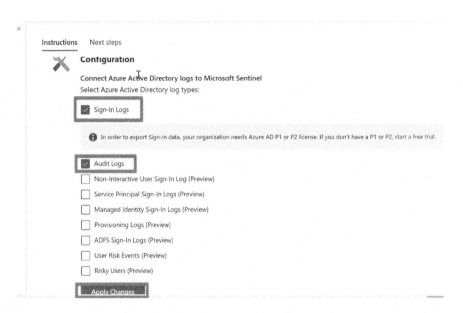

Figure 15.15 – Configure sign-in and activity logs

15. On the **Data connectors** page, **Azure Active Directory** will show as connected. This process may take some time. *Figure 15.16* shows the connector for Azure AD being successfully connected with the green bar:

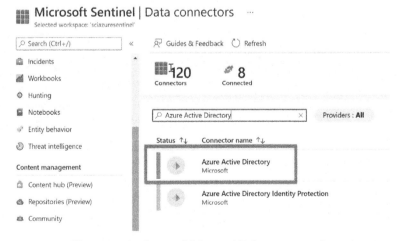

Figure 15.16 – Successful Azure AD data connected

You have now completed the creation of a Log Analytics workspace, connecting that workspace, creating a Microsoft Sentinel instance, and connecting Azure AD data to Microsoft Sentinel. In the *Reviewing Azure AD activity by using Log Analytics and Microsoft Sentinel* section of this chapter, we will go through the steps to review this activity through queries in Log Analytics and Microsoft Sentinel workbooks.

In the next section, we will discuss how to export sign-in and audit logs to an external SIEM.

Exporting sign-in and audit logs to a third-party SIEM

Azure Monitor is the Azure solution that most Azure services utilize for activity, event, and security logging. Azure AD, Azure Resource Manager, Azure Firewall, and Microsoft Defender for Cloud all utilize integration with Azure Monitor for monitoring and managing activity within Azure. The previous section discussed how to use and connect Microsoft Sentinel for monitoring, managing, and alerting on security activity based on these logs through Azure Monitor and Log Analytics. Companies that currently have a third-party SIEM and/or SOAR solution can also connect to Azure Monitor to monitor Azure AD activity. Azure Monitor routes the logs through Azure Event Hubs to deliver the log data to external applications.

More information on connecting Azure Monitor to third-party SIEM solutions for Azure AD logs can be found at this link: `https://docs.microsoft.com/en-us/azure/active-directory/reports-monitoring/overview-monitoring`.

Prior to Azure Monitor and Event Hubs, the only method to integrate logs with third-party SIEM solutions was to use **Azure log integration** (**AzLog**). This tool is currently still supported by Microsoft for customers using this for their SIEM integration, but the Azure Monitor and Event Hubs method is the preferred method for new integrations. The following is a list of three common SIEM tools and the current method supported to integrate these tools with Azure AD logs:

- **Splunk** uses the Azure Monitor add-on for Splunk for both log integration and log investigation. More information can be found at this link: `https://docs.microsoft.com/en-us/azure/active-directory/reports-monitoring/howto-integrate-activity-logs-with-splunk`.

- **IBM QRadar** log integration starts with migrating to the Microsoft Azure **Device Support Module (DSM)** and Microsoft Azure Event Hubs protocol. These tools are available from the IBM support website. The link to this information can be found here: `https://www.ibm.com/docs/en/dsm?topic=options-configuring-microsoft-azure-event-hubs-communicate-qradar`.

- **ArcSight** integrates with Azure Monitor logs through collecting Azure logs into JSON files and using **ArcSight JSON** connectors for JSON to CEF mapping. This provides integration for Azure activity logs only. A link to how to perform this integration can be found here: `https://docs.microsoft.com/en-us/azure/active-directory/reports-monitoring/howto-integrate-activity-logs-with-arcsight`.

More information on the integration with these third-party SIEM solutions can be found at this link: `https://azure.microsoft.com/en-us/blog/use-azure-monitor-to-integrate-with-siem-tools/`.

Additional step-by-step integration can be found at this link: `https://ifi.tech/2020/10/14/integrating-third-party-siem-through-azure-event-hub/`.

These are only three third-party SIEM solutions among many. If you are utilizing a SIEM or SOAR that is not one of these solutions, review the documentation that is provided by that solution as well as Microsoft Docs. If you are using Azure AD and require integration with these SIEM solutions, make sure that you verify with the SIEM and/or SOAR solution developer their integration capabilities for Azure Monitor.

The next section will discuss how to review Azure AD activity in Microsoft Sentinel using Log Analytics query tools and workbooks.

Reviewing Azure AD activity by using Log Analytics and Microsoft Sentinel

In this section, we will go through the step-by-step process of running a log query for Azure AD activity within Microsoft Sentinel. We will also step through how to review Azure AD workbooks and save the workbooks for monitoring, reviewing, and exporting:

1. Navigate to your Microsoft Sentinel workspace from within `portal.azure.com`:

Figure 15.17 – Microsoft Sentinel workspace

2. Select **Logs** under the **General** menu to access the Log Analytics workspace that is connected to Microsoft Sentinel. There is a video available here to provide an overview of Log Analytics. Select the **X** icon at the top right to close this video window:

Figure 15.18 – Microsoft Sentinel Logs screen

3. A tile of common queries opens. Select the **X** icon on the right to close this tile:

Figure 15.19 – Common queries tile

4. In the Log Analytics workspace, select the **Queries** tab, find the **Security** queries, expand the security list, and select **All SiginLogs events**, as shown in *Figure 15.20*:

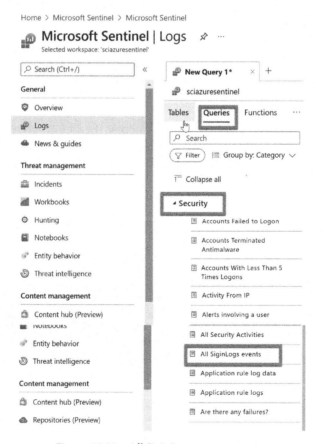

Figure 15.20 – All SiginLogs events query

5.   Select the **All SiginLogs events** query by double-clicking it and select **Run**:

Figure 15.21 – Run the query

6.   Results will appear in the pane below the query. *Figure 15.22* shows this activity:

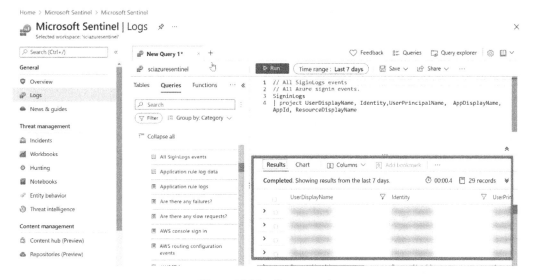

Figure 15.22 – Query results

7. If you want to run this query in the future, you can do so using the **Save** selection. You can also create an alert rule for this query for Azure Monitor or Microsoft Sentinel. These options are shown in *Figure 15.23*. Now that you have the data connector active for the log activity, you can try additional queries to see the results that are created:

Figure 15.23 – Query options to save, export, or create an alert rule

Important Note

For additional information on creating queries with **Kusto Query Language** (**KQL**), refer to the following links:

KQL tutorial: https://docs.microsoft.com/en-us/azure/data-explorer/kusto/query/tutorial?pivots=azuredataexplorer

Splunk KQL cheat sheet: https://docs.microsoft.com/en-us/azure/data-explorer/kusto/query/splunk-cheat-sheet

SQL cheat sheet: https://docs.microsoft.com/en-us/azure/data-explorer/kusto/query/sqlcheatsheet

8. Next, navigate to **Workbooks** under the **Threat management** section:

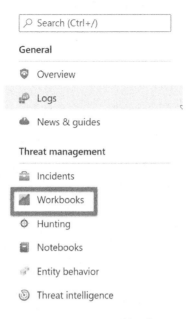

Figure 15.24 – Workbooks

9. Within **Workbooks**, use the search bar to find Azure AD workbook templates, as shown in *Figure 15.25*:

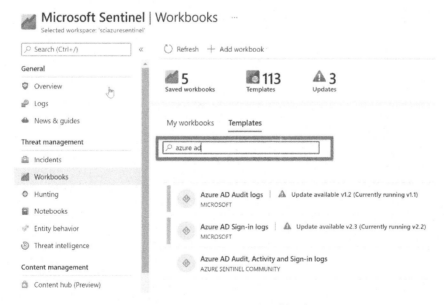

Figure 15.25 – Azure AD workbooks

10. Select **Azure AD Sign-in logs** to view the tile that opens on the right. From here, you can view the template and also save this workbook to your **Workbooks** section:

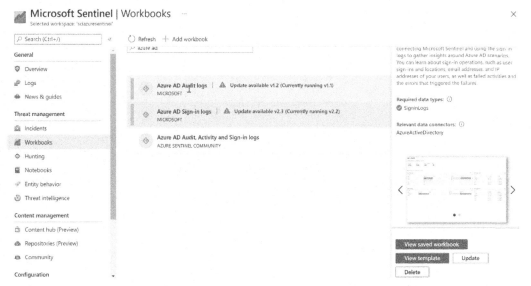

Figure 15.26 – Azure AD Sign-in logs workbook

11. Select **View template** to see the data that is provided. *Figure 15.27* shows a sample of the information that will be provided:

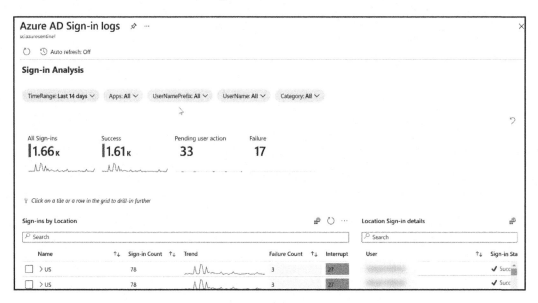

Figure 15.27 – Azure AD Sign-in logs workbook data

The data that populates is from the last 14 days within your Azure AD tenant. You can review this data to understand the sign-in activity taking place within your tenant.

Log Analytics queries and Microsoft Sentinel are not a highly tested objective area for this exam. If you want to learn more about Microsoft Sentinel, you can review Microsoft Learn content for the SC-200 Security Operations Analyst exam; here is the link: `https://docs.microsoft.com/en-us/learn/certifications/exams/sc-200`.

Next, we will provide a summary of what was discussed in this chapter.

Summary

In this chapter, we covered the integration of Azure Monitor with Microsoft Sentinel and other third-party SIEM and SOAR solutions. This included the configuration and setup of Microsoft Sentinel. Microsoft has provided the capability to integrate Azure Monitor with popular third-party SIEM and SOAR solutions, and we provided solutions and links to help with the integration process. The final section of the chapter provided steps to run Kusto queries with Log Analytics to review Azure AD activity, along with Azure AD workbooks for monitoring Azure AD activity.

The next chapter will provide practice questions to help you in your final preparation for the Identity and Access Administrator Associate exam.

16
Mock Test

Throughout this guide, you have learned about the objectives that you are required to master to pass the Microsoft Identity and Access Administrator Associate exam (SC-300). The exercises throughout the chapters in this book provide you with hands-on practice to prepare and references for performing the role of an identity and access administrator. The final assessment in this chapter can be used as additional preparation toward passing the SC-300 exam. For information regarding the exam structure and content, review *Chapter 1, Preparing for Your Microsoft Exam*.

In this assessment, you can expect the following:

- Number of questions: 80
- Question types: Multiple choice and true/false

Questions

For a true exam experience, attempt this assessment as a closed book and give yourself 190 minutes to take the assessment. Have a notepad to answer the questions and then review the answers to grade your exam and determine areas that need additional review. The recommendation for practice assessments is that you should be able to score 90% or better. Once you have attained this score, you should be ready to sit and pass the SC-300 exam. So, let's begi:.

1. When thinking about identity and access management, which is the most accurate statement?

    A. Identity is your password and access is your applications.

    B. Identity is who you are and access is the permission that is granted.

    C. Identity is the permission that is granted and access is who you are.

    D. Identity is your username and access is your administrative privileges.

2. What are some of the use cases that we use identity and access management for?

    A. Shopping on websites

    B. Email accounts

    C. Social media

    D. Business applications

    E. All of the above

3. The principle of least privilege is defined as _____.

    A. The concept that a user or resource only has access to the applications and information required to perform their specific duties

    B. The concept that a user has global administrator privileges to access all applications within the company

    C. The concept that a user must request access to applications and information every time they need to complete their duties

    D. The concept that a user has no administrator access regardless of their job role

4. There are three levels of identity and access management: traditional, advanced, and optimal. Which of the following characteristics is not included in optimal identity and access management?

    A. Password-less authentication.

    B. **Multi-factor authentication** (**MFA**) is enforced.

    C. **Single sign-on** (**SSO**) is not present.

    D. User behavior is analyzed in real time for possible risks.

    E. None of the above.

5. When creating your **Azure Active Directory** (**AAD**) tenant, which of the following is an example of the domain that you would create?

    A. `Tenantname.com`

    B. `Tenantname.onmicrosoft.com`

    C. `Sales.tenantname.com`

    D. `Tenantname.microsoft.com`

6. Which built-in AAD role has full control over the tenant and should be assigned to a limited number of select users?

    A. Billing Administrator

    B. Security Administrator

    C. Global Administrator

    D. User Administrator

    E. None of the above

7. Which of the following would *not* be considered an Azure RBAC role?

    A. Security Administrator

    B. Virtual Machine Owner

    C. Resource Group Contributor

    D. Virtual Network Reader

8. When adding a custom domain to the AAD tenant, you can use a domain from which of the following domain registrars?

    A.   Microsoft

    B.   GoDaddy

    C.   WordPress

    D.   Google

    E.   All of the above

9. How many custom domains can be added to AAD in a cloud-only infrastructure?

    A.   450

    B.   900

    C.   1,500

    D.   Unlimited

10. Which device registration option is commonly used for personal devices (BYOD)?

    A.   Hybrid AD-joined

    B.   AAD-joined

    C.   AAD-registered

    D.   None of the above

11. Which of the following is *not* a function of security defaults when enabled?

    A.   Require all users to register for AAD MFA.

    B.   Enforce and require the use of AAD MFA for all administrators.

    C.   Allow legacy authentication methods.

    D.   Protect privileged access activities.

    E.   Require MFA for accessing sensitive information.

12. In AAD, a user that is cloud-native on the AAD tenant is referred to as a(n) _____.

    A.   Guest user

    B.   External user

    C.   Windows user

    D.   Member user

13. When creating a new user in AAD, what are the *two* required fields to populate to allow the user to be created?

    A. User name

    B. Usage location

    C. Name

    D. Department

    E. Manager

14. Which is *not* a valid method to add a user to AAD?

    A. PowerShell

    B. CSV file

    C. AAD portal

    D. Microsoft 365 admin portal

    E. Microsoft 365 security portal

15. Which field or fields is/are required to invite a guest user to AAD?

    A. Name

    B. Usage location

    C. Email address

    D. Personal message

    E. All of the above

16. Within the AAD portal, what are the group type options available? Select all that apply.

    A. Microsoft 365

    B. Distribution

    C. Mail-enabled security

    D. Security

17. When creating a dynamic group, what AAD license is required? Select all that apply.

    A. AAD Free

    B. Office 365 Apps

    C. AAD Premium P1

D.   AAD Premium P2

E.   None of these

18. Dynamic groups can be used for which group type(s)? Select all that apply.

A.   Microsoft 365

B.   Distribution

C.   Mail-enabled security

D.   Security

19. You have created a user within the AAD portal. When you attempt to assign a license, you get an error. What information is missing that is required to assign a license?

A.   Department

B.   Manager

C.   Role

D.   Usage location

20. A partner relationship between two companies within AAD is known as

_____.

A.   B2C

B.   A2B

C.   B2B

D.   C2B

21. When you visit a shopping website and it gives you the option to use your Microsoft account to log in, this is an example of a(n) _____ relationship.

A.   B2C

B.   A2B

C.   B2B

D.   C2B

22. Which of the following is an option for guest invite restrictions?

    A.   Anyone in the organization can invite guest users, including guests and non-admins.

    B.   Member users and users assigned to specific admin roles can invite guest users, including guests with member permissions.

    C.   Only users assigned to specific admin roles can invite guest users.

    D.   No one in the organization can invite guest users, including admins.

    E.   All of the above.

23. What section of the **External collaboration** settings would you use to block someone from a specific domain from being invited to the AAD tenant?

    A.   Guest invite settings

    B.   Collaboration restrictions

    C.   Guest user access

    D.   None of the above

24. Which is *not* a valid method to use to invite a guest user to AAD?

    A.   PowerShell

    B.   CSV file

    C.   AAD portal

    D.   Microsoft 365 admin portal

    E.   Microsoft 365 security portal

25. True or false? Guest users can manage their passwords through **self-service password reset (SSPR)**.

    A.   True

    B.   False

26. True or false? Guest users can be configured to use AAD MFA within the tenant in which they are a guest.

    A.   True

    B.   False

27. Which of the following external identity providers can be configured directly within the AAD portal? Select all that apply.

    A.   Google

    B.   Facebook

    C.   Amazon Web Services

    D.   Any SAML/WS-fed identity provider

28. You have created an AAD tenant. You also have an on-premises Windows Active Directory that includes users and groups. What can you use to bring together a hybrid infrastructure for AAD cloud applications and synchronize on-premises users and groups for identity and access management?

    A.   Application Proxy

    B.   **Active Directory Federation Services (AD FS)**

    C.   AAD Connect

    D.   External identities

29. There are three AAD Connect synchronization options. Which is the least complex and can be configured with the Express settings?

    A.   Password hash synchronization

    B.   Pass-through authentication

    C.   AD FS

30. Which AAD Connect synchronization option would you choose if you have a third-party MFA solution?

    A.   Password hash synchronization

    B.   Pass-through authentication

    C.   AD FS

31. What is the best AAD Connect synchronization option if you do not have registered custom domains in your Active Directory organizational units?

    A.   Password hash synchronization

    B.   Pass-through authentication

    C.   AD FS

32. To configure AAD Connect while adhering to the principles of least privilege, what are the two roles that are required during setup?

    A. Hybrid Identity Administrator

    B. Global Administrator

    C. Domain Enterprise Administrator

    D. User Administrator

33. To utilize seamless SSO in a Hybrid Identity architecture with pass-through authentication, what option must be activated in AAD Connect?

    A. Device writeback

    B. Password writeback

    C. Password protection

    D. Account lockout

34. What is used to monitor the connection of AAD Connect to AAD?

    A. AAD Connect dashboard

    B. AAD Connect Health

    C. Windows Active Directory Connection Manager

    D. Synchronization Service Manager

35. Which of the following is *not* a factor that is part of MFA?

    A. Something you know

    B. Something you have

    C. Something you are

    D. Something you belong to

36. You have entered your username and password to log into the company intranet site. You are prompted to provide an additional form of verification. Which of the following would *not* be a proper second form of verification with MFA?

    A. Fingerprint

    B. Code from an authenticator app

    C. PIN

    D. Phone call to cell phone

37. SSPR uses many of the same forms of verification as MFA. Which of the following is used by SSPR but *not* MFA?

    A.   Mobile phone

    B.   Authenticator app

    C.   Security question

    D.   App code

38. Which of the following is *not* configured in AAD Password Protection?

    A.   Lockout threshold

    B.   Lockout duration

    C.   Global banned passwords

    D.   Custom banned passwords

    E.   Windows Active Directory password protection

39. True or false? Password-less authentication provides a high level of complexity without the benefit of added identity protection.

    A.   True

    B.   False

40. True or false? Password-less authentication, such as Windows Hello, is considered an authentication method with MFA.

    A.   True

    B.   False

41. The verification workflow of a zero-trust identity model includes which of the following? Select all that apply.

    A.   Signal

    B.   Trigger

    C.   Decision

    D.   Enforcement

42. What is the service that implements zero trust for identity within AAD?

    A.   AAD Identity Protection

    B.   Privileged Identity Management

    C.   Identity Governance

    D.   Conditional Access

43. What can be used to test your Conditional Access policies to verify that they are working as expected?

    A.   Report only

    B.   Turning on the policy

    C.   What If

    D.   None of the above

44. Smart lockout in AAD Identity Protection can protect users against what type of attack?

    A.   SQL injection

    B.   Cross-site scripting

    C.   Phishing

    D.   Brute-force dictionary

45. An alert in AAD Identity Protection based on atypical travel is a form of what type of risk?

    A.   User risk

    B.   Sign-in risk

    C.   Device risk

    D.   None of the above

46. An alert in AAD Identity Protection regarding potentially leaked credentials is what type of risk?

    A.   User risk

    B.   Sign-in risk

    C.   Device risk

    D.   None of the above

47. What are two ways of discovering applications that are being used by a company?

    A.   Ask IT

    B.   Microsoft Defender for Cloud Apps

    C.   Microsoft Intune

    D.   AD FS

48. True or false? Cloud and line-of-business applications that authenticate using AD FS can be migrated to AAD to provide cloud-only SSO.

    A.   True

    B.   False

49. For cloud-only SSO, what is used to integrate on-premises applications to AAD?

    A.   AAD Connect

    B.   AAD Application Proxy

    C.   AD FS

    D.   None of the above

50. What are the benefits of registering on-premises applications to AAD?

    A.   SSO creates a better user experience.

    B.   Decreased reliance on on-premises Active Directory.

    C.   Full use of AAD security features.

    D.   All of the above.

51. Third-party cloud applications that can be registered directly to AAD can be found where?

    A.   Software website

    B.   AAD gallery

    C.   Azure Marketplace

    D.   Microsoft 365 portal

52. What is the primary use of Microsoft Defender for Cloud Apps?

    A.   Discovery apps to monitor for shadow IT.

    B.   Assign cloud apps to users.

    C.   Register for cloud apps licensing.

    D.   All of the above.

53. Which of the following are Conditional Access policy types that have templates in Microsoft Defender for Cloud Apps?

   A.   Access policy

   B.   Activity policy

   C.   File policy

   D.   App discovery policy

   E.   OAuth app policy

   F.   All of the above

54. When creating a file policy in Microsoft Defender for Cloud Apps, the policy governs over what solutions? Select all that apply.

   A.   Outlook

   B.   SharePoint Online

   C.   OneDrive for Business

   D.   Dropbox

   E.   Google Drive

55. Which policy monitors applications that could be identified as shadow IT?

   A.   Activity policy

   B.   Session policy

   C.   App discovery policy

   D.   File policy

   E.   None of the above

56. Which policy is considered a threat protection policy and can approve or revoke permissions to an app?

   A.   Activity policy

   B.   Access policy

   C.   Session policy

   D.   OAuth policy

   E.   None of the above

57. The four sections of a discovered app score are what?

    A.   General

    B.   Security

    C.   Compliance

    D.   Legal

    E.   Identity

58. True or false? Entitlement management allows non-administrators to delegate access to users and groups.

    A.   True

    B.   False

59. Which of these is a collection of users and groups, applications, and SharePoint sites?

    A.   Access package

    B.   Catalog

    C.   Department

    D.   Entitlement

60. What defines the life cycle and how requests are handled when governing catalogs?

    A.   Departments

    B.   Entitlements

    C.   Access package

    D.   None of the above

61. Evaluating a guest or member user's need of continued membership with an access package is done using _____.

    A.   Catalogs

    B.   Entitlements

    C.   Administrator audits

    D.   Access reviews

62. True or false? Terms of use are company-provided documents on the proper processes and procedures for using an application or site. These can also be tied to Conditional Access policies to allow access to applications.

    A.   True

    B.   False

63. Which service provides just-in-time administrator access that is time-bound to decrease the attack surface of elevated privileges?

    A.   Identity Protection

    B.   Access packages

    C.   Privileged Identity Management

    D.   Microsoft Defender for Cloud

64. True or false? When creating a PIM role assignment, it is a best practice to make the role permanent.

    A.   True

    B.   False

65. When creating emergency access, or a break-glass account, what should you avoid using? Select all that apply.

    A.   MFA

    B.   Conditional Access policies

    C.   Strong passwords

    D.   Documented procedures

66. As a best practice, an access review for a guest user should be completed by who? Select all that apply.

    A.   Guest user

    B.   Manager

    C.   IT

    D.   Member user

67. True or false? Access reviews can be configured to remove access if the reviewer does not respond.

    A.   True

    B.   False

68. How is the reviewer notified that an access review has begun?

    A.   AAD portal

    B.   Text message

    C.   Authenticator app

    D.   Email

69. Which of the following logs are in the category of activity reporting? Select all that apply.

    A.   Risky sign-ins

    B.   Sign-ins

    C.   Audit logs

    D.   Provisioning logs

    E.   User risk

70. Which of the following logs are in the category of security reporting? Select all that apply.

    A.   Risky sign-ins

    B.   Sign-ins

    C.   Audit logs

    D.   Provisioning logs

    E.   User risk

71. In what section of the AAD menu would you find activity reporting logs?

    A.   Security

    B.   Overview

    C.   Manage

    D.   Monitoring

    E.   Troubleshooting + Support

72. In what areas of AAD can you find sign-in and audit logs? Select all that apply.

    A.   AAD portal

    B.   Enterprise applications

    C.   Users

    D.   Groups

    E.   All of the above

73. Workbooks provide graphical data on AAD activity for enterprise applications. Where can this be accessed in AAD?

    A.   Log analytics

    B.   Diagnostic settings

    C.   Usage & insights

    D.   Access reviews

74. True or false? Microsoft Sentinel is a scalable, cloud-native, **security information event management (SIEM)**, **extended detection and response (XDR)**, and **security orchestration automated response (SOAR)** solution.

    A.   True

    B.   False

75. Which of the following represents Microsoft Sentinel's workflow, in order?

    A.   Respond, collect, detect, investigate

    B.   Collect, detect, investigate, respond

    C.   Investigate, detect, collect, respond

    D.   Detect, collect, investigate, respond

76. The first thing that you need to do when setting up Microsoft Sentinel is what?

    A.   Connect data sources.

    B.   Run Kusto queries.

    C.   Connect a Log Analytics workspace.

    D.   Save workbooks.

77. What role is required to connect AAD log data to Microsoft Sentinel?

    A.   Security reader

    B.   Security operator

    C.   Security administrator

    D.   User administrator

78. Which third-party SIEM solution has integration with Azure Activity logs, but not audit logs?

    A.   Microsoft Sentinel

    B.   Splunk

    C.   IBM QRadar

    D.   ArcSight

79. Which third-party SIEM solution uses the Microsoft Azure Device Support Module and Microsoft Azure Event Hubs protocol to integrate with Azure Monitor?

    A.   Microsoft Sentinel

    B.   Splunk

    C.   IBM QRadar

    D.   ArcSight

80. Which third-party SIEM solution has an add-on for Azure Monitor built in for log integration and investigation?

    A.   Microsoft Sentinel

    B.   Splunk

    C.   IBM QRadar

    D.   ArcSight

Answers

We recommend that you review these answers after attempting to answer the questions. Check your answers and review the sections within the chapters for additional clarification:

1. B. The most accurate statement is that identity is who you are and access is the permission that is granted. Your identity may include your password and username, and access may include your authorized applications and administrative privileges, but these are not the most accurate statements in these responses. For additional details, see *Chapter 2, Defining Identity and Access Management*.

2. E. All of these choices are examples of where we would use identity and access management. For additional details, see *Chapter 2, Defining Identity and Access Management*.

3. A. The principle of least privilege is the concept that a user or resource only has access to the applications and information required to perform their specific duties. For additional details, see *Chapter 2, Defining Identity and Access Management*.

4. C. Within an optimal IAM infrastructure, SSO should be present for all cloud and on-premises applications. For additional details, see *Chapter 2, Defining Identity and Access Management*.

5. B. When creating a tenant in AAD, the initial tenant is the name that you assign and then `onmicrosoft.com`. This domain name will remain within your tenant and cannot be removed. After creating your tenant, you can then add a custom domain name that is more suited for business use. For additional details, see *Chapter 3, Implementing and Configuring Azure Active Directory*.

6. C. The Global Administrator has full administrative control over the tenant and subscription and should only be assigned to 3-5 select users. For additional details, see *Chapter 3, Implementing and Configuring Azure Active Directory*.

7. A. Azure RBAC roles are based on owner, contributor, and reader roles for Azure resources. When a role is administrator, this is an AAD role. Both AAD and RBAC have reader roles, but in this example, the reader role is for Azure resources, which makes it RBAC. For additional details, see *Chapter 3, Implementing and Configuring Azure Active Directory*.

8. E. It is not required that you purchase a domain from Microsoft to use it on the AAD tenant. You can use any domain registrar, including the ones that are in the list provided. For additional details, see *Chapter 3, Implementing and Configuring Azure Active Directory*.

9. B. For AAD tenants that are not federated with an on-premises Active Directory, the maximum number of custom domains is 900. If AAD is federated with an on-premises Active Directory, this number decreases to 450. For additional details, see *Chapter 3, Implementing and Configuring Azure Active Directory*.

10. C. The most common way to manage a personal device within AAD is to register the device in AAD. This allows the device to be managed with Microsoft Intune without requiring a full AAD join. For additional details, see *Chapter 3, Implementing and Configuring Azure Active Directory*.

11. C. A feature of security defaults is blocking legacy authentication, that is, not allowing it. All other choices are features of security defaults. For additional details, see *Chapter 3, Implementing and Configuring Azure Active Directory*.

12. D. A cloud-native user on AAD is a member user. A Windows user is a synchronized user from AAD Connect in a Hybrid Identity infrastructure. For additional details, see *Chapter 4, Creating, Configuring, and Managing Identities*.

13. A and C. The only fields that you are required to populate are User name and Name (display name). Usage location is required for assigning licenses to the user, but it is not required for user creation within AAD. It is a requirement when using the Microsoft 365 admin portal to create a user. For additional details, see *Chapter 4, Creating, Configuring, and Managing Identities*.

14. D. The Microsoft 365 security portal cannot be used to add users to AAD. All of the other options can be used, with PowerShell and CSV bulk import as ways to add multiple users simultaneously. For additional details, see *Chapter 4, Creating, Creating, Configuring, and Managing Identities*.

15. C. The only field that is required to invite a guest user to the AAD tenant is the email address of the person that is being invited. For additional details, see *Chapter 4, Creating, Configuring, and Managing Users*, and *Chapter 5, Implementing and Managing External Identities and Guests*.

16. A and D. Within the AAD portal, the group type options are Microsoft 365 and security groups only. Distribution and mail-enabled security groups are group options that are available *only* within the Microsoft 365 admin portal. For additional details, see *Chapter 4, Creating, Configuring, and Managing Identities*.

17. C and D. Dynamic groups are supported with AAD Premium P1 and Premium P2 licensing. They are not available with AAD Free or Office 365 Apps licensing. For additional details, see *Chapter 4, Creating, Configuring, and Managing Identities*.

18. A and D. Microsoft 365 and security group types support dynamic groups. For additional details, see *Chapter 4, Creating, Configuring, and Managing Identities*.

19. D. Since User name and Name are the only required fields to create a member user within the AAD portal, the user will be created without a usage location. However, this will cause an error when attempting to assign licenses to the user. For additional details, see *Chapter 4, Creating, Configuring, and Managing Identities*.

20. C. When a partner relationship is established between two companies within AAD, this is a B2B, or business-to-business, relationship. For additional details, see *Chapter 5, Implementing and Managing External Identities and Guests*.

21. A. This is an example of a B2C, or business-to-consumer, relationship. For additional details, see *Chapter 5, Implementing and Managing External Identities and Guests*.

22. E. All of these are options for guest invite restrictions. For additional details, see *Chapter 5, Implementing and Managing External Identities and Guests*.

23. B. Allowing and denying invitations to specific domains can be configured under Collaboration restrictions. For additional details, see *Chapter 5, Implementing and Managing External Identities and Guests*.

24. D. The Microsoft 365 security portal cannot be used to add guest users to AAD. All of the other options can be used, with PowerShell and CSV bulk import as ways to add multiple users simultaneously. For additional details, see *Chapter 5, Implementing and Managing External Identities and Guests*.

25. B. Since guest users are not provided a password within the AAD tenant, they cannot use SSPR to manage their password. If they need to reset their password, they will use the identity provider in which they are a member. For additional details, see *Chapter 5, Implementing and Managing External Identities and Guests*.

26. A. Guest users on the AAD tenant can be configured and required to use AAD MFA on the tenant. For additional details, see *Chapter 5, Implementing and Managing External Identities and Guests*.

27. A, B, and D. Google, Facebook, and SAML/WS-fed identity providers can be configured within the AAD portal. There is currently no direct configuration option for Amazon Web Services. However, by using AWS SAML roles for IAM, this option can be used. For additional details, see *Chapter 5, Implementing and Managing External Identities and Guests*.

28. C. AAD Connect is used to synchronize on-premises users and groups with AAD. Application Proxy can be used for hybrid infrastructures, but it utilizes AAD for identity and access, not on-premises directly. For additional details, see *Chapter 6, Implementing and Managing Hybrid Identities*.

29. A. Password Hash synchronization is the least complex and the option that would be configured with Express settings. For additional details, see *Chapter 6, Implementing and Managing Hybrid Identities*.

30. C. AD FS is required to synchronize with AAD when using a third-party MFA solution. For additional details, see *Chapter 6, Implementing and Managing Hybrid Identities.*

31. B. Pass-through should be used if authenticating with an unregistered domain name, such as `domain.local`. For additional details, see *Chapter 6, Implementing and Managing Hybrid Identities.*

32. A and C. Hybrid Identity Administrator in AAD and Domain Enterprise Administrator in Windows Active Directory are the best roles to have while adhering to the principle of least privilege. Global Administrator can be used instead of Hybrid Identity Administrator but assigning this role for this task is not a best practice. For additional details, see *Chapter 6, Implementing and Managing Hybrid Identities.*

33. B. Password writeback is required to utilize seamless SSO with pass-through authentication with AAD Connect. For additional details, see *Chapter 6, Implementing and Managing Hybrid Identities.*

34. B. AAD Connect Health is installed on the on-premises Windows Active Directory server to monitor the connection to AAD. For additional details, see *Chapter 6, Implementing and Managing Hybrid Identities.*

35. D. MFA consists of using two forms to verify identity. These can be a combination of something you know, something you have, and something you are. For additional details, see *Chapter 7, Planning and Implementing Azure Multi-Factor Authentication and Self-Service Password Reset.*

36. C. A PIN number is something that you know, and so is a password. Therefore, it does not meet the requirements for MFA. For additional details, see *Chapter 7, Planning and Implementing Azure Multi-Factor Authentication and Self-Service Password Reset.*

37. C. MFA does not use security questions as a valid factor for verification but can be used for SSPR. For additional details, see *Chapter 7, Planning and Implementing Azure Multi-Factor Authentication and Self-Service Password Reset.*

38. C. Global banned passwords are included by default within your AAD tenant and there is no need to configure this list. For additional details, see *Chapter 7, Planning and Implementing Azure Multi-Factor Authentication and Self-Service Password Reset.*

39. B. This statement is false. Using password-less authentication provides a high level of usability and security without additional complexity. For additional details, see *Chapter 8, Planning and Managing Password-Less Authentication Methods.*

40. A. Forms of password-less authentication, Windows Hello, FIDO/2, and an authenticator app, all require two factors of verification for authentication. In FIDO/2 and an authenticator app, these are something you are and something you have. Windows Hello has a PIN embedded behind BitLocker on the hardware and facial recognition. For additional details, see *Chapter 8, Planning and Managing Password-Less Authentication Methods.*

41. A, C, and D. The zero-trust model for identity has a workflow that includes a signal that initiates a decision that enforces the final result of authorizing or denying access. For additional details, see *Chapter 9, Planning, Implementing, and Administering Conditional Access and Azure Identity Protection.*

42. D. Conditional Access policies follow the zero-trust workflow to enforce zero-trust verification of identities. For additional details, see *Chapter 9, Planning, Implementing, and Administering Conditional Access and Azure Identity Protection.*

43. C. Running the What If feature against users, locations, applications, and devices will show which Conditional Access policies will and won't apply. If you receive a result that you did not expect, you can reconfigure the policy before turning it on. For additional details, see *Chapter 9, Planning, Implementing, and Administering Conditional Access and Azure Identity Protection.*

44. D. Configuring smart lockout in AAD Identity Protection protects users against a brute-force dictionary attack where an attacker is attempting to guess the user password by running multiple attempts. For additional details, see *Chapter 9, Planning, Implementing, and Administering Conditional Access and Azure Identity Protection.*

45. B. Atypical travel identifies a potential sign-in risk. For additional details, see *Chapter 9, Planning, Implementing, and Administering Conditional Access and Azure Identity Protection.*

46. A. Leaked credentials identify a potential user risk. For additional details, see *Chapter 9, Planning, Implementing, and Administering Conditional Access and Azure Identity Protection.*

47. B and D. Microsoft Defender for Cloud Apps and AD FS can be used to identify applications that are being accessed by users. For additional details, see *Chapter 10, Planning and Implementing Enterprise Apps for Single Sign-On (SSO).*

48. A. This is a true statement. For additional details, see *Chapter 10, Planning and Implementing Enterprise Apps for Single Sign-On (SSO).*

49. B. AAD Application Proxy can be installed on-premises to create a cloud-only SSO experience for on-premises applications. For additional details, see *Chapter 10, Planning and Implementing Enterprise Apps for Single Sign-On (SSO).*

50. D. All of these are reasons to register on-premises applications into AAD. For additional details, see *Chapter 10, Planning and Implementing Enterprise Apps for Single Sign-On (SSO)*.

51. B. The current list of cloud applications that are available to be registered to AAD can be found in the AAD gallery. For additional details, see *Chapter 10, Planning and Implementing Enterprise Apps for Single Sign-On (SSO)*.

52. A. Microsoft Defender for Cloud Apps can discovery apps that are being used on your network and help you monitor and protect against shadow IT. For additional details, see *Chapter 11, Monitoring Enterprise Apps with Microsoft Defender for Cloud Apps*.

53. F. These are all Conditional Access policies within Microsoft Defender for Cloud Apps. For additional details, see *Chapter 11, Monitoring Enterprise Apps with Microsoft Defender for Cloud Apps*.

54. B and C. File policies govern over SharePoint and OneDrive for Business. For additional details, see *Chapter 11, Monitoring Enterprise Apps with Microsoft Defender for Cloud Apps*.

55. C. There are two policies that monitor potential shadow IT applications. These are app discovery policies and Cloud Discovery anomaly detection policies. For additional details, see *Chapter 11, Monitoring Enterprise Apps with Microsoft Defender for Cloud Apps*.

56. D. The OAuth policy investigates permissions to an app and can approve or revoke permissions and access to the app to mitigate against potential threats. For additional details, see *Chapter 11, Monitoring Enterprise Apps with Microsoft Defender for Cloud Apps*.

57. A, B, C, and D. Identity is not a section that is scored in Microsoft Defender for Cloud Apps. For additional details, see *Chapter 11, Monitoring Enterprise Apps with Microsoft Defender for Cloud Apps*.

58. A. Entitlement management allows non-administrators to assign access to applications and SharePoint sites for specific uses, such as a project. For additional details, see *Chapter 12, Planning and Implementing Entitlement Management*.

59. B. A catalog is a collection of users and groups, applications, and SharePoint sites. For additional details, see *Chapter 12, Planning and Implementing Entitlement Management*.

60. C. The access package defines the catalog, how to handle requests, and the life cycle of user and group access. For additional details, see *Chapter 12, Planning and Implementing Entitlement Management*.

61. D. Access reviews provide life cycle management and can be configured to take place regularly to evaluate and govern over continued membership to an access package. For additional details, see *Chapter 12, Planning and Implementing Entitlement Management.*

62. A. Terms of use are company-provided documents that can be used for user understanding and compliance to application or site use. For additional details, see *Chapter 12, Planning and Implementing Entitlement Management.*

63. C. Privileged Identity Management provides just-in-time access to administrator roles. For additional details, see *Chapter 13, Planning and Implementing Privileged Access and Access Reviews.*

64. B. All assignments to privileged administrator roles should have a time-bound expiration. For additional details, see *Chapter 13, Planning and Implementing Privileged Access and Access Reviews.*

65. A and B. Break-glass accounts should never have MFA enforced and should also be excluded from all Conditional Access policies. You should have a strong password for these accounts and a documented procedure for how to access and use these accounts. For additional details, see *Chapter 13, Planning and Implementing Privileged Access and Access Reviews.*

66. B, C, and D. A guest user should never self-review their access review. This should be performed by someone from the host company. For additional details, see *Chapter 13, Planning and Implementing Privileged Access and Access Reviews.*

67. A. When you configure automated tasks for an access review, there is an option to remove a user's access if the reviewer does not respond. For additional details, see *Chapter 13, Planning and Implementing Privileged Access and Access Reviews.*

68. D. When an access review begins, the reviewer is notified through email. For additional details, see *Chapter 13, Planning and Implementing Privileged Access and Access Reviews.*

69. B, C, and D. Risky sign-ins and user risk are in the security reporting category. For additional details, see *Chapter 14, Analyzing and Investigating Sign-in Logs and Elevated Risk Users.*

70. A and E. Risky sign-ins and user risk are in the security reporting category. For additional details, see *Chapter 14, Analyzing and Investigating Sign-in Logs and Elevated Risk Users.*

71. D. Activity reporting logs can be found under the Monitoring header in the AAD menu. These can also be found under Activity under the User and Groups section of AAD, for more specific information. For additional details, see *Chapter 14, Analyzing and Investigating Sign-in Logs and Elevated Risk Users.*

72. E. You can find sign-in and audit logs for all of these services. The AAD portal provides the most comprehensive data. For additional details, see *Chapter 14, Analyzing and Investigating Sign-in Logs and Elevated Risk Users.*

73. C. Usage and insights can be used to access this information for specific applications within enterprise applications. There are also templates that can be accessed in the AAD portal under Monitoring – Workbooks. For additional details, see *Chapter 14, Analyzing and Investigating Sign-in Logs and Elevated Risk Users.*

74. B. Microsoft Sentinel is not an **XDR** solution. Microsoft Defender provides XDR solutions that can be used with Sentinel SIEM and SOAR solutions. For additional details, see *Chapter 15, Enabling and Integrating Azure AD Logs with SIEM Solutions.*

75. B. Microsoft Sentinel's workflow is to collect, detect, investigate, and respond. For additional details, see *Chapter 15, Enabling and Integrating Azure AD Logs with SIEM Solutions.*

76. C. Before you can set up Microsoft Sentinel, you must connect a Log Analytics workspace to Microsoft Sentinel. For additional details, see *Chapter 15, Enabling and Integrating Azure AD Logs with SIEM Solutions.*

77. C. Security Administrator is required to connect AAD log data to Microsoft Sentinel. Global Administrator can also complete this task. For additional details, see *Chapter 15, Enabling and Integrating Azure AD Logs with SIEM Solutions.*

78. D. ArcSight does not have integration with AAD audit logs, only activity logs. For additional details, see *Chapter 15, Enabling and Integrating Azure AD Logs with SIEM Solutions.*

79. C. This is the process for integrating IBM QRadar with Azure Monitor. For additional details, see *Chapter 15, Enabling and Integrating Azure AD Logs with SIEM Solutions.*

80. B. Splunk has a direct add-on for Azure Monitor. For additional details, see *Chapter 15, Enabling and Integrating Azure AD Logs with SIEM Solutions.*

Summary

This completes your assessment and preparation for the SC-300 Microsoft Identity and Access Administrator Associate exam. Good luck and I hope you see continued success in your certification and professional journey.

Index

Packt.com

Subscribe to our online digital library for full access to over 7,000 books and videos, as well as industry leading tools to help you plan your personal development and advance your career. For more information, please visit our website.

Why subscribe?

- Spend less time learning and more time coding with practical eBooks and Videos from over 4,000 industry professionals

- Improve your learning with Skill Plans built especially for you

- Get a free eBook or video every month

- Fully searchable for easy access to vital information

- Copy and paste, print, and bookmark content

Did you know that Packt offers eBook versions of every book published, with PDF and ePub files available? You can upgrade to the eBook version at packt.com and as a print book customer, you are entitled to a discount on the eBook copy. Get in touch with us at customercare@packtpub.com for more details.

At www.packt.com, you can also read a collection of free technical articles, sign up for a range of free newsletters, and receive exclusive discounts and offers on Packt books and eBooks.

Other Books You May Enjoy

If you enjoyed this book, you may be interested in these other books by Packt:

Microsoft Security Operations Analyst Exam Ref SC-200 Certification Guide

Trevor Stuart, Joe Anich

ISBN: 9781803231891

- Discover how to secure information technology systems for your organization

- Manage cross-domain investigations in the Microsoft 365 Defender portal

- Plan and implement the use of data connectors in Microsoft Defender for Cloud

- Get to grips with designing and configuring Microsoft Sentinel Workspace

- Configure SOAR in Microsoft Sentinel

- Find out how to use Microsoft Sentinel workbooks to analyze and interpret data

- Solve mock tests at the end of the book to test your knowledge

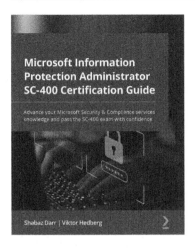

Microsoft Information Protection Administrator SC-400 Certification Guide

Shabaz Darr, Viktor Hedberg

ISBN: 9781801811491

- Understand core exam objectives to pass the SC-400 exam with ease
- Find out how to create and manage sensitive information types for different types of data
- Create and manage policies and learn how to apply these to Microsoft 365 SaaS applications
- Broaden your knowledge of data protection on M365
- Discover how to configure and manage the protection of your data in M365
- Monitor activity regarding data access in M365
- Understand and implement Data Governance in M365

Packt is searching for authors like you

If you're interested in becoming an author for Packt, please visit `authors.packtpub.com` and apply today. We have worked with thousands of developers and tech professionals, just like you, to help them share their insight with the global tech community. You can make a general application, apply for a specific hot topic that we are recruiting an author for, or submit your own idea.

Share Your Thoughts

Now you've finished *Microsoft Identity and Access Administrator Exam Guide*, we'd love to hear your thoughts! Scan the QR code below to go straight to the Amazon review page for this book and share your feedback or leave a review on the site that you purchased it from.

`https://packt.link/r/1-801-81804-5`

Your review is important to us and the tech community and will help us make sure we're delivering excellent quality content.

Made in the USA
Las Vegas, NV
05 January 2023

65076901R00249